Performing the Politics of Translation in Modern Japan

Performing the Politics of Translation in Modern Japan sheds new light on the adoption of concepts that motivated political theatres of resistance for nearly a century and even now underpin the collective understanding of the Japanese nation.

Grounded in the aftermath of the Meiji Restoration in 1868 and analyzing its legacy on stage, this book tells the story of the crucial role that performance and specifically embodied memory played in the changing understanding of the imported Western concepts of "liberty" (jiyū) and "revolution" (kakumei). Tracing the role of the post-Restoration movement itself as an important touchstone for later performances, it examines two key moments of political crisis. The first of these is the Proletarian Theater Movement of the 1920s and '30s, in which the post-Restoration years were important for theorizing the Japanese communist revolution. The second is in the postwar years when Rights Movement theatre and thought again featured as a vehicle for understanding the present through the past. As such, this book presents the translation of "liberty" and "revolution", not through a one-to-one correspondence model, but rather as a many-to-many relationship. In doing so, it presents a century of evolution in the dramaturgy of resistance in Japan.

This book will be useful to students and scholars of Japanese history, society and culture, as well as literature and translation studies alike.

Aragorn Quinn is assistant professor of Japanese at the University of Wisconsin-Milwaukee, USA.

Routledge Studies in the Modern History of Asia

Borneo in the Cold War, 1950–1990
Ooi Keat Gin

International Rivalry and Secret Diplomacy in East Asia, 1896–1950
Bruce A. Elleman

Women Warriors in Southeast Asia
Edited by Vina A. Lanzona and Frederik Rettig

The Russian Discovery of Japan, 1670–1800
David N.Wells

Singapore—Two Hundred Years of the Lion City
Edited by Anthony Webster and Nicholas J. White

Borneo and Sulawesi
Indigenous Peoples, Empires and Area Studies
Edited by Ooi Keat Gin

Tuberculosis—The Singapore Experience, 1867–2018
Disease, Society and the State
Kah Seng Loh and Li Yang Hsu

Caste in Early Modern Japan
Danzaemon and the Edo Outcaste Order
Timothy D. Amos

Performing the Politics of Translation in Modern Japan
Staging the Resistance
Aragorn Quinn

For a full list of available titles please visit: www.routledge.com/Routledge-Studies-in-the-Modern-History-of-Asia/book-series/MODHISTASIA

Performing the Politics of Translation in Modern Japan
Staging the Resistance

Aragorn Quinn

LONDON AND NEW YORK

First published 2020
by Routledge
2 Park Square, Milton Park, Abingdon, Oxon OX14 4RN

and by Routledge
52 Vanderbilt Avenue, New York, NY 10017

Routledge is an imprint of the Taylor & Francis Group, an informa business

First issued in paperback 2021

© 2020 Aragorn Quinn

The right of Aragorn Quinn to be identified as author of this work has been asserted by him in accordance with sections 77 and 78 of the Copyright, Designs and Patents Act 1988.

All rights reserved. No part of this book may be reprinted or reproduced or utilised in any form or by any electronic, mechanical, or other means, now known or hereafter invented, including photocopying and recording, or in any information storage or retrieval system, without permission in writing from the publishers.

Trademark notice: Product or corporate names may be trademarks or registered trademarks, and are used only for identification and explanation without intent to infringe.

British Library Cataloguing-in-Publication Data
A catalogue record for this book is available from the British Library

Library of Congress Cataloging-in-Publication Data
A catalog record for this book has been requested

ISBN: 978-0-367-19240-2 (hbk)
ISBN: 978-1-03-208200-4 (pbk)
ISBN: 978-0-429-20126-4 (ebk)

Typeset in Times New Roman
by Apex CoVantage, LLC

For my father

Contents

	List of figures	viii
	Acknowledgments	ix
	Introduction	1
1	Weaponizing Meiji liberty	12
2	There is a specter haunting Communism	44
3	Democracy dies in Gifu	80
4	Shinsengumi live!	111
5	The last sōshi	142
	Index	165

Figures

1.1	The final battle at Philipi as rendered in the book publication of Kawashima Keizō's translation of *Julius Caesar*	19
1.2	Menenius Agrippa faces down the mob in Itakura Kotarō's translation of *Coriolanus*	25
1.3	Nishikie of Kawakami Otojirō's *Oppekepe*, 1891	34
2.1	Scene from Sasaki Takamaru's *The Secret Account from Tsukuba*	45
2.2	Cartoon from *Theater News*	66
3.1	Nishikie of the Kawakami Ichiza troupe's production of *Itagaki Taisuke sōnan jikki*, with Aoyagi Sutesaburō (left) as Itagaki and Kawakami Otojirō (right) as his would-be assassin, Aihara Naobumi	81
3.2	Nishikie of the dramatic final scene from Kawakami Otojirō's *A Record of the Saga Disturbance*	96
3.3	Scene from Sasaki Takamaru's play *Itagaki Taisuke*	103
3.4	Sōshi confronting a traitor in their midst in a scene from Sasaki Takamaru's play *Itagaki Taisuke*	104
4.1	Final scene from the production of *Shinsengumi: A Talkie Rensageki*; this scene features Kondō Isami both live on stage and on the screen behind him	123
4.2	Kubo Sakae's *The Blood Oath at Goryokaku*	123
4.3	Kondō Isami played by Kawasaki Chōjūrō in the final scene of Murayama Tomoyoshi's *Shinsengumi*. The projected image of Kondō appears on screen at the same time as the actor performing the same scene live	135
5.1	Scene from Fukuda Yoshiyuki's *Oppekepe* (1963); Shiroyama performs for his audience in this play-within-a-play that is itself within a play	145
5.2	A blind shakuhachi player sees Sudō's lost mirror in Inagaki Hiroshi's *Sōshi gekijō*	147
5.3	In this four image sequence from *Sōshi Theater*, an intoxicated audience member disrupts the troupe's performance, is subjected to a "trial" on the stage, and is sentenced to banishment from the theater in *Sōshi gekijō*	154

Acknowledgments

All first books are as much a product of the mentors who fostered the new scholar as they are the efforts of said scholar. This book is no exception. I am primarily, overwhelmingly, unceasingly, and in every other way in debt to my doctoral advisor, Indra Levy. Her clear and insightful feedback through every stage of my research and writing is central to the completion of this project. She is and will always be the model of scholarly and teaching excellence by which I measure my own professional development. Her unwavering support and guidance is indicative of the rigorous yet mutually supportive culture fostered by the faculty in the East Asian Languages and Cultures Department at Stanford University, and I am forever grateful to all of those who helped create this intellectual community. Melinda Takeuchi's warmth and generosity helped foster a latent love of teaching, and all of my research going forward will bear the mark of her guidance and inexhaustible patience. I am indebted to Steven Carter and James Reichert for teaching me the literary and scholarly canon.

I also thank the many friends and colleagues who strengthened this project with feedback and suggestions for avenues of research I had not even considered. A far-from-inclusive list must begin with my senpai Andre Haag, for his invariably insightful guidance as well as unflagging support, and Molly Valor for feedback on early versions of this manuscript. Other colleagues who provided criticism and support include Michael Wert, Hilary Snow, Kevin Mulholland, Jason Protass, Adrian Thieret, Nicholas Witkowski, Andre Deckrow, Allain Daigle, the members of the Midwest Japan Seminar, the members of the junior faculty writing group at the University of Wisconsin-Milwaukee, and members of the Association for Asian Performance, who have been supportive of this project from its very beginning. I am indebted to Yoshihara Yukari of Tsukuba University for her mentorship during my Fulbright fellowship, for organizing public talks during my fellowship, and for insights and guidance on my research. I am also grateful for fellowship support from the Center for 21st Century Studies. Director Richard Grusin and my cohort of fellows offered the invaluable gift of perspectives from fields far removed from my own bubble, and this project is stronger for their insights. For foundational guidance early in my academic career, my deep thanks to Maria Tymoczko, as well as the East Asian and Translation and Interpreting Studies faculty at the University of Massachusetts-Amherst.

x *Acknowledgments*

This project is also only possible through the generous institutional funding, both public and private, which allows research in the humanities to continue during these challenging times. This includes the Fulbright IIE fellowship, the Center for East Asian Studies at Stanford University, and Title VI National Resource Center. During times of increasing political, ideological, and financial pressure on the humanities, these and other institutions allow for the creation of new knowledge and pay back to society far more than they cost.

Finally, my deepest thanks to my family, without whom none of this work would have any meaning.

Introduction

No regrets! Struggle is the seed of happiness
That will cause liberty to bloom
The rights of the citizens must increase
To nourish the power of the people
If not, dynamite: *boom*![1]

So goes the song "Ballad of Dynamite" (ダイノマイト節) performed by politically active sōshi youth in the early and mid Meiji Period (1868–1912). The lyric's idealistic cry, couched within a threat of terrorism, encapsulates the imbricated virtue and violence motivating the political performance and music of the Freedom and People's Rights Movement in the years after the Meiji Restoration in 1868. Tsuchitori Toshiyuki (土取利行, 1950–) recorded "Ballad of Dynamite" for his 2013 album of popular political Meiji Period songs which highlight the role played by music in shaping newly introduced notions of rights and liberty. In its chronology of politically resistant tunes reaching from deep into the past and extending into years well after the Meiji Period, Tsuchitori's album tells a story in song of the Rights Movement which could serve as the soundtrack of the argument of this book.[2] My aim in the chapters which follow is to shed new light on the adoption of concepts that motivated political theaters of resistance for nearly a century and even now undergird the collective understanding of the Japanese nation. Grounded in the aftermath of the Restoration, this monograph tells the story of the crucial role that performance—specifically embodied memory—played in the translation and changing understanding of the imported Western concepts of "liberty" (自由 *jiyū*) and "revolution" (革命 *kakumei*).

The players in this story are not simply or even primarily the names that typically drive historical narratives of Japanese performance, translation, and political history for the century after the Restoration. Certainly, leading intellectuals such as Nakae Chōmin and Nakamura Keiu were central figures in introducing new political philosophy through their translations of the work of Rousseau and J.S. Mill, respectively. Likewise, leading political figures including Itagaki Taisuke

2 Introduction

and other elites in the oligarchy worked with various competing agendas to implement new policies, including the Meiji Constitution itself. In the common historical narrative, the translation of "liberty" and "revolution" was both a textual and political process overseen by these cultural and political elites. However, the Freedom and People's Rights Movement, the retroactive term for a broad swath of people and groups involved in post-Meiji Restoration cultural and political change, was also made up of disenfranchised youth and others who occupied some of the lowest rungs of society's hierarchy. This book shows how performers at all levels of society engaged in the process of determining how new political terms which articulated the relationship of the people to the state were understood in their new context. In other words, performance and performance texts enlisted elite and plebian circles in order to enact translation of new political philosophy. Indeed, the music and theater of the sōshi youth (sampled in Tsuchitori's album) proved popular across boundaries of class, status, and geography.

The "memory" part of the embodied memory in play in this book has two components. The historical moment between the Meiji Restoration and the adoption of the constitution was a key political, national, and cultural touchstone as future generations continued to contest the meaning of liberty and revolution in a Japanese context. The stories and performances of the Rights Movement inspired a century's worth of content in performance which in turn traced the translation history of liberty and revolution through performances in and about the Meiji Period in three key moments of political resistance in the development of modern Japan. The story begins during the Meiji Period itself in theater by members of the Freedom and People's Rights Movement in the 1870s and 1880s. It then rediscovers how the Meiji Period became a topic of performance in socialist plays that featured the aftermath of the Restoration by members of the Proletarian Theater Movement in the 1920s and '30s. Finally, it demonstrates how the Restoration Period became a lens through which to understand the post-war period in film and stage productions about early Meiji theater performed during the Occupation and postwar period after 1945. Thus, these performances represented new interpretations of a shared moment at the birth of the Japanese nation.

In addition to this function of memory for understanding the transformative role of the Restoration in later decades, the historiography of the Rights Movement was even framed as embodied memory at the very moment it played out on stage during the Restoration Period itself. In other words, before they became a subject in popular memory, Rights Movement dramatists themselves looked to the past to define their present. The first three Japanese translations of Shakespeare, for example, were Roman Plays. These scripts were doubly refracted historical imaginings: the memory of Rome seen through the lens of Elizabethan England transported to Meiji Japan. Dramatists and other performers looked to the history of Europe, Japan, and China to make sense of the momentous socio-political changes facing their new nation. As Marvin Carlson makes clear, the stage is a memory machine. In the case of the early Meiji Period, sometimes this machine produced "memories" which were brand new to both viewer and performer.

Introduction 3

By seeing performance as a vehicle of translation, I highlight the synergistic relationship of these two seemingly discrete activities. Throughout the century of theater and translation history in these chapters, theater and film professionals produced performances that directly engaged with the historiography of the Restoration in order to understand questions introduced through translation that were fundamental to the national project begun in 1868. This study argues that the role of modern Japanese political performance was more than just a means of agit-prop, but that it served as a tool for political movements to engage in translation in non-textual venues. The process of translation here is thus multivalent. It involves traditional interlingual translation of scripts, including translation into Japanese of Western language scripts; it also examines intra-lingual translations of history across time; and it takes as its subject inter-semiotic translations across genre and boundaries of mediation and liveness. In doing so it presents an example that troubles the traditional one-to-one correspondence of meaning. By examining the translation of liberty and revolution in multiple places and times with myriad ideological interests, this study sees translation as a many-to-many relationship. Further, by viewing translation as a performative process, it highlights the ways in which performance and translation served as a central hub for the generation, contestation, and propagation of foundational national narratives and concepts. Alternatively, viewing translation as a performative process allows for new ways to understand the emergence of modern Japanese theater. In contrast to conventional theater scholarship's focus on the development of Japanese theater from within the context of the theatrical world, I attempt to broaden our understanding of Japanese theater through its historical relationship to translation (literary and otherwise) and internationally informed domestic politics.

The historiography which served as the subject of this embodied memory proved conveniently pliable over time. The three periods of performance examined here, that of the Freedom and People's Rights Movement, the Proletarian Movement, and the Occupation/postwar period, span an entire century. As such, it is not surprising that theater practitioners in each period would espouse different political ideals. Yet in the 1920s and '30s, and again in the 1950s and '60s, performers looked to the Meiji Period and the Freedom and People's Rights Movement to understand existential challenges on a national scale. Key figures in the Proletarian Movement and the postwar period developed strands of thought that were first approached during the aftermath of the Meiji Restoration. Key questions included: What is the nature and role of revolution? Can the Meiji Restoration be thought of as a revolution that parallels 1789 France, 1688 England, and other European models? What is the relationship of the subject to the state? Where is the locus of authority in an ideal governing system? Fundamentally, to what extent should the translation/importation of foreign ideals be reshaped by domestic context, and to what extent should it be mobilized to restructure the same?

These questions over the nature of liberty and the locus of authority remain contested and relevant in our current context, perhaps even more so now than in most of our lifetimes. The recent global emergence of notions of "illiberal democracy", "authoritarian capitalism", and similar notions trouble the principles which

4 Introduction

undergird the foundation of post-Renaissance political ideals and ostensibly motivate the actions of the post-World War II international order. These anti-liberal ideologies which reduce liberalism to economic prosperity find themselves prominently featured in the current political and intellectual landscape in Japan as well. Iwata Atsushi, for example, argues that the very notion of liberty which was introduced in the Meiji Period was and remains incompatible with Japanese political and cultural tradition.[3] This resistance to the ideals of liberalism, and a re-framing of the very notion of "liberty" and "freedom", unsurprisingly emerged shortly after the fall of the Berlin Wall, the collapse of the Japanese economic bubble, and the death of Showa emperor at the end of the 1980s. The current re-negotiation of Japanese liberal democracy can be traced at least as far back as the 1990s, when calls for a "liberalist view of history" (自由主義史観) reframed notions of "liberalism". Right-wing figures argued that the Japanese should be "free" to view their history in ways that were not "masochistic"—in other words, citizens should feel at liberty to deny uncomfortable and inconvenient historical truths, particularly in relation to war guilt.

This reframing of the concept of liberalism in the 1990s coincided with the emergence of the new katakana word "*riberaru*" (リベラル) as a new translation word for "liberal". This new term, ostensibly a redundant translation word for the already widely used *jiyū* which had been the codified translation of "liberty" and "freedom" for well over a century since the Meiji Period, is more focused in meaning than *jiyū*. It is defined in large part by its antonym, "conservative" (保守), and it describes left-of-center political leanings which represents a smaller subset of the territory carved out from the existing lexical field of *jiyū*'s broader philosophical principles of human rights. In that sense, this new translation word disambiguates underlying assumptions of the relationship of citizen to government which *jiyū* put into play in the early Meiji Period (1868–1912).

The use of katakana in the rendering of this nuance of the notion of "liberal" accentuates the conceptual split between old and newer notions of liberalism by visually and conceptually separating notions (left-leaning politics from liberal democracy) that had previously been semantically and orthographically linked. As Chapter 1 of this book details, because the normative practice was for translators to use kanji compounds for new translation words in the Meiji Period, the use of katakana as an orthographic translation choice was unavailable to Nakamura Keiu in his translation of J.S. Mill's *On Liberty*. It was this text, and ultimately the word that he settled on in this translation, which served as the nucleus of the debate over the meaning of liberty in a Japanese context. It is thus significant that the term was partially re-translated in the 1990s when notions of liberty became newly contested. This new term *riberaru* does not carry any obvious etymological links to its Japanese root word. The katakana word, in contrast to the character compound jiyū, is an orthographic blank slate upon which a new lexical field was mapped without the interference of prior associations.

In the void left by this orthographic shift and obfuscation of the etymological familial links of the sign, the socio-political referent of liberty is as contested a term in contemporary Japan as it was in the Meiji Period. An article in the October

Introduction   5

8, 2017, Asashi News (朝日新聞) goes so far as to ask, "What Exactly Does 'Liberal' Mean?" ("「リベラル」って何？"), and it wrestles with the way that liberty is claimed as a motivating principle for a wide range of political parties and politicians. The article points out that the word is understood in a variety of ways (解釈は多様だ) and that *riberaru* cannot be easily defined. Like libertarians and left-wing liberals in the United States, the term is claimed by Japanese politicians of diametrically opposing viewpoints.[4] Edano Yukio of the Constitutional Democratic Party particularly crystallizes this dichotomy in words which recall the rhetoric of the 2016 US presidential election in calling for "a return via liberalism to the golden era of Japanese society" (リベラルによって日本が輝いていた時代の日本社会を取り戻す). In other words, it is a conservative call for liberalism using language which resonates with the current global right-wing nationalist movement, a movement which also entertains notions of illiberal democracy.

This serves as just one current example of the historically fraught nature, as far back as the coining of the word, of the concept of liberty in Japan outlined throughout the following chapters. The fact that *jiyū* has its roots in what we now have labeled the early Meiji Period's Freedom and People's Rights Movement should not suggest that the wide range of figures and groups that fall under this umbrella represented a unified resistance movement demanding a liberal democratic political agenda. The title of Tsuchitori's album cited at the beginning of this introduction speaks to the challenge of framing the ideals of Meiji Period performers of resistance. It carries the mixed Japanese and English title "明治の壮士演歌と革命歌: the song of civil rights movement at Meiji Period in Japan (1868–1926) by Toshi Tsuchitori [sic]".[5] The title suggests a close connection between the sōshi, the notion of *kakumei* (revolution), and Western notions of rights (in the sense that those rights are literally rendered in English). It seems to suggest that the Rights Movement was a movement for civil rights, but also it suggests some degree of ambivalence with this equivalence by displacing the explanation across a linguistic divide. In other words, how exactly we should think of the Rights Movement is a muddy question. Central figures such as Itagaki Taisuke, for instance, were as concerned with the creation of a constitution based on liberal principles as they were in pursuing a colonial, expansionist foreign policy. Performers such as Sudō Sadanori and Kawakami Otojirō (along with their audiences), were as concerned about domestic income inequality as they were with the encroachment of Western culture into Japanese life and victory in the Russo-Japanese War. The broad lexical field included in the word *jiyū* allowed the newly imported notion to be put into use in pursuit of all of these political ends and more. This heteroglossia is mirrored in fragmented Western political notions of the term. The United States Constitution, for example, houses competing Western conceptions of political representation, with direct election for the House of Representatives and election by state legislatures for the Senate. Thus, the status of liberty as a translation word has always been contested terrain, even in its source contexts. The century of performance rooted in the embodied memory of the Rights Movement around which this book

6   *Introduction*

revolves may be largely fuzzy and forgotten. Yet the implications of the Rights Movement–contested translation of liberty and the locus of authority over which the performances in the following chapters wrestled is very much relevant today.

The "embodied" quality of the embodied memory in this book is partly rooted in the fact that the stage was a key mode through which collective memory was created and shared. In the early twentieth century, liberty and revolution were sites of divisive conflict and rupture within the Japanese Proletarian Movement and prompted a newfound interest in the historiography of the Restoration. This enthusiasm manifested itself on stage in a genre of what I call "Restoration Plays" produced for the Proletarian stage that would later play an instrumental role in shaping post-war historical dramas made for film and television. This book looks at well-studied figures such as Kubo Sakae and Murayama Tomoyoshi, who were just two of many who produced examples of this genre. It also examines the work of Sasaki Takamaru, an often overlooked but influential translator, actor, director, and political activist who led both the Trunk Theater and the Avant-Garde Theater in the 1920s and '30s. In the postwar period, prominent film maker Inagaki Hiroshi, screenwriter Mishō Kingo, and playwright Fukuda Yoshiyuki picked up these threads in helping to understand the meaning of 1945 through the lens of 1868.

Throughout most of this nearly 100 years of Rights Movement performance, government and Occupation censorship policies dictated dramaturgical choices. To accommodate these challenges, performers actively sought alternative ways to embody the new notions of liberty and revolution. Could the ideologies of the present and future be performed using the conventions of the past? Alternatively, could the performance conventions of the past help to forge a path for a radically unstable future? What is at stake when actors modify, or even more drastically reject entirely, inherited performance conventions that had developed over centuries? In what ways can the performance traditions of the past be coupled with new modes to leverage liveness for political ends in an increasingly codified and mediated performance environment?

In other words, the "embodiment" of the embodied memory at play in this book is grounded in a specific kind of liveness in pursuit of a particular mode of inquiry. Meiji performers and their artistic descendants interested in the performance of resistance operated on the cutting edge of formal and legal challenges that had never before been addressed in Japan's long, sophisticated performance tradition. In the early Meiji Period, numerous barriers hindered politically motivated would-be thespians from co-opting the kabuki stage for political resistance. Yet mainstream kabuki was not the only available performance mode for political expression in the early and mid Meiji Period. The earliest translations of Shakespeare were drawing room dramas read collectively by friends or closet dramas read at home. The sōshi performances and songs of Rights Movement youths utilized street corners and informal *yose* performance halls. Performances of Kawakami Otojirō's song *Oppekepe* and his performances of the story of Rights Movement Leader Itagaki Taisuke's attempted assassination, which appear in Chapters 1 and 3, rely for their success upon audience engagement and unscripted violence by the audience and authorities. These performances utilize informal

Introduction 7

spaces and blur boundaries between audience and performer, and these formal properties are as central as the content to their political effectiveness. In later years, when Rights Movement performance became the subject of its own embodied memory, theaters of the Proletarian Movement strove for that same level of spontaneity and chance by seeking ways to dismantle the fourth wall and to make the audience a more active contributor to the performative event. The Trunk Theater and the "moveable theater" movement, for example, looked to dislocate performance from what was seen as the confining space of the formal stage.

Concern over the threat posed by codified, script-driven performances appeared in new performance genres, and even productions in highly scripted forms featured representations of spontaneous performance and violent demonstrations. In other words, spontaneity was valued in both form and content. Beginning in the 1930s, the threat of increased mediation to the political effectiveness of performance prompted formal experimentation such as the stage-film hybrid genre of the "talkie *rensa-geki*" which puts liveness and mediation in dialog and works to theorize the role of liveness in an increasingly mediatized world. The unscripted and confrontational nature of Rights Movement performance was foregrounded even in performances which espoused more traditional dramaturgies. Sasaki Takamaru's *The Secret Account from Tsukuba*, explored in Chapter 2 features communal performances on stage of Rights Movement songs while those performers are preparing for certain defeat to government forces in the Chichibu Incident. Chapter 5 features three postwar backstage dramas of the sōshi theater which foreground the way that Rights Movement theater and song eschews the restrictions of the fourth wall. The performances in this chapter suggest a political impact on society at large that the loss of this kind of dramaturgy through the codification of passive viewing of theater has upon the political potency of performance. In this sense, too, Tsuchitori's album mentioned previously provides a musical companion argument to that in this book. His song selection spans a range, from tunes that originated in the Edo Period, to "Oppekepe" which was recently called the "origin of rap music", to music of the early socialist movement in the twentieth century.[6] These songs, which in performance embraced the freewheeling nature of Meiji political performance, create an ideological and performative continuity across decades of change in political resistance. The political and artistic legacy of performance traced in this book thus finds a corresponding trajectory in political music.

Each of the three of pillars of Japanese culture at the center of this book—translation, performance, and politics—looms large in histories of the modern Japanese nation. Pairs of this triad undergird a strong body of scholarship, in both Japanese and English, which examines the political nature of translation in modern Japan, the performative element of politics in modern Japanese theater, and the role of performance in Japanese translation. Some of this work that *Staging the Resistance* is indebted to include Ayako Kano's *Acting Like a Woman in Modern Japan*, which explores the intersection of politics and early modern Japanese performance; Douglas Howland's *Translating the West*, which focuses on the political role of translation in modern Japan; and Indra Levy's *Sirens on*

8 *Introduction*

the Western Shore, which explores the role of performance in Meiji Period translation. Yet, *Staging the Resistance* is located at the node of all three of these components of Japanese culture. As such, it is the first work to highlight the prominent space occupied at the overlap in Japanese society of performance, translation, and politics. In not recognizing this intricately imbricated condition, we risk an incomplete understanding of all three pieces of this puzzle, and by extension the larger context in which they operate. For example, the Proletarian Theater Movement, indeed the Proletarian cultural movement generally, is now almost exclusively remembered as a theater of socialist realism and avant-garde performance (as seen in two of the most widely noted examples of the movement, *The Crab Cannery Boat* based on the novel by Kobayashi Takiji and *The Skeleton Dance* by Akita Ujaku). The tri-pronged approach in this book helps to highlight the degree to which political resistance for at least a century after the Restoration was deeply concerned with the question of Japan's past in relation to its present.

Organization and chapter outline

This monograph follows the performative history of the Rights Movement, and as such is roughly chronological in its narrative. Yet there is inevitably some degree of rushing ahead and moving back to fill in the blanks. Chapters 1 and 2 share some texts and together tell a narrative spanning from the Meiji to early Showa periods. Chapter 3 backtracks in time to trace within a single chapter a similar temporal trajectory in a series of performances from Meiji to Showa. Chapter 4 focuses on a relatively narrow time span in the 1930s. Chapter 5 focuses on postwar performances from the early Occupation to the 1960s. In other words, this book is organized both chronologically and thematically.

Chapter 1 examines the translation history of "liberty" in the Meiji Period. It is a curious fact that the first three translations of Shakespeare into Japanese were the Roman Plays—*Julius Caesar* twice, followed by *Coriolanus*. By eschewing entries in the canon such as *Hamlet* and *A Midsummernight's Dream* that are more highly praised for their dramaturgical and literary qualities, not to mention their appeal with audiences, these translation choices foreground the nexus of translation, politics, and performance in Meiji Japan. Theater was widely seen by Meiji intellectuals as a key measure of European modernity and as a tool with which to advance the consciousness of the Japanese nation. These three scripts in particular were valued as a way to think through the newly imported notion of liberty. This chapter sets these translations of Shakespeare in dialog with Kawakami Otojirō's hit song *Oppekepe*, demonstrating the impact of performance across class divides.

While the Japanese word for "liberty", *jiyū*, was first coined in the translation of John Stuart Mill's *On Liberty*, the translation was complicated on both ends of the translation process. The concept for the word "liberty", and its associated "liberal democracy", has undergone radical change throughout the centuries in Europe after its first incarnation in the Greek city states. The Athenian notion of democracy required the participation of all citizens in governance. Mill's notion, however, reflects a competing notion of liberal democracy that relies upon representation

Introduction   9

by the best and brightest of society. Yet, while these competing notions developed and changed over centuries, understanding of the original notion was complicated by the fact that both were introduced into Japan at the same time. The translation process was compounded by questions of how to incorporate these disparate notions of liberty with a Japanese intellectual tradition very different from the philosophical traditions of the West. This chapter argues that these debates broke down generally between two main political parties of the Freedom and People's Rights Movement, and that both of these concepts of liberty are at play in these translations. The translations of *Julius Caesar* and *Coriolanus* worked to understand what liberty might look like in a Japanese political environment. In what ways can the seemingly incompatible foreign notions of liberty be reconciled with the tradition of a domestic political philosophy? Perhaps more crucially, just as Shakespeare looked to classical history to understand his own present, these Japanese translations work to situate Japan within a global history which offers the promise of modernity.

While Chapter 1 focuses on the translation of liberty in the Meiji Period, Chapter 2 probes the emergence of the new notion of "revolution" (*kakumei*). The chapter begins in the Meiji Period and examines some of the same texts as in Chapter 1, but it also moves forward to the Proletarian Theater Movement of the 1920s and '30s. It looks to the members of the Trunk Theater and the Avant Garde Theater, particularly Sasaki Takamaru, who, although being the leader of both troupes, has been completely forgotten in the story of Japanese Proletarian Theater. This chapter introduces the genre of history plays I call "Restoration Plays", or plays by proletarian playwrights and troupes about the period surrounding the Meiji Restoration. Bringing these plays to light serves to expand our picture of the Proletarian Theater Movement as a theater of socialist realism, such as in the theater of Kobayashi Takiji, and theater informed by European avant-garde aesthetics such as that by Murayama Tomoyoshi.

In this prewar moment, the key conflict that these productions seek to resolve is actually *within* the movement itself rather than against the authorities. Debate raged within the Japanese Marxist community generally over the meaning of the Restoration in the Marxist trajectory of history. Is the Restoration a bourgeois revolution? If not, what does that mean for the Marxist movement in early twentieth-century Japan? At the center of this debate was the schism between the Yamakawaists and the Fukumotoists—a schism that split the political structure of the Japanese Communist movement as well as the theaters of the Proletarian Movement.

Chapter 3 looks to problematize narratives of modern Japanese theater history which highlight artistic rupture. The translations of Shakespeare in Chapters 1 and 2 represented one way in which liberty and revolution were translated through performance. Yet the elites involved in those translations—one of the *Ceasars* was translated by Tsubouchi Shōyō, a giant in literary and dramatic circles, and *Coriolanus* received a prologue from the great Ichikawa Danjurō IX—were not the only arbiters of how liberty would be translated into a Japanese context. The performance of the *sōshi*, the politically radical youth associated with the

10 *Introduction*

Freedom and People's Rights Movement, had very different notions of liberty and very different expectations from the forthcoming Meiji Constitution.

The performances of the sōshi introduced in this chapter differ markedly from the Shakespeare scripts in Chapters 1 and 2. While the drawing room dramas of *Caesar* and *Coriolanus* represent one kind of political theater—one that engages intellectually with political ideas—the performances of the sōshi were political theater of a very different kind. Yet their confrontational form of guerilla theater served as a mode of resistance. They share a performative mode I call "paratheatrical performance", a term I use to refer to a wide variety of informal performance practices that extend back in the Edo Period and earlier. One of the most famous events encapsulated in the sōshi performances was the attempted assassination of Rights Movement leader Itagaki Taisuke. The chapter closes by examining the Itagaki story in sōshi performance and the Restoration play *Itagaki Taisuke* by Sasaki Takamaru.

Chapter 4 changes pace to look at a very different kind of Restoration Play from that in Chapters 2 and 3. While the work of the Avant Garde Theater (前衛 座 *Zen'eiza*) in those earlier chapters looks back to the Restoration for stories of resistance that pre-figure the proletarian movement in Japan, other theaters in the movement used the past in ways that are perhaps less expected. Kubo Sakae and Murayama Tomoyoshi, both prominent figures in the Avant Garde Theater and Proletarian Theater Movement generally, each produced plays that featured the Shinsengumi, the pro-shogunate brute squad that fought in the last years of the Shogun's rule. These performances come in the context of an existential crisis of live performance in the face of an increasingly mediatized environment. While there had long been a performance genre called *rensa-geki* which mixed silent film and live performance, the advent of recorded sound in film represented a new challenge to live performance. Moves by film companies to reduce the numbers and salaries of *benshi* film narrators resulted in takeovers of theaters and violent strikes. Under similar threat from talkie films, theater practitioners, including Kubo and Murayama, worked to theorize a new place for liveness. A key question at play was whether and how performance could maintain its political effectiveness without the element of liveness which was so central to earlier modes of performance. This chapter focuses on Kubo's and Murayama's "talkie *rensa-geki*" productions about the Shinsengumi, as well as their companion stage and film productions about the group. The materials examined in this chapter demonstrate the variety of perspectives in the various theaters under the Proletarian umbrella, and the analysis works to complicate the very notion of performed resistance in the Proletarian Theater Movement.

The final chapter looks at the legacy of the sōshi in the immediate postwar period through the lens of film, stage, and novelistic representations of the Rights Movement–affiliated sōshi. Representations such as Inagaki Hiroshi's 1947 film *Sōshi gekijō*, Misho Kingō's 1957 *Oppekepe*, and Fukuda Yoshiyuki's 1963 play *Oppekepe* represent a conflicted view of the Rights Movement. On the one hand, they serve to re-think the Restoration and hold out a potential alternate history—one in which presumably the devastation wrought both in Japan and across

Introduction 11

Asia by Japan's militarism might not have occurred had the country followed the vision of these stalwart defenders of liberty. Yet these representations also portray the sōshi as being deeply flawed human beings whose personal values were in blatant opposition to their supposed political ideals. The case of the sōshi is a sharp contrast to the postwar legacy of the Shinsengumi touched on in Chapter 4. Although the Shinsengumi have widespread appeal and appear throughout popular culture even into contemporary Japan, the sōshi have disappeared from popular memory. This chapter argues that the re-appearance of Restoration Plays in the post-war period was an attempt to understand the disaster of 1945 through the lens of 1868.

Notes

1　悔やむまいぞや苦は楽の種　やがて自由の花が咲く
コクリミンプクゾウシンシテ　ミンリョクキョウヨウセ
若しもならなきゃダイナマイトどん
2　Tsuchitori Toshiyuki's (土取利行, 1950-) album is titled *Sōshi Enka and Revolution Songs of the Meiji Period* (明治の壮士演歌と革命歌). It included "The Ballad of Dynamite" along with 13 other Meiji Period political songs. The album is a rare instance of the once widely popular performance art and music of the sōshi receiving contemporary attention, and it wrestles as an artistic project with very similar threads that trace through this book.
3　Although this stance may seem reactionary and extreme, Iwata's book, titled *The Disease of Liberalism* (「リベラル」という病), and others expressing similar distaste for liberal values are not relegated to the cultural fringe. His book received high visibility marketing in mainstream newspapers. On a recent trip to Japan, I found Iwata's book and those of his ideological allies (or alternatively, books reacting with consternation to the prevalence of books like Iwata's) featured prominently on shelves and end caps in bookstores across Japan. This is hardly a rigorous sampling, but it does indicate that the questioning of liberal values occupies a space in mainstream, rather than fringe, cultural discourse. See Iwata Atsushi, *"Riberaru" to iu yamai*, Saizusha, 2018.
4　Hokkaido University professor Yoshida Tōru points out, for example, the post-Cold War ideological dissonance between social liberalism and economic liberalism, a divide that he sees as also manifesting in the United States and Europe.
5　The Japanese translates as "Sōshi and revolutionary songs of Meiji". Thus, the album title is not just confusing in its dates for the Meiji Period (which ended in 1912, not 1926 as suggested by the English), it is also redundant in naming Meiji in both the Japanese and English. It is thus difficult to decipher if the English is meant to supplement the Japanese as a subtitle or to loosely translate the Japanese.
6　Nagamine Shigetoshi, *Oppekepebushi to Meiji* (Tōkyō: Bungei Shunjū, 2018).

1 Weaponizing Meiji liberty

The Freedom and People's Rights Movement (自由民権運動), a retroactive label applied to a broad spectrum of groups and individuals working in resistance to the Meiji oligarchy to define the modern nation in the wake of the Meiji Restoration, has been largely forgotten in the popular imagination of the early Meiji Period. Yet the Rights Movement, with all its ideologically eclectic self-contradictions, is largely responsible for introducing the concept now encompassed with the Japanese term *jiyū* ("liberty", alternatively "freedom") which defines the location of sovereignty and the relationship of the subject to the state in a modern democratic political system. For citizens of the newly emergent Japanese nation, their investment in the future empowered the European concept of liberty with ideological work beyond its role in political philosophy. It did more than describe a theory of social justice at the base of a system of government built on an assumption of equality. Liberty also served as a metonym for modernity, Westernization, and an attendant national power towards which citizens of the new nation strived. The term was thus the subject of keen interest not just to Rights Movement figures at all strata of society, but also to the nation as a whole. Its popularity beyond the relatively limited number of the politically attuned is highlighted by the way that "*jiyū*" became a buzzword which appeared on marketing campaigns for a wide range of commercial products, including branding for alcoholic beverages. In other words, the new notion of liberty was not simply an esoteric concept of interest to elite scholars of foreign languages and law (although it was certainly that), but rather appealed to a broad range of citizens, all in very different ways.

Myriad implications of the notion of liberty in Japan led to a contested translation process—one in which various terms were in play before the translation pair of "liberty/freedom = *jiyū*" became codified in everyday usage and continued in the mapping of the semantic field of the term even after the translation pair became settled. On the source language side of the translation, the term "liberty" (and its related term "democracy") was a contested philosophical concept in its own European context. Yet as a synecdoche for modernity, the translation of *jiyū* took on connotations with existential stakes which were tied to notions of progress that simultaneously were in concert and competition with nationalist goals of civilization and enlightenment. The translation of liberty into Japanese, then, is not a linear process of one to one (source word to target word) but rather of many to many, with competing notions of the term being translated separately into Japanese target texts representing competing expectations and uses of the term *jiyū*.

Nakamura Keiū's translation of Mill's *On Liberty* and Nakae Chōmin's translation of Rousseau's *Social Contract* introduced the character compound and the central philosophical tenets that are used now as the standard translation and definitions of "liberty" and "freedom". As such, they played a central role in the introduction of liberty in the Meiji Period. Yet, while scholarship on the introduction of Western political theory into Japan in the Meiji Period generally focuses on the translation of written texts in (often) erudite tomes by educated men of status like Nakamura and Chōmin, this chapter makes the case that the meaning of *jiyū* was also negotiated through performance texts for audiences both educated and not and for both high and low classes. Specifically, this chapter brings together the first three translations of Shakespeare into Japanese—texts which were explicitly about the political Meiji context and which also placed Japan within a modern and Western historical narrative—into dialog with the *sōshi* theater of Kawakami Otojirō. These performance texts are located at the center of the contested discourse over the locus of authority in the new modern state. Yet a newfound appreciation of the cultural power of performance, along with an attention to the dangers of performance to existing power structures, led to policies which prevented these discussions from being performed in large scale, mainstream performance spaces. Diplomatic missions to Europe shortly after the establishment of the Meiji government, the most famous being the Iwakura Mission in 1871, brought back a heightened appreciation of and methods for controlling political discourses, as well as highlighting the potentiality of theater as a venue for disseminating the official agenda of nation building. As a result, the oligarchy made concerted efforts to co-opt the theater, granting greater official sanction to kabuki actors than they had ever known, and having the emperor himself attend a kabuki production in 1887. In addition, through censorship laws enacted in 1875 and 1880, the state exerted greater control over performance as part of the "Occidental techniques, Oriental morals" policy. Westernization of theatrical space and tools was part and parcel of this effort. Above all, the state pushed the kabuki theater to project messages that supported their agenda.[1]

Thus, government policies effectively stymied the presentation of oppositional political views in traditional, mainstream theatrical spaces. In addition, while the translation of Western works spurred radical innovations in prose and poetry, the Japanese stage in early Meiji generally resisted translated theater.[2] Yet all of this does not mean that Japanese performance lacked innovation in the decades after 1868 or that discussion of politics was absent from the Meiji performance world. However, it does require looking to alternative performance spaces for examples of oppositional political performance and translated theater in the 1870s and 1880s. Hence, this chapter examines performances of the *sōshi* (politically motivated young toughs) and the first Japanese translations of Shakespeare's Roman Plays as examples of the use of alternative spaces for the performance of political messages.

14 *Weaponizing Meiji liberty*

Defining liberty

A fundamental point of contention between the two main factions of the Freedom and People's Rights Movement stems from their views of whether the sovereignty of the nation resided in the populace or in the authority of the government.[3] Ideas of popular sovereignty and individual freedom originating in ancient Greece arrived in Japan through a circuitous route, having been significantly transformed along the way. In her study of nineteenth-century political discourse, Alexandra Lianeri tracks the development of English conceptions of liberal democracy through the translation of the term "democracy" from ancient Greek sources, primarily Thucydides' *History*. Thucydides quotes a speech by Pericles which characterizes Athenian democracy as being founded upon principles that include the following: the government is in the hands of the many; all citizens are equal participants in the decision-making process; and all citizens are expected to be engaged with and knowledgeable about the political issues of the day. Indeed, those who do not keep themselves up on the issues are "good for nothing".[4]

These fairly straightforward criteria which locate sovereignty in the participation of each and every citizen undergo a series of shifts, additions, and elisions in their English translations, and Lianeri pegs these transformations to contemporary consensuses and deliberations over the nature of liberal democracy. Seventeenth- and eighteenth-century thinkers feared rule by the people as a "menace to social order and coherence" that "threaten[ed] prosperity and cultural development".[5] Thomas Hobbes translated Thucydides' *History* in 1629, a time when the monarch occupied a central and unifying place in government. Given this context and Hobbes's pessimistic view of the unchecked individual, it is not surprising that his translation promoted the concept of a ruling class:

> The essence of democracy in this translation is found not in the power of the people but in the fact that government has regard to the multitude . . . that is, it has consideration for the majority in the administration of social issues. In other words, people do not govern themselves, but their views and interests are taken into account by the government.[6]

Thus, Hobbes's translation substantiates his understanding of government as an institution into which people freely enter and to which they surrender their sovereignty. Reprinted three times from the seventeenth to the mid-eighteenth century, Hobbes's translation partially informed the principles of English liberal democracy as outlined by Jeremy Bentham and J.S. Mill. These two, and the Utilitarians generally, argued for a definition of liberty that allowed for individual freedom. They saw liberal democracy as antithetical to rule by the masses and feared the tyranny of the majority.

Continuing in this vein, George Grote translated extensive passages of Thucydides' *History* in his *History of Greece* (1846–56), and his translation worked to restore some acceptability for the concept of democracy among Utilitarians by eliding the concept of equality of the citizen participants. Unlike the historical Greek context in which all citizens are equal parties in governing, and

Weaponizing Meiji liberty 15

unlike Hobbes's endorsement of an aristocracy, the Utilitarian Mill embraced Grote's translation because of the way it characterized democracy as including a divide between the rulers and the ruled. While this notion of a ruling class is similar to an aristocracy, Mill (and Grote's translation of *History*) endorses a ruling class that can be chosen from among "only those citizens of 'real worth'", and thus differed from an aristocracy by changing the qualifications for membership from pedigree to ability. In theory, this opened up participation to all classes of individuals.[7] These developments, which simultaneously allowed for popular representation but built in protections against the tyranny of the masses, were influential in popularizing and legitimizing the concept of democracy in England. Stripped of its requirement for widespread social equality, democracy enjoyed a much more friendly reception in nineteenth-century England than it had previously.

Further, while Hobbes envisioned the rulers as taking the concerns of the many into account, by the nineteenth century there was a growing feeling that there were conflicting interests between the many and the few. In this context, Mill argued that a democratic government's *aim* (but, significantly, not its basis of legitimacy) was to satisfy the needs of the many. These divisions between the many and few, the rulers and the ruled, were absent from the source text but markedly present in discussions of political theory in nineteenth-century England. Such discussions had direct relevance to the development of political discourse in Meiji Japan, since ideas of liberal democracy developed by such writers as Mill and Hobbes were introduced through sources that included Nakamura Keiu's translation of Mills's *On Liberty* (1871) and Fukuzawa Yukichi's *Conditions of the West* (1866–1870).[8] Euro-American political theory and practice contemporary to the Restoration revealed traces, like geologic layers, of these competing visions of liberal democracy.[9] However, the early Meiji thinkers simultaneously encountered iterations of these concepts from a variety of historical contexts, a fact that blurred the historicity of the European concepts behind the words.[10]

Understanding and acceptance of Western concepts of democracy and liberty were also complicated by conditions in the target culture, as has been examined by Yanabu Akira in his 1976 work *What is Translation—Japanese and the Culture of Translation* (翻訳とはなにか ― 日本語と翻訳文化). Yanabu notes that Japanese reception of liberal democratic ideals faced linguistic challenges that were only partially related to the source-culture understandings of the term. The range of words used to translate "liberty" and "liberal politics" in the early Meiji Period included 自主 (*jishu*), 自在 (*jizai*), 不羈 (*fuki*), 寛弘 (*kankō*), and even 我儘 (*wagamama*).[11,12] Ultimately, Nakamura's translation of *On Liberty* as *Jiyū no ri* helped to cement the adoption of *jiyū* as the established equivalent word, but Yanabu notes that Nakamura expressed ambivalence about this translation choice. Yanabu argues that the etymology and cultural history of the word *jiyū* actually obscured the source word's meaning for Japanese readers. In fact, *jiyū* initially had more negative connotations than positive: it meant something like "incorrigible" and was usually used to describe someone with a difficult personality. When it had positive connotations, it tended to be within religious contexts.[13]

16   *Weaponizing Meiji liberty*

Yanabu's analysis adds another twist to the story of the evolution of the idea of liberal democracy in Japan: not only did it evolve within the English context from its Greek roots, and not only were the various historical understandings of the term imported in a wholesale fashion into Japan, but also the use of an established word (as opposed to a neologism, calque, or the like) as a translation for "liberty" invited Japanese writers and readers to graft a wide range of Japanese and Confucian ideas onto the concept. Yanabu notes that the word *jiyū* became something of a buzzword and was adopted in a wide range of contexts. Indeed, the Freedom and People's Rights Movement was less of a united movement in pursuit of political representation (although some members of the group agitated for this), than it was a coalition of anti-oligarchy groups. In other words, *jiyū* was interpreted broadly and co-opted for causes not necessarily focused on individual rights and political representation.

Douglas Howland adds to our understanding of the adoption of the concept of liberty in Meiji Japan.[14] Like Lianeri, he notes the split in European understanding of the concept of liberty between an individual's freedom from arbitrary government interference such as Hobbes argued for ("negative freedom"), and political enfranchisement as nominally argued for by Mill ("positive freedom").[15] Adoption of popular representation, even when limited to the elites as Mill proposed, faced resistance from many in the Meiji intelligentsia. Among other issues, many were uncomfortable with the idea of "positive freedom", because it ran contrary to the Neoconfucian concept of duty as they understood it. They were more sympathetic to a Hobbesian view of democracy, or "negative freedom", where the law acted as a check upon unrestricted personal freedoms that would infringe upon the freedom of the people as a whole.

These are just some of the factors that played a role in creating plural understandings of political enfranchisement in Meiji Japan, and so it is perhaps not surprising that the Freedom and People's Rights Movement comprised an umbrella group for a wide range of smaller political parties, rather than a highly focused and disciplined opposition party. Some of the groups were more populist in nature and engaged in violent protest; some were highly enfranchised intelligentsia; and some favored an expansionist military policy and had no obvious sympathies with popular political empowerment at all.

These internal divisions were very clearly illustrated in the rift that emerged in 1881 between Itagaki Taisuke (1837–1919), leader of the Liberal Party (*Jiyūtō*), and Ōkuma Shigenobu (1838–1922), leader of the Constitutional Reform Party (*Rikken Kaishintō*). While both were "progressive" in some sense, their views of political enfranchisement reflected the class differences of their respective constituencies. The Liberal Party represented large groups of the unenfranchised and pressed for a constitution that would place sovereignty in the hands of the people—a position that went significantly beyond those of most contemporary Western political philosophers. The Constitutional Reform Party represented the urban elite who were moderately liberal but were disturbed by the more radical Liberal Party partisans. Rather than all citizens having a direct voice in their government, the Constitutional Reform Party argued for sovereignty being shared by the emperor and the people's representatives in a British manner.[16]

Romanized Meiji, Meiji-ized Rome

One example where this heterogeneous semantic field of the new term *jiyū* is particularly prominent is in the adoption of Shakespeare into Meiji Japan. Shakespeare, as a key cultural marker of English (and by extension European) modernity, served as a popular lens through which to understand Japan's hoped-for future. The popularity of Shakespeare among early Meiji thinkers and writers of belles-lettres is neither surprising nor unique to late nineteenth-century Japan, yet the choice of texts for the first full translations into Japanese is notable. While there were many partial translations and adaptations of many of the more popularly and critically acclaimed plays, it was *Julius Caesar* (twice within one year in 1883 and 1884 by different translators) that became the first full translations of Shakespeare into Japanese.[17] This was followed by *Coriolanus* (1888), highlighting an interest in the Roman Plays that is far greater than the level of popular and critical acclaim typically enjoyed by those plays. Yet it is the Roman Plays, as Robert Luongo points out, that are Shakespeare's most overtly political and which in unmasked ways grapple with the relationship of the people to the state. They ask what liberty looks like in actual practice, and they explore what it means to change a government when the people are denied liberty. The Meiji translations of these plays make it clear that this facet of these plays was the primary source of interest in these texts.

To pursue this line of inquiry, these translations apply a temporally, spatially, and culturally distant history to explain the local contemporary political situation in Meiji Japan between the Restoration and the adoption of the Meiji Constitution. In other words, these translated texts are not simply reflections from the source culture. Taken as a group, these translations suggest a range of formal possibilities in negotiating the interaction of Western and Japanese dramaturgy and political philosophy. These scripts, and the concept of liberty which they were meant to explicate, were introduced from a source culture in which liberty encompassed competing conceptualizations and infused into a target culture context with a long received tradition of its own that was very different from the theatrical and political makeup of the source texts.

Julius Caesar in particular is an appropriate vehicle for thinking through these competing conceptualizations of liberty for reasons that go beyond its political content. The source play's structure is ambiguous and self-contradictory even before its meaning is complicated through the production of a target text via the dislocating process of translation. Shakespeare wrote the play at the tail end of his history plays and just before *Hamlet* and the other great tragedies, and the text possesses qualities of both genres. One clear example of this split is that, in its publication in the first folio in 1623, it is listed in the table of contents with the tragedies but is titled *The Life and Death of Julius Caesar*, a title that resembles many of the histories and none of the tragedies. The title in the text in the first folio, however, does not match its listing in the table of contents. Rather, it reads the way it has now been standardized as *The Tragedy of Julius Caesar*. Reflecting this title discrepancy, the text does not easily conform to the structural

18 *Weaponizing Meiji liberty*

conventions of the Greek tragedy as adhered to in Elizabethan theater, but neither is it a typical history play. Because of the relatively free-wheeling nature of Elizabethan performance, it is certainly possible that the play may have been performed under both titles during Shakespeare's lifetime, and that it may have seen iterations that fit into both genres. In short, this source text remains problematic from a generic perspective.

The ambiguous nature of the drama has clear and meaningful ramifications for both productions and translations because directors and translators have the opportunity to come down on one side or the other of the genre question. If the text is to be treated as a tragedy (as it usually is in performance), steps must be taken to resolve the fact that it lacks a clear tragic hero in the Aristotelian sense. Yet the ambiguous tragic hero question is a key component of the play's appeal, and it motivated nineteenth-century interest in *Caesar*. Productions of the play and scholarship on the text have a long history of treating it as a tragedy and choosing a tragic hero. Schlegel, for example, sees Brutus as the tragic hero. Yet common as this practice is, the text itself does not easily support either choice.

Often, this interest in choosing a tragic hero is motivated by a drive to see current events and people in not-so-thinly disguised analogs of those in the play. The famous Orson Wells production in 1937, for example, set the play in fascist Italy. John Wilkes Booth compared himself to Brutus after assassinating Abraham Lincoln.[18] In a more recent example, the Public Theater's Shakespeare in the Park production of *Caesar* after the 2016 presidential election stirred controversy with a production that placed a Donald Trump–like figure in the role of Caesar. Yet as easily as this play maps over contemporary events and people from almost any time period and location, Shakespeare seems to have been doing something different (or to have masked his contemporary critique in more subtle ways than subsequent productions often have). While numerous scholars have attempted to locate political analogs among Shakespeare's contemporaries, no critical consensus has emerged as to any of the possible Elizabethan Caesars or Brutuses. Nevertheless, productions such as Wells' and the Public Theater's, which set the play within a new political context, have appeared frequently throughout the play's production history.

All three of the translations examined here disassociate the source plays from both the purported original context in ancient Rome and the performative context of Elizabethan England. Kawashima Keizō's translation does not use his characters as transparent ciphers for contemporary figures, but rather uses Caesar and Brutus as metonymic examples of other historical moments. In addition to his introduction described later, the cover of the published edition of his translation features a mounted nineteenth-century colonial soldier in the midst of battle, complete with pith hat and firearms (Figure 1.1). Shōyō cites his own contemporary politics as the primary motivating factor in his choice of text.[19] Like the paratextual material in Shōyō's *Caesar*, Itakura's *Coriolanus* re-locates the play within a Japanese context in a way that complements its re-writing in the format of *jōruri/ kabuki* performance text.[20] While these texts take very different strategies to dislocate the source text, all three explicitly engage with their contemporary moment.

Weaponizing Meiji liberty 19

Figure 1.1 The final battle at Philipi as rendered in the book publication of Kawashima Keizō's translation of *Julius Caesar*

Most importantly, divorced from a performative tradition of Aristotelean tragedy, all three of these texts see their plays as a form of historiography into which the translators seek to insert the Japanese story. In short, at play in these three translations are dual notions of liberty in the source culture and a received political philosophical tradition all placing Japan within a modernizing and Western stream of history using textual artifacts of Japanese and Western theatrical traditions.

Liberty's Sword, Liberty's Scourge, and the Rise and Fall of Rome

Tsubouchi Shōyō published his translation of *Caesar* in 1884 under the title *The Amazing Story of Caesar: The Legacy of the Sharpness of Liberty's Sword* (*Jiyū no tachi nagori no kireaji: Shiizaru kidan*, 自由太刀余波鋭鋒：該撒奇談)—a title which reflects his stated desire to write a translation that was more appealing to his audience and far more fleshed out than its minimalistic source text. With a preface written in Sino-Japanese (*kanbun*) by Yoda Hyakusen (Yoda Gakkai), as well as Shōyō's own contextual commentary that frames the text (a passage which

20 Weaponizing Meiji liberty

does not appear in the source text), *Liberty's Sword* employs a translation strategy that linguistically naturalizes the text and deploys Japanese points of reference. The play is translated in the popular jōruri style, the names are written in Chinese characters, and the paratextual material draws a visual parallel between the subject matter of the play and the contemporary Japanese political scene. These localizing linguistic and paratextual translation choices manifest in the text itself.

Yoda Hyakusen's preface frames the text as an alternative form of historiography. *Caesar*, he argues, is akin to the Chinese classic *The Romance of the Three Kingdoms* in that they work to blur the boundary between fictional narrative and the writing of history. The former, he argues, enhances the historical record in ways that standard histories alone cannot. By this view, fictional narrative does not exist in an ahistorical environment, and neither does it operate in a de-politicized context. Yoda Hyakusen thus sees Shōyō's translation as a way to blend histories and also Shakespeare's view of liberty together with Confucian political philosophy. At the core of Shōyō's approach to this text is an attempt to cast Brutus in the role of the protagonist versus the antagonist Caesar. Shōyō's preamble leads with a description of the general collapse of the political order when evil leaders take over, and then smoothly transitions into a description of Caesar himself. In introducing the scene in this way, Shōyō leads the reader to understand Caesar as representative of these evil leaders. Shōyō also goes out of his way to highlight Brutus's virtues. In Act V (in the original) after the death of Brutus, Antony delivers a magnanimous eulogy to his fallen foe:

> This was the noblest Roman of them all:
> All the conspirators, save only he,
> Did that they did in envy of great Caesar;
> He only, in a general-honest thought
> And common good to all, made one of them.
> His life was gentle; and the elements
> So mix'd in him that Nature might stand up
> And say to all the world, "This was a man!"
> (Act 5, Scene 5)[21]

As flowery as this eulogy is, Shōyō expands upon the praise given to Brutus in the original and makes it more specific. His eulogy praises Brutus as the one conspirator among 30 who was willing to sacrifice himself for greater liberty for all (*zenpan no jiyū no tame*) and the benefit of the country (*kokka no rifuku*). This stands in stark contrast to the evil leaders described in Shōyō's introduction (including, by suggestion, Caesar) who pursue policies for self-benefit (*shiri*). Although the conspirators are ultimately unsuccessful, Shōyō leads the audience to see Brutus as the protagonist of his translated text.

Establishing Brutus as a tragic hero is central to Shōyō's working through the notion of liberty that pits the rule by the many against the rule by the most deserving. Beginning with the title, which inserts "*jiyū*" in the target text when none is in the source, to the final line, which speaks about the "sword of liberty", Shōyō frames the motivations of the conspirators in terms of a fight for liberty.

Weaponizing Meiji liberty 21

There are far more instances of the word "*jiyū*" in the target text than uses of the words "freedom" and "liberty" in the source.[22] Further, Shōyō inserts the word "*kyōwakoku*" (republic) at times to underscore the democratic ideals he sees in the text. One example is when Brutus gives his speech to the people of Rome to justify the assassination and delivers the famous line:

> If then that friend demand
> why Brutus rose against Caesar, this is my answer:
> Not that I loved Caesar less, but that I loved
> Rome more.

Shōyō renders this in Japanese as:

> 誠と舞妻多須は獅威差を、愛慕なすこと薄きにあらねど、偏に*羅馬の共和国*を、愛する心のそのそれにもまして、尚一層厚きが故なり。。。。但しは稀稀世の豪傑たる獅威差が、露の命は脆くとも、*羅馬の共和*は大磐石、子々孫々に傳わるを、幸福なりと思わるるや。[23]

(Shakespeare and Tsubouchi 1884, 164)

A back translation of Shōyō's rendering would read something like:

> It is not that my love for Caesar was lacking, but that my love for the Roman Republic [*kyōwakoku*] was even greater . . . but though the magnificent Caesar's life was as fragile as dew, if the Roman Republic [*kyōwa*] remained solid as stone for succeeding generations, wouldn't he think that this is good fortune?[24]

The threat of Caesar, then, is to the specific form of government that Brutus sees as essential to the idea of Rome. It is republicanism versus imperialism rather than a sense of patriotism versus treason.

The Rise and Fall of Rome

Kawashima Keizō's translation of *Julius Caesar*, titled *The Rise and Fall of Rome* (*Rōma seisuikan*, 羅馬盛衰鑒, 1883), came out just before Tsubouchi Shōyō's and contrasts with *Liberty's Sword* in a number of key ways. While Kawashima, like Shōyō, brings the text out of its original context, Kawashima writes the text more explicitly into a modern milieu and a larger Western historiography. His translation strategy also contrasts with Shōyō's in that he employs a much greater degree of formal equivalence both in the text itself and in the text type into which he renders the language. In other words, comprehension errors aside, Kawashima's text reads more closely like Shakespeare's dialog and is couched in the format of a Western script.

Although it was the first full translation of Shakespeare into Japanese, being serialized from February 16 to April 11, 1883, it has been brushed aside in favor of the much more popular translation by the much more famous Shōyō. For instance,

22 *Weaponizing Meiji liberty*

Furuhara Yoshiaki notes that the book version of *Liberty's Sword* was published before the book version of *The Rise and Fall of Rome* (1884 and 1886, respectively) and states that Shōyō's version was the first full translation of *Caesar*.[25] An otherwise comprehensive chronological listing of Shakespeare translations in *Nihon Sheikusupia sōran* seemingly uses the same criteria in listing Shōyō's translation first. Other critics such as Kaieda Susumu disparage the translation by pointing to Kawashima's limited resources: a Webster's dictionary, a German translation of the text, and a missionary whom he happened to know were apparently the only references available to him. Such scholars focus primarily on the errors in Kawashima's translation.[26] Additionally, even at the time of its publication, a review of Shōyō's translation in the *Yomiuri Shinbun* led with the headline "A First Translation in Japan".[27] In short, the critical consensus has never favored Kawashima's translation. Whatever the linguistic failings of the text, though, the translation occupies an important position within its contemporary political milieu that is central to this study.

Kawashima's text presents a fundamentally different take on *Caesar* than that of Shōyō's. While his text also resituates the text and the reader, it does so in very different ways. For example, he foreignizes his translation in ways that Shōyō does not—names are rendered in katakana and the form of the script is not naturalized into an established Japanese theatrical tradition as is *Liberty's Sword*. To use the spatial analogies that are often employed to locate a translator or translation vis-à-vis the source and target texts and cultures, Kawashima's translation situates the text away from the target culture and near the source culture. The most dramatic shift away from the source context comes not in the text itself but in the paratext of the published translation. In the images accompanying Kawashima's version, the characters are located in a nineteenth-century setting—in a modern Rome, at the beginning of the text, and later in the text with battles rendered as nineteenth-century warfare. The cover features an officer dressed in modern nineteenth-century attire; the pages of images at the front of the book include one of a fountain in a nineteenth century Rome; and the final climactic battle is portrayed as nineteenth-century warfare. Accompanying this rendering, the techniques used to create the images in these two *Caesar* translations reflect the difference in their content. While *Liberty's Sword* renders its images using a traditional woodblock print, *Rise and Fall* uses a modern form of image production. Yet, despite their obvious differences, Kawashima's text was received in a similarly politicized context as *Liberty's Sword*. It was serialized in *Nihon rikkenseitō shinbun* precisely because of the timely nature of the plot (coincidentally, at the same time that Kawakami Otojirō worked there). The editors of the paper saw the story as one of the fall of corrupt governments, a story that fits their political ideology.[28]

Rise and Fall also contrasts with *Liberty's Sword* in its approach to the task of translation. While Shōyō took considerable creative license in rendering his text, at least in the text itself Kawashima generally attempted to adhere to a relatively strict standard of formal equivalence.[29] Yet even in the text, differences of interpretation emerge. Shōyō assigns the title of *daisōsai* to Caesar (rendering the English "consul" into the term that was used for the position of the head of the Meiji oligarchy), setting the translation within a political context. By contrast, Kawashima sets his translation in a military context by assigning Caesar the title of *gensui* (元帥) or *daigensui*, meaning "general" (the term *gensui* is close in meaning to the word "shogun"). Further, whereas Shōyō inserts the word *kyōwakoku* into his translation and increases the number of occurrences of the term *jiyū* over the frequency of the terms "liberty" and "freedom" in the source text, Kawashima does not employ the word *kyōwakoku* at all, and actually decreases the frequency of the word *jiyū* over the corresponding words in the source text. There is more to this translation, then, than is suggested by scholars who criticize it as nothing more than a dictionary exercise.

In fact, a closer examination of the term *jiyū* in Kawashima's translation shows that the text inscribes a different set of meanings onto the word than does Shōyō's text. Immediately following the assassination of Caesar, Cinna and Cassius utter the following lines in the original:

> CINNA: Liberty! Freedom! Tyranny is dead!
> Run hence, proclaim, cry it about the streets.
> CASSIUS: Come to the common pulpits, and cry out
> 'Liberty, freedom, and enfranchisement!'

Kawashima renders this as:

> 支：嗚呼、自由よ自由よ壓制家は斃れたり
> 軻：誰か演壇に上りて壓制の區域は免れたりと呼ばれよ[30]

This back translates as:

> CINNA: Hurrah! Liberty! Liberty! The tyrant has fallen!
> CASSIUS: Let someone go to the rostrums and shout out that we have been spared from the realm of oppression.

In this sequence in the original, liberty means both freedom from tyranny (negative freedom) according to Cinna as well as enfranchisement (with the possible connotation of positive freedom) according to Cassius. While Shōyō conveys both of these lines in full, Kawashima leaves out Cassius's call for enfranchisement. Not only does this elide any connotation of rule by the people, but it also works to qualify Cinna's call for *jiyū*. In other words, Kawashima's Cassius offers up a reserved response to the assassination and frames the political change within terms of despotic and benevolent rule.

Kawashima, like Shōyō, values the text in large part as a form of historiography. During its initial serialization in *Nihon rikkenseitō shinbun*, the translation was titled *The Drama of Julius Caesar* (*Jūriasu Shiizaru no gikyoku* ジュリアスシーザーの戯曲), but when republished as a book it was retitled *The Rise and Fall of Rome: Shakespeare's Drama* (*Rōma seisuikan: Sheikusupia gikyoku* 羅馬盛衰鑒:沙吉比亜戯曲). While the text retains the form of a theatrical script, it was never actually performed, and there is no indication that Kawashima intended

24 *Weaponizing Meiji liberty*

it to be. Indeed, the orality of the source text is muted in the prose translation compared with Shōyō's rendering the text in meter. In other words, Kawashima seems to see this text as more historiography than performance. To the extent that this is a dramatic script, the space for the "performance" of this text was within the reader's mind, or perhaps the room in which it was quietly read. This is a marked difference from the group readings to which Shōyō's translation availed itself. Such an approach eschews the performance of the drama in favor of the textual recounting of history. Yet they share the fact that neither appeared on a public stage upon their publication.

Further, while Shōyō's (and Itakura's discussed later) title borrows from the titles of popular Chinese historical fiction, Kawashima's title resonates with the Western historiography *Rōma seisuiki*, the Japanese title given to Montesquieu's *Considerations on the Causes of the Grandeur and Decadence of the Romans* (1734), translated in a three-volume set just three years before *Rise and Fall*.[31] The writing of history was a contested activity at this time, splitting down lines that reflected views of political reforms generally and jiyū specifically.[32] Montesquieu's text, written during Louis XIV's reign, speaks to a flowering of culture and also argues for the inevitable necessity of a powerful central state to maintain a large and successful nation—both goals that were closely aligned with the agenda of the Meiji government. Kawashima's preface confirms this, situating the disorder of Rome at the time of the play as one of many conflicts in Western history between the establishment (represented by Caesar) and agents of change (represented by Brutus). Other examples he gives include King George III and the American colonies, the Bourbons and the Jacobins, the Romanovs and the anarchists, Charles I and Oliver Cromwell, and most curiously, Pope Leo X and Martin Luther. In contrast with the preface of *Liberty's Sword*, Kawashima also frames his translation as a way to write history, but his history is more deliberately situated within the source-culture.

Liberty's Scourge

In contrast to *Caesar*, Shakespeare's *Coriolanus* has somewhat less structural and formal ambiguity. It was, after all, written very late in Shakespeare's career, after he had mastered the Elizabethan/Aristotelean tragic model. It also contrasts with *Caesar* and other Shakespeare plays, which tend to render the crowd as highly suspect and granted rather little in the way of agency. The commoners in *Coriolanus* stand out in contrast, with specific members of the crowd having individual names and agency in the plot in ways that they do not in many of Shakespeare's earlier works. This has clear implications for the kind of liberty at play in the title.

Itakura Kōtaro published his translation of *Coriolanus* in Meiji 21 (1888), just a few years after Shōyō's and Kawashima's translations (Figure 1.2). Like Kawashima, Itakura is an obscure figure, and this forgotten text is his only contribution to the Meiji cultural and political landscape. Itakura was only a 15-year-old

Weaponizing Meiji liberty 25

Figure 1.2 Menenius Agrippa faces down the mob in Itakura Kotarō's translation of *Coriolanus*

college student at Keio Gijuku (later Keio University) from Hiroshima when he published this translation, yet he must have shown some kind of academic or linguistic promise. When his *senpai* Ono Tomojirō, who was originally commissioned to do the translation, suffered an injury, he passed it on to his junior Itakura and acted only as proofreader. After this translation, both Ono and Itakura faded into obscurity. All we know is that Itakura went on to a career in business, and Ono went on to become the branch manager of Mitsui Bank in Kobe (Terada 413–416).[33] Itakura's title *Gōketsu isse no kagami: Jiyū no shimoto on'ai no kizuna* (豪傑一世鏡:自由の笞恩愛の紲) can be translated into English as *Liberty's Scourge and the Bonds of Affection: The Tale of the Greatest Hero of the Age*, and it clearly resonates with Shōyō's *Liberty's Sword*. Both emulate the titles of Chinese histories that were popular at the time, and both share a very similar translation strategy and formal approach.

Visually, *Liberty's Scourge* merges the approaches of both *Liberty's Sword* and *Rise and Fall* by using traditional woodblock printing to co-mingle European modernity, European antiquity, and contemporary Japan. Coriolanus is depicted as living in a modern Rome, indicated by showing modern soldiers marching in the Forum in ruins, as it would only have looked in contemporary nineteenth-century

26 *Weaponizing Meiji liberty*

pictures of Italy. In not depicting the modern areas of the city, as does *Rise and Fall*, the Rome in *Liberty's Scourge* foregrounds its antiquity. Added to this temporal pastiche, in a crowd of angry citizens march peasants dressed in contemporary Japanese clothing. Thus, the visuals set the story in an anachronous modern Rome, as *Rise and Fall* does, whilst also placing contemporary Japanese into the narrative and giving a nod to Western antiquity.

The text of *Liberty's Scourge* is introduced by four prefaces. The first is by the renowned kabuki actor Ichikawa Danshū (Ichikawa Danjurō), printed in a handwritten script. The second is by Chikugai Koji, written in kanbun style. The last two are by Itakura himself, written in a literary Japanese (gabun) style. Three of the four prefaces make reference to "*engeki kairyō*" or "theater reform", a reference to the Association for Theater Reform (*Engeki kairyō kai*). The Association for Theater Reform was founded in 1886, and included members Ichikawa Danjurō and Yoda Gakkai (author of the introduction to *Liberty's Sword*) and advocated for raising the status and standards of kabuki—both in production values (but not fundamentally altering their "kabuki-ness") and in the cultural value and morals of the plays.

Thus, *Liberty's Scourge* shares more in common with Shōyō's translation than just their similar titles. Both also rewrite the text to conform to Japanese performative norms. Shōyō's stated effort to make the text more interesting by fleshing out the minimalist original text into a *jōruri* script is mirrored by Itakura's transformation of his text into one that follows kabuki performance conventions. Kabuki permeates every facet of *Freedom's Scourge*, from the language and performance styles to the stage directions and scenic instructions. The standard Shakespearean five-act structure is replaced by seven acts with no specifically numbered scenes within them. As in *Liberty's Sword*, stage directions are given a great deal of attention and elaborated upon from what is in the source material. Whereas Shakespeare's stage directions are characteristically minimalistic, Itakura gives long and detailed descriptions of his scenes. They are written for a kabuki stage: entrances and exits come from the *shimo-te* (stage left), *kami-te* (stage right), and the *hanamichi* (runway entrance that begins downstage right and exits house left), and the stage revolves to change scenes. These extended narrative scenes also help to locate the action in a decidedly Japanese environment, such as one scene that begins with the characters looking at the autumn leaves (*momiji*) under the moonlight, in a pensive moment while Coriolanus is off stage meeting with the city government.

The lines of the actors also reflect this attempt to render the play as kabuki, and like *Liberty's Sword* they bring the orality of performance into the text. Actors employ *watari-serifu*, a technique from traditional theater where one line is broken into phrases and spoken in succession by multiple speakers. This technique can have many different dramatic functions depending on the way it is used, but in this play it is generally used for emphasis and to indicate the fact that characters are speaking simultaneously and in agreement. One example is at the end of Act III. The senators and the tribunes have approved Coriolanus's

Weaponizing Meiji liberty 27

bid to become consul, and over his complaints they urge him to bow to tradition and humble himself before the commoners to get their approval. Itakura ends the scene with:

BRUTUS: Request the consent of the citizens
SICINIUS: and with it the consulship
MENENIUS: position will joyfully be
ALL: Bestowed upon you!

不盧多須： 平民の一致をお求めなされ
西齋紐士： その上にて執政の
麥尼紐士： 職に目出度
一同： お登り召され[34]

Through the performative text type as well as through the orality of a technique like watari-serifu, both Shōyō's and Itakura's translations bring the liveness of a performative event into an environment outside of the stage. This use of *watari-serifu* also indicates a key understanding of liberty—a central notion in the performance—and cues the audience to pay attention. The liberal government at stake here is one where the locus of state authority rests with the people.

We see the notion of liberty again foregrounded early in Act I, when the commoners riot against income inequality. The commoners complain to Menenius that the aristocracy is inflating the price of grain and passing laws that allow the practice of usury. In response, Menenius defends the aristocracy by saying that while it may appear that they are rich with rice (corn in the original), their wealth trickles down and benefits everyone. Coriolanus is then much less diplomatic than Menenius in castigating the unworthy "takers" who do not contribute with taxes or military valor. Itakura renders all of this relatively closely but then tacks on his own lines between Menenius and Marcius following the end of Coriolanus's speech:

MARCIUS: Even today, these commoners make selfish demands and are quick to riot, causing great trouble for the aristocracy.
MENENIUS: If we give liberty to the people, these kinds of things are bound to happen.
MARCIUS: But if we do not grant it to them
MENENIUS: The carnage in the streets
MARCIUS: Here in the city
MENENIUS: Would be a tragedy.

Both strike an omoi-ire [a dramatic pose used in kabuki]:

（馬爾士亜） 今日ですら平民は　気儘気随を申立て動もすれば　一揆三昧　貴族の心痛少なからぬ
（麥尼紐士） その上自由を与えなば　いかなる珍事起こるも知れず

28 *Weaponizing Meiji liberty*

（馬爾士亜）とは言へ それを許さぬときは
（麥尼紐士）その街道は修羅の道
（馬爾士亜）遂にここだ
（麥尼紐士）考え所で御座るわい
ト両人よろしく思入れ在る[35]

Throwing in an exchange like this, particularly one that has no counterpart in the source text, and using the buzzword *jiyū*, is clearly a deliberate comment upon the larger societal debates over political representation in the forthcoming constitution. And just to hammer home who exactly should have the reader's sympathies, the corresponding illustration in the published text depicts the commoners revolting, and dresses some of them in clothing reminiscent of nineteenth-century Japanese commoners. There is an adage that the past is a foreign country, but in this particular case the people of a foreign past are remarkably similar to those of the nearby present. While textually Itakura's translation resonates with *Liberty's Sword*, it offers up a competing vision of liberty and the authority of the state.

All of these formal properties of the play places *Liberty's Scourge* in dialog with *Liberty's Sword* and in contrast with *Rise and Fall*. By rendering their texts as jōruri/kabuki scripts, Shōyō and Itakura are able to expand upon and interpret the play in ways that Kawashima cannot. Kawashima, by contrast, sticks to formal equivalence in both linguistic and extra-linguistic elements. Yet in their understanding of *jiyū*, *Liberty's Sword* and *Liberty's Scourge* take contrasting views on where the locus state authority should reside. As one example, Shōyō concludes the play with commentary that, paired with the introduction, helps to situate the political agenda of his translation. The commentary has no corresponding text in the original.

> The country of Rome became peaceful and the waves rocking the nation were quelled. For laying the foundation of the empire and for the wisdom he possessed, he will be praised and his name will be remembered as part of the dawn of the age and in the history books. It must serve as a warning to all generations of the frivolous and fickle citizens of the country that this peace followed the unfortunate snapping of the sword of freedom.

> 四海波、静しずく治まる羅馬国、其帝政の基礎を、開きし君の身の内に、備はる智略末長く、朝日時代と竹帛に、ほまれを残し名を残し、憾みを残す自由の太刀、折れて治治まる時勢こそ、軽佻浮薄の國人の、萬古の誡となりにけれ。[36]

This suspicious stance towards the "fickle and frivolous" (*keichō* and *fuhaku*) citizens, was certainly not an anachronous way to end the translation even if this text had no corresponding text in the original. Neither Shōyō nor Shakespeare espoused a conceptualization of liberty that endorsed full, universal enfranchisement or that located the authority of the state in the people. Shakespeare (1564–1616) shared a contemporary political context with Hobbes (1588–1679), and a Hobbesian fear of the crowd is evident not only in *Julius Caesar* but also in Shakespeare's plays generally—although much less so in *Coriolanus* than elsewhere. *Caesar* actually makes a mockery of the fickleness of the mob. Rather than riding a wave of popular support, Brutus assassinates a popular leader and is only able to win the populace to his side for a brief part of one scene in the third act (with the famous "Friends, Romans, countrymen" speech). In fact, the fortunes of the masses do not play into the calculations of the conspirators at all. Yet the message is also clear that authority of the state rests at least to some degree with the people. This sensibility also seems to have meshed with the ideals of the *Kaishintō* and head of Shōyō's Waseda University, Ōkuma Shigenobu. Among his many achievements in his long political career, Ōkuma was involved in working out the compromise with the oligarchy that gave suffrage only to approximately the top 1 percent of the country who paid the highest property taxes. The choice of this particular text, along with his agenda that he grafted onto it, is indicative of Shōyō's political leanings beyond just his affiliation with the People's Rights Movement. His liberal democratic affinity must not be confused with an endorsement of full democratic reforms that empower the masses.

Shōyō's use of translation to advance a political agenda, even one that is not disruptively radical, may seem surprising to readers of Atsuko Ueda's *Concealment of Politics, Politics of Concealment* (2007). She argues that Shōyō opposed both the Freedom and People's Rights Movement and the use of literature for political ends. However, her argument is based upon the close reading of only a single text by Shōyō and fails to take into account his political affiliations, his politically oriented translations and fiction, or the distinctions among different factions within the Freedom and People's Rights Movement. In particular, her argument that Shōyō implicitly rejected the practice of communal reading suggests that the practice itself was somehow particular to the radical wing of the movement. While Ueda does not address *Liberty's Sword* in her project, it is exactly the kind of text that was read aloud, and it was written precisely with such a performance with his college friends in mind. Yanagida Izumi notes that Shōyō began translating *Liberty's Sword* almost on a lark when he produced a monologue by Brutus in conjunction with his friend Toyoda Ichirō.[37] Unlike the radical *sōshi* discussed later in this chapter, communal reading among Shōyō and his friends took place out of the public view and was a popular form of entertainment. Communal reading was thus more widely practiced than Ueda's project suggests, and Shōyō's rejection of *Jiyūtō* politics did not necessarily amount to a rejection of their reading practices or of politics in general.[38]

Thus, at many levels, these translations pose very different possibilities for the scope of jiyū in its new context. The notion of liberty at issue in Itakura's translation is much more sympathetic to the masses than either of the two *Caesar* translations discussed in this chapter. In terms of the locus of state authority, *Liberty's Scourge* asks the reader to see the text in terms of the competing interests of the elites and the commoners, and it calls the reader to sympathize with the masses. While two of these translators have disappeared into obscurity,

30 *Weaponizing Meiji liberty*

these three translations bear the mark of their translators in unobscured ways that Japanese translations would soon cease to do. When Shōyō re-translated *Caesar* for production by the Literary Arts Society (*Bungei Kyōkai*) and for inclusion in his translation of the complete works of Shakespeare, for example, his translation bears none of the stylistic characteristics in *Liberty's Sword*. Yet through the paratextual material and the translation strategies, these texts highlight competing ways to conceptualize *jiyū*. Yet it is also significant that these texts were introduced through the unusual medium of performance texts that were not meant for the stage. In this way they share a context with the sōshi performances discussed subsequently. Yet in almost every other way, these Shakespeare translations stand in stark contrast, particularly in the kind of liberty which they perform.

Liberty and *Oppekepe*

While he would gain greater fame in the early twentieth century with performances in the *shinpa* style that were far removed from his roots in the Freedom and People's Rights Movement, the young Kawakami Otojirō (川上音二郎 1864–1911) was affiliated with the movement's activist wing as a young *sōshi*. The term "*sōshi*" was an early Meiji neologism used to describe a type of political activist who was usually male, young, rebellious, and generally lower class.

Scholars of Kawakami such as Egashira Kō generally represent the *sōshi* as energetic, politically motivated, and rowdy youth whose clashes with the law were motivated by playful attempts at pushing the boundaries of censorship and political suppression by the police in particular and the Meiji government in general. It is true that the "oppositional mobilization of cultural expression"[39] in a public arena was one means by which they voiced their politics. Yet focusing solely on their creative activities does not do justice to the wide variety of people who were included under the name "*sōshi*", nor does it acknowledge the degree to which violence and confrontation were integral to who they were.[40]

Eiko Maruko Siniawer offers a different description of the *sōshi*. She sees the *sōshi* as part of a tradition of political violence in Japan that extended back to the Edo period and would continue into the post-World War II period.[41] Their status on the periphery accounts for the paucity of documentation on the *sōshi*, but Siniawer notes that their membership was eclectic and seems to have comprised former samurai, farmers, merchants, industrialists, *bakuto* (gamblers), student ruffians, as well as drifters and toughs with no fixed occupation.[42] Siniawer makes it clear that lawlessness, violence, and ruffianism were central to the culture of the sōshi. They were involved in violent incidents (*gekka jiken*) such as the Chichibu Uprising and the Fukushima Incident.[43] Politicians hired *sōshi* as bodyguards and small-scale personal security forces to inflict intimidation and physical violence upon their enemies. In one particularly brutal episode, Hoshi Tōru sent his sōshi to assuage a personal affront by a political rival, and the resulting brawl ended with the death of said rival.[44] Even when their activities did not include outright violence, Siniawer notes that their culture was infused with masculine bravado.

Yet, however important violent masculinity was to the conception of the sōshi, it was not the only unifying ethic that held this rowdy youth movement together. Siniawer stops short of using the term "violence specialists" to describe the *sōshi* of the 1880s, since their activities were at least ostensibly motivated by political commitments, and they produced creative material that both earned them money and some degree of fame.[45,46] To a significant degree the sōshi were both a creative *and* a disruptive entity. Thus, while Siniawer is interested in the culture of violence that was central to the sōshi, Kawakami scholars focus upon their creative activities. A comprehensive account of the sōshi that takes into account the imbrication of *both* violence and creativity in their activities is central to my understanding of their performance art during Meiji. Even when their events such as political speeches and eventually, political theater (*sōshi-shibai*) were ostensibly non-violent, the threat of violence was always present. Likewise, brawls among Kawakami's audience, even involving the actors themselves, were common (Ameroku, 48).[47] Violence was a tool for establishing dominance over rival sōshi, and not just through the physical act of winning a fight in a theater.[48] Violent conflict with the authorities served as a badge of honor among sōshi. In his work for the newspaper as well as his early years as a performer, Kawakami claimed to have been arrested more than 170 times during the first few years of his association with the movement, and he made maximum use of this (likely inflated) number as a boastful point of pride.[49]

Even when this violence had the effect of inviting restriction by the authorities, violence and performance remained imbricated for the sōshi. In Meiji 13 (1880) the government passed laws restricting assembly that aimed to crack down on the political speeches popular with members of the Freedom and People's Rights Movement. In response, the sōshi gradually adopted more theatrical and creative modes of performance as part of their strategy to push the limits of legality and as creative experiments in avoiding censorship. For example, when the government specifically banned "political orations" (*seiji enzetsu*), Kawakami's troupe simply changed the name of their gatherings to "ridiculous orations" (*kokkei enzetsu*). Another time he was arrested for the common sōshi practice of selling parody songsheets in the streets that were based on old war songs.[50] The picture of the sōshi that emerges is not just a group of violent thugs that some representations make them out to be, but also not just the merry pranksters that theater scholars tend to paint them as. Further, while they often invoked the buzzwords of "freedom" and "liberty", their diversity meant that they were motivated by a wide range of contemporary issues, such as reformation of the unequal treaties with the West, which had nothing to do with personal freedom or political representation.

This kind of performance, particularly in the spaces in which they performed (informal *yose* and on the street), problematizes the way we can think of these performances as theater. In that sense, the Shakespeare translations discussed earlier which were never produced on stage share a peripheral performance space in common with the lowbrow, violent sōshi performances. The slippery,

32 *Weaponizing Meiji liberty*

multivalent nature of performance makes it difficult to comment upon in precise ways, and sōshi performance is inherently ephemeral: improvisational by nature, seen in each iteration by very few viewers, and largely overlooked by the taste makers and elite. Yet this challenge is not limited to sōshi performance. Even in the best-recorded of cases, in the most highly publicized performances by famous actors which are widely reported on, the study of "performance" and "performativity" themselves can be elusive concepts from a theoretical perspective. This is at least partly a disciplinary challenge. Performance studies scholars have expanded our understanding of performance and theatricality far beyond the stage into the realms of ritual, festivals, and even ordinary everyday life. Discourse analysis and gender studies have examined how the formal properties of theater are evident in constructing our lived experience, with the mixed benefit of shedding new light on the nature of performance as well as stretching the term to cover so many kinds of acts that the word risks losing specificity. This situation has inspired Thomas Postlewait and Tracy C. Davis to lament that, "To some people, [theatricality] is that which is quintessentially the theater, while to others it is the theater subsumed in the whole world. Apparently, the concept is comprehensive of all meanings yet empty of all specific sense".[51] The examination of the sōshi's use of impromptu performance spaces benefits in obvious ways from the reach of performance studies into non-traditional spaces, but it also faces challenges.

These challenges also raise questions of the rhetorical efficacy of political performances like those of the sōshi. In light of these challenges of theatrical space that is semi-public and highly varied, texts which are for the most part not extant, and performers who lacked formal training, an examination of audience is perhaps a productive mode in examining the mechanisms by which sōshi performance operates in a political mode in society. Michael Warner's discussion of publics and counterpublics in his 2002 book by that title is particularly enlightening in this regard. He builds on Habermas's concept of the public sphere to examine the role of audiences that emerge through discursive practices surrounding texts. While Warner himself is interested in written texts and tends to give them priority in his argument, he also discusses audiences of live texts and the analysis that he applies to audiences of written texts are equally applicable to audiences of performance. For Warner, a counterpublic is a public that is defined in relation to the individual members who make up that public as well as their collective relationship to one or more dominant publics. Such an audience emerges around a text through the readers' engagement with that text, and crucially is excluded from entry into the dominant public sphere. It is neither a stable nor precisely quantifiable entity, but the discursive exchange between audience and text establishes a counterpublic that works to influence public opinion. This is a useful model for describing the *sōshi* and their guerilla theater. In fact, the very nature of Kawakami's performances offers a stark contrast to the Shakespeare translations in this chapter. Unlike those private performances, the *sōshi* were active and visible players in their own publics and in the wider public to which they represented a counterpublic. This fact gave them perhaps a more instrumental role in shaping the public opinion of others

Weaponizing Meiji liberty 33

despite their under-privileged status. Indeed, while Warner stipulates that audiences must consciously act, even in the weakest of ways, to join a counterpublic, the guerilla nature of Kawakami's street theater actually co-opts members of the public to become unwitting members of his counterpublic, even temporarily. This engagement with their audience and the threat of public disorder, while certainly not unique to the sōshi's performances, provoked the ire of the authorities. When the Meiji government tightened censorship on publications in Meiji 8 (1875) and increased restrictions on assembly in Meiji 13 (1880), the People's Rights Movement turned to alternative modes of performance in order to bypass the censors' scrutiny.[52]

Kawakami despite not being the only, or even first, successful sōshi performer was certainly the most successful and best remembered.[53] His path to success was guided in large part and ironically by government efforts at silencing the sōshi. Kawakami was and is most known for his breakout hit song *Oppekepe* (おっぺけぺ) in the late 1980s, yet the song began as a group effort and only became "his" through his versions of live performances and through the sales of lyrics pamphlets with his image on them. After politically resistant groups, including *sōshi* performance, were banned under the Peace Preservation Law of 1887, Kawakami shifted performance genres to rakugo (comic storytelling). Upon joining the troupe of Sorori Shinzaemon (曾呂利新左衛門 1842–1923), Kawakami took on the stage name Ukiyotei Marumaru (浮世亭○○). *Oppekepe* was initially a song which was performed around Kansai and on tour by a number of members of Sorori's troupe. However, Kawakami began to attract increasing national attention with performances of his versions of the song, and it was his name that was associated with *Oppekepe* when it became a nationwide hit.[54] In 1889, he brought his act from Kansai to the political center in Tokyo, eventually performing in the proper theatrical space of the Nakamura Theater. Even though his audience consisted primarily of fellow sōshi and violence remained a key element of the performance experience, the success of his act marked the beginning of Kawakami's rise to celebrity.

Kawakami's ballad inscribed specific conceptions upon the "jewelry box word" jiyū that contrast with those at play in the contemporary translations of Shakespeare.[55] In other words, traditional translated texts are not the only venue through which ideas were translated from Western source cultures. While Kawakami's text was not a translation per se, he and his fellow sōshi actively negotiated the signification and importance of translated political terms and were therefore integral players in the "translation" of Western concepts of freedom. For many, there was a strong association between newly translated concepts and the fashions of the source culture from which those words were imported. Because the trappings of Western society with which these concepts were associated were expensive and difficult to attain, the adoption of Western customs was an expensive prospect that was only available to those of high status and wealth. Kawakami's interpretation of *jiyū* worked to decouple the concept from the associations with class and status that were attached to Western material and intellectual objects.

Figure 1.3 is a *nishikie* of Kawakami performing *Oppekepe*:

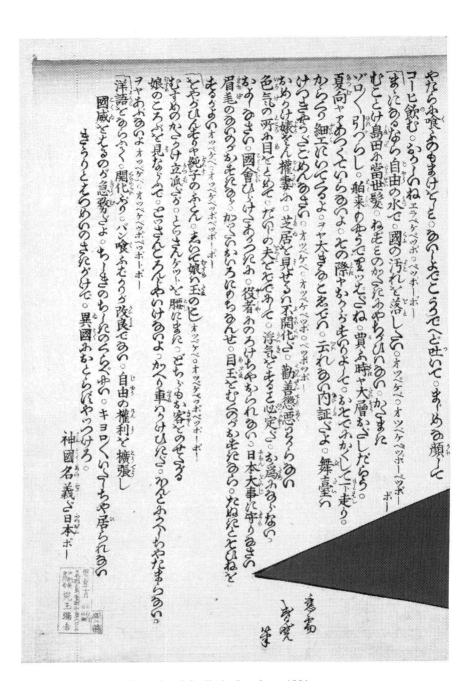

Figure 1.3 Nishikie of Kawakami Otojirō's *Oppekepe*, 1891
Source: Reproduced with permission from the National Theater of Japan.

Figure 1.3 (Continued)

36 *Weaponizing Meiji liberty*

The lyrics printed to the left of the image read:[56]

I want to make those who resent rights and happiness chug shots of freedom-booze[57] *oppekepe, oppekepeppōppeppoppō.*

He takes off his fancy *kamishimo* and puts on a cloak and pants and rides in a rickshaw. With her dashing *sokuhatsu*[58] hairdo and a bonnet, they look the consummate lady and gentleman. They look impeccable, but their political thought is lacking. They just don't get the truth of the world.[59] Plant the seed of freedom in their heart. *Oppekepe, oppekeppeppō.*

Ignoring the plight of the poor citizens when the cost of rice rises, he pulls his top hat over his eyes. He wears a gold ring and gold watch. He bows and scrapes in front of the powerful, and he throws money at geisha and their attendants. He stores up rice at home, and he stands by while his dearest companions die. He has a merciless and insatiable greed, he has no morals, and no compassion.

He wants to bring a gift, to bribe Emma[60] in hell, to let him go to heaven. Think it will work? Think again! *Oppekepe oppekeppo peppopo.*

I don't know the husband's occupation, but the wife wears a contemporary *sokuhatsu* 'do. She uses foreign words.[61] She carries a pooch[62] but begs off her debts on the last day of the month.[63] It is unbecoming. She should stop! She acts like she knows things when really she knows nothing, and she goes overboard putting on Occidental airs. She won't drink *sake*, only beer, brandy, and vermouth. She stuffs herself with Western food that her stomach isn't used to. She will secretly throw it up, but she drinks coffee with a straight face. She looks the fool.

If I could do it myself, I would wash the filth from our country with the water of liberty. *Oppekepe oppekepeppopo.*

She has a chic shimada hairdo. She is the mouse's enemy, dragging along an imported shawl with a fancy pattern that she dropped a wad of cash on.[64] But it's summer now and it is too hot for shawls. So her mother hides the shawl inside her sleeves and sneaks away to pawn it into cash.[65] So sorry for spilling your secret on this public stage! *Oppekepe oppekeppo peppopō.*

Don't take your lady to the theater—it's uncivilized. She doesn't understand the moral of the story, she just ogles the actors. She neglects her husband and will undoubtedly cheat on him. It is useless to bring her in the first place. With our parliament established, now isn't the time to waste dreaming about actors. We should support our country. If you like men with no eyebrows, go find a lover among the lepers. If you find wide open eyes attractive, go sleep with a badger.[66] *Oppekepe oppekepeppo peppopo.*

Although the parents are poor, their daughter married into money and sleeps on silk damask.[67] *Oppekepe oppekepeppopo.*

The daughter wears a fancy shawl, but her father wraps himself in a blanket. Both of them want to "carry" customers. Don't "fall" like your daughter has, father![68] He pulls the returning rickshaw, but it is truly unbearable. Be careful, parents! *Oppekepe oppekepopeppopo.*

You learn Western words and seem so enlightened, but eating bread is not reforming. Spread the rights of the liberty.[69] Raising our national prestige is urgent business! We can't be looking around restlessly to compare our knowledge. Leading the way in science and invention, we will not fall behind other countries. Let's go get 'em!

In the name of the sacred nation of Japan: *po*.

権利幸福きらいな人に、自由湯をば飲ましたい
オッペケペ、オッペケペッポー、ペッポッポー
堅い裃かど取れて、マンテル　（マント）、
ヅボンに人力車、粋な束髪、ボンネット
貴女や紳士のいでたちで、外部の飾りはよいけれど
政治の思想が欠乏だ、天地の真理がわからない
心に自由の種をまけ
オッペケペ、オッペケペッポー、ペッポッポー
　米価騰貴の今日に　細民困窮省らず　目深にかぶった高帽子　金の指輪に金時計　権門貴顕に膝を曲げ　芸者たいこに金を蒔き　内には米を倉につみ　同朋兄弟見殺しに　いくらじひなき欲心も　余り非道な　薄情な　但し冥土のおみやげか　じごくで閻魔に面会し　わいろ使うて極楽へ　行けるかえ　ゆけないよ
　オッペケペー、オッペケペッポー、ペッポッポー
　亭主の職業は知らないが、おつむは当世の束髪で、言葉は開化の漢語にて
　晦日の断り洋犬抱いて、不似合いだ、およしなさい
　なんにも知らずに知った顔、むやみに西洋鼻にかけ、日本酒なんぞは飲まれない
　ビールにブランデ、ベルモット、腹にも慣れない洋食を、やたらに食うのも負け惜しみ、内緒でそっと反吐ついて、真面目な顔してコーヒ飲む、おかしいな　エラペケペッポ　ペッポーポー
　ままになるなら自由の水で　国の汚れをおとしたい
　オッペケペ、　オッペケペッポー、ペッポーポー
　むことけ島田に当世髪　ねずみのかたきにやちがいない　かたまきゾロゾロ引きづらし　舶来もやうでりっぱだね　買う時や大層おだしだらう　夏向ヤアあつくていらないよ　その際（とき）ヤおかかがすいりよして　おそでにかくして下走り（ひとはしり）　からくり細工にいてくるよ　オヤ大きな声では　云われない内証だよ　舞台はけつきやうだごめんなさい　オペケペ　オッペケペッポ　ペッポッポー
　お妾嬢さん権妻に　芝居見せるは不開化だ　勧善懲悪わからない　色気の所に目をとめて　だいじの夫をそでにして　浮気すること必定だ　お為にならない　およしなさい　国会ひらけたあかつきに　役者にのろけちゃいられない　日本大事に守りなさい　眉毛のないのがおすきなら　かったいお色にもちなんせ　目玉むくのがおすきなら　たぬきとそいねをするがよい
　オッペケペー、オッペケペッポ、ペッポーポー

38 *Weaponizing Meiji liberty*

おやがひんすりヤ頓子（とんす）のふとん　しいて娘は玉のこし
オッペケペ　オッペケペッポペッポーポー
娘のかたかけ立派だが
とうさんケットを腰にまき　どちらもお客をのせたがる　娘のこ
ろぶを見ならうて　とおさんころんじゃいけないよ　かえり車はう
けひきだ　ほんとにかえしちゃたまらない　オヤあぶないよ　オッ
ペケペ、オッペケペッポー、ペッポーポー
洋語なろうて開化ぶり　パン食うばかりが改良じゃない　自由の
権利を拡張し　国威を張るのが急務だよ　知識の知識の競（くら）ベ
合い キョロキョロいたしちゃ居られない 究理と発明の先がけで　異
国に劣らず やっつけろ 神国めいぎだ 日本ポー

The humor is invariably at the expense of the elites and the rich for their fad-dish adoption of Western customs, a facet of the song that essentially remained true throughout the decades in which Kawakami continued to rewrite and perform the song. The "jiyū" in these verses is rooted in an economic and social equality, which importantly is available to the common man (the notion of liberty, like the humor in the text, is highly gendered). This notion of liberty is free of much of the academic complexity and overtones at play in the more intellectual exercises in the Shakespeare plays examined earlier. Unlike those plays, which were produced with an audience of intellectual elites and college students in mind, Kawakami's performances were accessible to his fellow sōshi and popular with people in all classes of society. His performance mode underscores an understanding of liberty which runs counter to the Hobbesian view of democracy as a means for governing the masses, and even contradicts Mill and the Utilitarians, who viewed democracy as a government which is responsive to the needs of the people but maintains a hierarchical distinction between the rulers and the ruled. Kawakami articulated a view of government in which officials were in fact *subject* to the citizens of the country when he said, "The People are second to the emperor, and high govern-ment officials/chancellors (*dajōdaijin* 太政大臣) are below the People (*shita ni zasu* 下に座す)".[70] A government that was subject to the hoi polloi in this way would have terrified Hobbes, and it was not popular with the Meiji oligarchy either: this comment earned Kawakami a punishment of 45 days in jail and a five-yen fine.

With such radical, destabilizing political ideals, it is not surprising that the Meiji authorities would exert a heavy-handed censorship on the Rights Move-ment's chosen performative mode of expression. Yet it is also not surprising that Kawakami's ballad would appeal to a wide swath of disenfranchised Japanese citizens.

Conclusions

The performances and translations in this chapter represent an engagement with the translation of liberty in the Meiji Period that goes beyond the textual model by which this fraught political term is typically understood to have been brought into the Japanese political discourse. They also represent a performative tradition that sits outside of the mainstream, formal theater world. Eschewing the formal stage worked to neuter the Meiji government's project to control the political messages coming out of Rights Movement performances. The kind of performance explored in this chapter, in other words, ways in which translated texts and ideas were deployed in alternative performance spaces, resulted in effects ranging from vibrant oppositional modes of discourse to a more reasoned reflection on the meaning and role of liberty in a Japanese context. These performance modes inspired the performances recounted in the following chapters which looked back to the resistance of the Rights Movement as models for their own brands of political resistance.

The varying performance modes examined here all represent a relationship between creator and audience that interacts with and enhances their political agenda. The radical political activism of Kawakami Otojirō is embodied in his brash guerilla theater that embraced violence and operated on the border of legality. Such a mode of performance inspired the kind of activism that true radicals require. Tsubouchi Shōyō's and Itakura Kōtarō's translations are written for oral presentation, with meter and *jōruri* and kabuki conventions, but the group readings in a closed setting were more suitable for the cautious liberalism of elite college friends who had much to lose personally from a true disruption of the status quo. Kawashima's translation retains none of the oral properties of the source text (such as meter), and as such is most properly suited for silent and solitary reading. Such a setting tends not to inspire political fervor to the degree of the group settings of the other two, and the text is more likely to be read for its historiography than for a liberal political agenda, which in any event is effaced in his text.

The Shakespeare translations examined here see the events of the early Meiji Period through the lens of Western historiography in a broader strategy that continues in the ensuing decades. The concepts at play in these translations remain relevant into the 1920s and '30s, when the Japanese Proletarian Movement would again look to the Rights Movement through the lens of Western historiography to understand their place in history.

Notes

1 Matsumoto Shinko, *Meiji zenki engeki ronshi* (Tōkyō: Engeki Shuppansha, 1974).
2 Indra A. Levy, *Sirens of the Western Shore: The Westernesque Femme Fatale, Translation, and Vernacular Style in Modern Japanese Literature* (New York: Columbia University Press, 2006), 202.
3 R. L. Sims, *Japanese Political History Since the Meiji Renovation, 1868–2000* (New York: Palgrave, 2001), 59.
4 Alexandra Lianeri, "Translation and the Establishment of Liberal Democracy in Nineteenth-Century England: Constructing the Political as an Interpretive Act," in *Translation and Power*, eds. Maria Tymoczko and Edwin Gentzler (Amherst: University of Massachusetts Press, 2002), 5; William Shakespeare and Shōyō Tsubouchi, *Juriyasu Shīzā* [Julius Caesar.], Vol. dai 26-kan (Tōkyō: Chūō Kōronsha, 1934), 9, 4, 204.
5 Ibid., 6.
6 Ibid.

40 *Weaponizing Meiji liberty*

7 Ibid., 18.

8 There were also ideas of utopian and socialist writers who were contemporary with Mill, such as William Morris, who argued for governmental systems that were similar in many respects to those of ancient Greece. However, these writers did not have influence on the discussion in Japan in the early Meiji period.

9 The United States Constitution, for example, paired a popularly elected House of Representatives with a Senate that was elected by state legislatures.

10 Douglas Howland, "Translating Liberty in Nineteenth-Century Japan," *Journal of the History of Ideas* 62, no. 1 (University of Pennsylvania Press, 2001), 170.

11 *Jishu*: "independence" or "autonomy"; *jizai*: "freely", "at will", "being able to do as one desires"; *fuki*: "freedom from restraint", also "unconventional"; *kankō*: "tolerant (politics)"; and *wagamama*: "self-indulgence" or "willfulness" (note that this is very similar to the original meaning of *jiyū*).

12 Yanabu Akira, *Hon'yaku to Wa Nani Ka: Nihongo to Hon'yaku Bunka* (Tokyo: Hōsei Daigaku Shuppankyoku, 1976), 110–114.

13 Akira Yanabu, *Hon'yaku to wa nani ka: Nihongo to hon'yaku bunka* (Tōkyō: Hōsei Daigaku Shuppankyoku, 1976), 118.

14 Howland, "Translating Liberty in Nineteenth-Century Japan".

15 Ibid., 264.

16 Richard Sims, *Japanese Political History Since the Meiji Renovation* (New York: Palgrave, 2001), 56–59.

17 Other partial translations include, for instance, parts of *Hamlet* which were translated by Kanagaki Robun in 1875 and Wadagaki Kenzō in 1881; Charles Lamb's adaptation of *The Merchant of Venice* was adapted into Japanese by Inoue Tsutomu and published in 1883 under the title *The Lawsuit for a Pound of Human Flesh* (*Jinniku shichiire saiban: Seiyō chinsetsu*, 人肉質入裁判:西洋珍説); and in May 1885 *Merchant* became the first Shakespearean production by Japanese actors, this time titled *A Season of Cherry Blossoms, a World of Money* (*Sakuradoki zeni no yononaka: Hanamushiro shichimai*, 何桜彼桜銭世中:花莚七枚). This partial translation was performed in *kabuki* style by the troupe Nakamura Sōjūrō Ichiza. See timelines in Sasaki Takashi, *Nihon sheikusupia sōran*, Erupisu, 1990; Takashi Sasayama, J.R. Mulryne, and Margaret Shewring, eds., *Shakespeare and the Japanese Stage* (Cambridge: Cambridge University Press, 1998); and Ueno Yoshiko, *Hamlet and Japan*, The Hamlet Collection, No. 2 (New York: AMS Press, 1995).

18 And in an even further tragic coincidence, Booth, an actor himself and brother of the more famous American actor Edwin, was the son of Junius Brutus Booth, the renowned English Shakespearean actor. He was named after Shakespeare's character in *Caesar*.

19 Yanagida Izumi and Nakamura Kan, *Wakaki tsubouchi shōyō: Meiji bungaku kenkyū I*, Nihon Tosho Senta, 1984, 14, 308, 8.

20 *Jōruri* is the ballad drama style that was spoken in meter and employed in *bunraku* puppet theater performances and closely tied to kabuki performance texts.

21 This is rendered in Shōyō's text as: アッこれぞ誠に羅馬國の、賢士の賢賢士、義人の義人、たぐひ稀なる蓋世の、英傑なりしを惜しむべし、敢えなく黄泉の鬼となりしか、往る日獅威差（シイザル）殿下をば、陰かに謀って刺殺なせし、三十余名の徒党の中にて、誠と国家の利福の為に、只々全般の自由の為に、身を犠牲にして企に、興せし者は只一人、此マアカス舞妻多須（ブルタス）あるるのみ、其余は総て悉く、或は嫉妬偏執執より、或は私怨私憤憤より、彼の挙に興せし者のみなり、彼れれ舞妻多須の一生こそ、まことに貴人紳士と称して、恥しからぬ振舞多し、彼レ舞妻多須の如きをこそ、上天も又人人間の、雛形なりとて誇らせ給はん、アッ流石は人に慕はれし、羅馬古今の名士ぢやよなア. William Shakespeare and Shōyō Tsubouchi, *Jiyū No Tachi Nagori No Kireaji: Shiizaru Kidan* (Tōkyō: Yūshōdō Shoten, 1978), 302–303.

22 Yoshiko Kawachi, "Shakespeare in Nineteenth Century Japan," in *The Globalization of Shakespeare in the Nineteenth Century*, eds. Krystyna Kujawińska-Courtney and John Moore Mercer (Lewiston, NY: Edwin Mellen Press, 2003), 72.

Weaponizing Meiji liberty 41

23 Shakespeare and Tsubouchi, *Jiyū No Tachi Nagori No Kireaji*, 164.
24 Translations throughout this book, including back translations of Shakespeare here, are my own unless otherwise noted.
25 Yoshiaki Furuhara, "The Caesar Kidan: The Earliest Japanese Translation of Shakespeare's Julius Caesar and Its Performance," *Hitotsubashi Journal of Arts and Sciences* 4, no. 1 (1964), 22–38.
26 Kaieda Susumu, "*Julius Caesar:* Nihon ni okeru shakespeare geki," *Area and Culture Studies* 9 (1962), 69–79.
27 Ashihara Sei, "Nihon hajimete yakusho ari," *Yomiuri Shinbun* 6 June 1884.
28 Kawachi, "Shakespeare in Nineteenth Century Japan," 71.
29 In contrast to Kawashima's adherence to Shakespeare's script, Tetsuo Kishi describes Shōyō's translation as "Shakespeare's *Julius Caesar* with chorus played by Shoyo Tsubouchi"; see Tetsuo Kishi and Graham Bradshaw, *Shakespeare in Japan*, Continuum, 2006, 111.
30 William Shakespeare and Keizō Kawashima, *Rōma seisuikan: Shiēkusupia gikyoku* (Ōsaka: Shinshindō, 1886), 86.
31 Masao Murayama and Shūichi Katō, "Translation and Japanese Modernity," in *Translation in Modern Japan* (Abingdon, UK: Routledge, 2012), 28.
32 Christopher Hill, "How to Write a Second Restoration: The Political Novel and Meiji Historiography," *The Journal of Japanese Studies* 33, no. 2 (2007), 337–356.
33 Terada Yoshinori 寺田芳徳. 日本英学発達史の基礎研究：庄原英学校, 萩藩の英学および慶応義塾を中心に. (Zōhoban ed. Hiroshima-shi: Keisuisha, 1999), 413–416.
34 William Shakespeare and Kōtarō Itakura, *Minarezao: Wada Mankichi yaku. Jiyū no shimoto On'ai no kizuna Gōketsu isse kagami: Itakura Kōtarō yaku* (Tōkyō: Ōzorasha, 2000), 108.
35 William Shakespeare and Kōtarō Itakura, *Jiyū no shimoto On'ai no kizuna Gōketsu isse kagami: Itakura Kōtarō yaku* (Tōkyō: Ōzorasha, 2000), 29.
36 Ibid., 304.
37 Yanagida and Nakamura, *Wakaki tsubouchi shōyō*, 120.
38 However, it is certainly true as Ueda argues that the political and what was seen as the "literary" gradually came to occupy very different cultural spheres. As a benchmark of this shift in literary values, Shōyō re-translated *Caesar* in the Taishō period and made every effort to dissociate it from local political circumstances in the Bungei Kyōkai production at the Imperial Theater in 1913. Interestingly, this was after *Liberty's Sword* took on a bit of a life of its own at the beginning of the twentieth century. Building upon the political nature written into the text, *Liberty's Sword* was again re-situated into a new local context when it was first performed in 1901, more than a decade after the adoption of the constitution and the dissipation of the Freedom and People's Rights Movement. It was performed at Meijiza and was a not-so-subtle send-up of the assassination of the political boss Hoshi Tōru. There is a great deal of irony involved here, as Hoshi had been a member of the Rights Movement when *Liberty's Sword* was first published, but at the time of its performance Hoshi represented the corrupt establishment that the translation critiques. The production faced the close scrutiny of the censors because of its obviously political nature; see Kimura Kinosuke, *Meijiza monogatari*, Kabuki Shuppanbu, 1928. Shōyō was not involved with this performance, however, and he had moved away from the politics of his youth by the time this performance was staged.
39 I borrow this term from Miriam Silverberg's book *Erotic Grotesque Nonsense* (2007).
40 Kawakami Otojirō et al., *Jiden Otojirō Sadayakko*, Dai 1-han ed. (Tōkyō: San'ichi Shobō, 1984), 39.
41 Eiko Maruko Siniawer, *Ruffians, Yakuza, Nationalists: The Violent Politics of Modern Japan, 1860–1960* (Ithaca, NY: Cornell University Press, 2008), 270.
42 Ibid., 51.
43 Ibid., 44.
44 Ibid., 47.

42 *Weaponizing Meiji liberty*

45 Siniawer reserves this term to describe individuals who acted more like mercenaries, and it would not be until the decade after the adoption of the constitution and the emergence of party-controlled cabinets that the *sōshi* would become less politically idealistic and closer to what might be considered a gangster for hire (Yakuza Ruffians, *Nationalists: The Violent Politics of Modern Japan*, Eiko Maruko Siniawer, (Cornell) 5–8, 52).

46 A description of one of the most popular enka singers of his day, Soeda Azembō, is included in his memoir titled *A Life Adrift* (2009), translated by Michael Lewis.

47 Kawakami et al., *Jiden Otojirō Sadayakko*, 38–39. Ameroku Sei 雨六生. 1907. Jūgonen mae no sōshi shibai 十五年前の壮士芝居. In Engei gahō 演芸画報. (May): 48.

48 Jason Karlin, *Gender and Nation in Meiji Japan: Modernity, Loss, and the Doing of History (Honolulu: University of Hawai'i Press, 2014), 60.*

49 Kō Egashira Kō, *Hakata Kawakami Otojirō* (Fukuoka-shi: Nishi Nihon Shinbunsha, 1996), 59.

50 Ibid., 62.

51 Tracy C. Davis and Thomas Postlewait, *Theatricality* (New York: Cambridge University Press, 2003), 243.

52 Matsumoto, *Meiji zenki engeki ronshi*, 19.

53 Benito Ortolani notes that Sudō Sadanori was involved in much the same kind of political theater before Kawakami was and that Kawakami likely borrowed ideas from him. See Benito Ortolani, *The Japanese Theater: From Shamanistic Ritual to Modern Pluralism* (Princeton, NJ: University of Princeton, 1995).

54 Nagamine Shigetoshi, *Oppekepe bushi to Meiji* (Bunshun Shinsho, 2018).

55 "Jewelry box word" is a term used by Yanabu Akira to describe borrowed words whose original meanings are not clearly understood in the target culture. The jewelry box word is an empty signifier, in other words, that by virtue of its foreign origins and indeterminate meaning, has great appeal in the target culture. See Yanabu Akira, "Translation Words: Formation and Background (excerpts)," trans. Thomas Gaubatz and Andre Haag, *Review of Japanese Culture and Society, Vol. 20, The Culture of Translation in Modern Japan* (December 2008), 47.

56 The timely nature of the social commentary in *Oppekepe*, which Kawakami sang throughout the course of his performing career, resulted in a highly unstable textual artifact. Kawakami added and rewrote lines and whole stanzas from the song to speak to new current events and dropped significant parts of the text when events such as the Sino-Japanese War had ceased to be current news. Taguchi Chikashi has found 38 different stanzas in various printed editions of the song, and undoubtedly there were many more which Kawakami performed live (see Taguchi Chikashi 田口親, "*Oppekepe* nit suite" オッペケペ節について. Waseda Daigaku Toshokan kiyō 早稲田大学図書館紀要, 125–166). Despite the fluid nature of the text, portions of the text, such as the first stanza, seem to be core components which appear in all or most of the various renderings. The text used in this translation comes from the nishikie published in July 1891. It represents a widely disseminated version of the text when the song was at the height of its popularity, and it includes the central components of the song as it has been recorded in print and audio reproductions.

57 The original plays on slang words for "alcohol" and "Chinese medicine" with the name of the Liberal Party. See Egashira (1996).

58 A Western-style hairdo.

59 Literally: Heaven and earth.

60 The Buddhist god who rules over the underworld and judges the dead.

61 The original refers to compounds of Chinese characters that were commonly used as translations of Western words.

62 The original uses the characters for "occidental" and "dog" (洋犬), and the reading is glossed "*kame*" (a variant of the English "come here"). A Japanese person who saw an English speaker summon a dog with "come here" and thought that the English for

Weaponizing Meiji liberty 43

"dog" was "come here" was a story often invoked to make fun of Japanese who tried to pretend they were more cosmopolitan and multilingual than they actually were.

63 The pun here is that she has no money (*kane*) to pay bills, but she is carrying *kame*.

64 This is a visual pun that highlights her gauche pretentions at sophistication: her expensive scarf is draped inelegantly over her shoulder so that it looks like a rat tail. There may also be a verbal pun here, but the reference is unclear.

65 The original uses "*karakuri saiku*", suggesting the technological skill in, for example, wind-up automotons, as a euphemism for "pawn shop". It suggests that the mother has come up with a clever scheme to make the expensive, unwanted shawl turn into money.

66 The dramatic makeup (*kumadori*) of a kabuki actor paints over the eyebrows, and in making the eyes appear large and fierce resembles the coloring on a badger's (*tanuki*) face.

67 This line plays on the saying, "A poor person is a dumb person" (貧すれば鈍す). The line puns on "*donsu*", meaning both expensive silk damask and stupid.

68 In the daughter's case, the fall is a moral one, but in the father's case he literally should not fall while pulling the rickshaw.

69 Alternate versions of this line call for spreading the rights of the "Empire" (*teikoku*). It is a striking change which highlights the degree to which the meaning of "liberty" was in flux.

70 Egashira Kō, *Hakata Kawakami Otojirō*, Nishi Nihon Shinbunsha, 1996, 59.

2 There is a specter haunting Communism

The late 1920s and early 1930s simultaneously and paradoxically saw both the height of the prewar Japanese leftist culture movement (the so-called Red Decade) and a crippling schism within the leftist movement at large. Channeling these seemingly conflicting contexts, the Popular Theater (*Taishūza* 大衆座) ran a production of *The Secret Account from Tsukuba* (*Tsukuba hiroku*, 筑波秘録) by Sasaki Takamaru (佐々木孝丸, 1898–1986) from January 27 to 29, 1930. The play looks back to the performative and historical past to understand the confusing present moment, and it is perhaps for both of these reasons that this play is elided from the contemporary historiography of Japanese Proletarian Theater (Figure 2.1). Yet the production itself was innovative both as dramaturgy and ideology, and on top of that it was a popular example of the many leftist plays (likewise forgotten in the contemporary narrative of the movement) which reached back to the past for lessons about the present. Yet these historical dramas set during the Restoration Period, often featuring members of the Freedom and People's Rights Movement, were popular precisely because of the content and performance conventions that have seemingly led to their being forgotten. *Tsukuba* and plays like it represent important attempts to challenge assumptions in the Proletarian Theater Movement about the relationship of content to form and history to the present in ways that attempted to rationalize the ideological conflicts that plagued the movement at the end of the 1920s.

While historians have long wrestled with Japanese Marxist intellectuals' interest in the Meiji Restoration, the narrative of the prewar Japanese leftist culture movement has been that it was exclusively concerned both artistically and ideologically with the present and future. This narrative is reflected in both scholarship and in works selected for modern anthologies. Yet *Tsukuba* was just one example of a particularly popular production in this genre that I call "Restoration Plays", plays written in the 1920s and '30s for proletarian theaters and featuring the Restoration and its aftermath.[1] In addition to participating in productions he did not author, Sasaki himself wrote four of his own Restoration Plays between 1929 and 1939: *The Death of Danton* (*Danton no shi*, ダントンの死, 1929), *The Secret Account from Tsukuba* (*Tsukuba hiroku*, 筑波秘録, 1930, and restaged at least four times in the following years), *Itagaki Taisuke* (*Itagaki Taisuke*, 板垣退助, published in *Nihon hyōron* in 1935 and produced by the New Tsukiji

Figure 2.1 Scene from Sasaki Takamaru's *The Secret Account from Tsukuba*
Source: Reproduced with permission from the Tsubouchi Memorial Theater Museum.

Theater in 1937), and *The Brothers of the House of Oki* (*Okike no kyōdai*, 沖家の兄弟, 1939). Other examples of Restoration Plays include Mayama Seika's production of *Sakamoto Ryōma* (*Sakamoto Ryōma*, 坂本竜馬, 1928), Kubo Sakae's[2] *The Blood Oath of Goryōkaku* (*Goryōkaku kessho*, 五稜郭血書, 1933), Miyoshi Jūrō's *Slain Senta* (*Kirareta Senta*, 斬られた仙太, 1934), Kubo Sakae's and Murayama Tomoyoshi's *rensa-geki* productions of *Shinsengumi: A Talkie Rensa-geki* (*Toki rensa-geki Shinsengumi*, トーキー連鎖劇新撰組, 1937), and Wada Katsuichi's play *The Boat Heading to Shore* (*Riku wo yuku fune*, 陸を往く船, 1937). In other words, there were a host of plays that broadly fall under the category of Proletarian Theater which focused on the Restoration Period. The interest in Japan's recent history was strong, motivated by the existential-level stakes of staging the political aftermath of the Meiji Restoration in a socialist context, both for the movement as a whole and for the Proletarian Theater Movement in particular.

A shared resistance to the Japanese state in the early years of Meiji and Shōwa surely accounts for part of the Proletarian playwrights' interest in the genre, even if they approached that resistance from an ideological standpoint that differed from their Meiji predecessors. For Marxists, violent revolt is, of course, a key mechanism for propelling society to the next stage of history, and while groups who feature in these plays, including the Shinsengumi (the violent band that policed Kyoto, dealt with in more detail in Chapter 4) and the violent revolts of the Freedom and People's Rights Movement, failed in their ostensible aims, they represented valiant and principled Japanese models of resistance to what all leftists regarded as oppressive regimes.

46   *There is a specter haunting Communism*

Yet the point of putting this material on stage was more than a simple call to arms. Rather, these plays are concerned with Marxist conceptions of progress and stages of development, particularly as used to understand the Japanese context. Is there a possibility of "uneven temporality" of Marxist historical stages which would allow Japan's context to more smoothly integrate into the theoretical framework of the global proletarian movement?[3] Was this a way to move beyond "stage-ism", that affliction of Marxist ideologues to prescriptively apply Marx's historical determinist stages of history to every situation, which obstructed Japan's possibilities of a Communist future? A large part of *Tsukuba*'s success must be understood in terms of how the production addressed these questions.

Specifically, Sasaki employs references to temporally and spatially distant revolutions in order to reflect on contemporary crises. Analogy, primarily through the mode of translation, was a device through which the plays presented in this chapter worked to understand the Restoration as a revolution. Since source and target texts of translations are often presumed to have an analogous relationship, this use of analogy also manifested itself at the level of text type. The texts in question here are thus analogs in two senses: in their status as translations and in their presentation of histories that are meant to be read as corollaries to the audience's own recent past.[4] Analogy, while admittedly a blunt and imperfect instrument to communicate meaning, is a crucial tool for these dramatists to understand their recent past in a global historical context and to manufacture what Eric Selbin calls "revolutionary stories".[5]

This use of analog to explain the Restoration Period was neither new nor rare. The Proletarian Theater Movement's plays mirrored narrative practice in the post-Restoration period. The Freedom and People's Rights Movement itself made liberal use of foreign (i.e. Western) revolutions to serve as analogs for the Japanese situation, including historical accounts of the French, English, and American revolutions, as well as historical and literary references to ancient Rome. European philosophy informed the resistance to the Meiji government as well, through Nakamura Keiu's translation of Mill's *On Liberty* and Nakae Chōmin's introduction of Rousseau's writing on natural rights. The examples that these intellectuals brought in through translation permeated all varieties of written and performance art in Japan, including song, *rakugo* storytelling, and theater.[6]

The Restoration Plays in this chapter are either set in the early Meiji Period or are translations of narratives about revolution seen by their translators as analogs to the Meiji situation. They are, in other words, attempts to reframe and re-evaluate the Restoration to alternatively serve a nationalistic project that on the one hand placed Japan within a historical trajectory where modernity had been achieved, or on the other situated it as an ideological objective where the bourgeois revolution had already paved the way for a Japanese Communist Revolution. The Meiji Period translations of Shakespeare's Roman Plays pursue the first goal, and the latter is the aim of Sasaki's Restoration Plays, which span a significant stretch of his career and relationship with the movement. This analysis of these now-forgotten plays highlights the degree to which Sasaki's productions went beyond agit-prop, and they involved innovative performative approaches to tradition and modernity.

Sasaki's Restoration Plays look back to the past and out to distant lands through multiple refracting lenses, yet they are fundamentally grounded in their own present context, as is the case with any writing of history. Set in the early Meiji Period, these plays perform the unsettled meaning of revolution in this key moment of the Japanese Proletarian movement in the late 1920s. Thus, Sasaki's plays embody the proletarian revolution through the analogy of the Restoration, which in the 1880s was itself understood and interpreted by means of analogy to Western precedents. *Tsukuba* was an example of the Proletarian Theater's engagement with its political and performative past and present, as well as its struggle with the problematics of revolution and the Restoration.

The Meiji revolution

The events of 1868, which have come to be referred to by the terms "*ishin*" (維新) in Japanese and "Restoration" in English, sit uncomfortably in any taxonomy of violent overthrow. The fact that 1868 is not commonly referred to in English as a "revolution", or any other number of terms which describe internal regime change, and that the Boshin War is not usually described as a "civil war" (although the later, unsuccessful Seinan War often is), serves to craft a very specific interpretation of the events that led to the fall of the shogun. It also places 1868 within an ambivalent place in any attempt to define and theorize revolution. In unpacking the ontology of the term, Hannah Arendt describes revolution in its Western context as housing competing forces of rupture and continuity.[7] While internal regime change has existed for as long as there have been rulers with whom their subjects could be dissatisfied, Arendt sees revolution as irrevocably wedded to modernity. The French Revolution is the quintessential example of this shift as the one which changed the relationship of authority with time itself. 1789 represented such an extreme break with history for its instigators that it justified its being marked as year one in an entirely new measurement of time. Turning this focus in an about-face, the logic of authority is rooted in a break with all that has come before rather than a connection to the past through lineage or the like. This rupture pulled the word "revolution" out of the heavens—from speaking about the cyclical movement of celestial bodies which serve as temporal markers and metaphorically about the cyclical change of political systems back to a point of origins—into an earthly setting that referred instead to the irresistible nature of that celestial change. In this now commonly used sense of the term, what had once been a synonymous pair shifts so that a revolution is now the opposite of a restoration. Yet the trace of that shared original meaning of revolution—a return to origins—is embedded in both the semantic fields of the words and in the political events that they are used to describe. Arendt points out that even the purest examples of revolution—1789 and 1776—began as returns to originary greatness that had been lost. Revolution thus encompasses two competing, polar opposite processes which pull in progressive and conservative directions—the former rooted in modernity and the latter in antiquity.

48 *There is a specter haunting Communism*

This marriage of an internally conflicted model of Western revolution with the events of 1868 highlighted in the plays in this chapter foregrounds the lacunae in the Japanese historiography that is so often papered over through the act of translation. Inscribed into the inter-lingual gap between "*kakumei*" and "*ishin*", the meanings of which have evolved into the former being grounded in rupture and newness and the latter in continuity and tradition, is the fundamental challenge of conceptualizing 1868 in a way which balanced incongruous progressive and conservative nation-building rationales. Thus in the rush to define what has become codified as a "Restoration", both during the immediate aftermath and in generations following it, 1868 was retroactively framed as a 1789-style revolution. Other formulations that lie in and around the space between "*ishin*" and "Restoration" highlight competing theorizations of the highly contested discourse of 1868.

The reliance on 1789 to understand 1868 highlights points of contact in the new thinking about rebellion and regime change that resonated in both premodern Japan and premodern Europe. After all, angst felt by the ruled towards their rulers, spurred on by top-down policies deemed unfair, is not a sentiment that European peasants can claim as uniquely their own. Indeed, small-scale violent revolts can be traced throughout the ostensibly peaceful rule of the Tokugawa from the seventeenth to nineteenth centuries. Likewise, the local domains preceding the establishment of the Tokugawa Shogunate certainly were not devoid of violent conflicts, up to and including efforts to depose rulers in power in significant instances such as the Genpei War and Battle of Sekigahara. Yet both these small- and large-scale examples of violent resistance fundamentally differed from the change that came in 1868 and also from post-Enlightenment European notions of revolution. The Genpei Wars, the Hōgen Disturbance, and other large-scale violence left the political order largely unchanged, with the emperor and court as the nominal head of state. In other words, authority was still grounded in ties to an ancient past. Peasant revolts (一揆 *ikki*) in the seventeenth, eighteenth, and nineteenth centuries likewise did not seek fundamental change of the system but rather were organized around specific demands for policy reform. Indeed, these peasant uprisings were in fact a tacitly accepted mode of political negotiation (albeit as a last resort) with predetermined protocols by both the peasants and the authorities.[8] These modes of resistance all resonate with methods of regime change that Arendt sees in pre-revolutionary Europe.

The introduction of the word "revolution" into Japan through the translation word "*kakumei*", and the attendant examination of foreign models of revolution, offered a new framework through which to view the facts and repercussions of the Restoration. However, as with the introduction of jiyū discussed in Chapter 1, there was no broad consensus on either the meaning or ramifications of revolution in a Japanese context. Like its Western counterpart, the word kakumei itself uncomfortably housed both new and old ideas about governmental change. The variety of Western models that was held up in both text and on stage as ideals with which to compare 1868 highlighted the degree to which discourse on the Restoration remained contested throughout and beyond the Meiji Period.

There is a specter haunting Communism   49

The distinction between a "restoration" and a "revolution" was a new notion in Meiji Japan in ways very similar to those Arendt describes in her analysis of 1789. Like its European partner word "revolution", which both was and was not the opposite of "restoration", there was at best a fuzzy distinction between an *ishin* and a *kakumei* in these categories.[9] Even now, Mitani Hiroshi notes the contemporary scholarly ambivalence in calling the "*Meiji ishin*" a "Restoration". Mitani suggests that the contemporary equivalence of "restoration" with "*ishin*" elides substantial difference in the terms. He posits that *ōsei fukko* (王政復古, "the restoration of the monarchy") is a closer approximation of what is implied by the English word (i.e. a change limited to the political reinstatement of a head of government) and suggests that *ishin* operates on a larger scale, both politically and socially, than does the English term "restoration". However, he also disagrees with scholars who have translated the term as "revolution". Unlike Arendt, Mitani sees this term as primarily rooted in class warfare and bottom-up change. This, according to Mitani, does not describe the social position or motivations of those leading the toppling of the bakufu. To circle this square, some historians have used the term "conservative revolution", but Mitani sees this as something of an oxymoron. Ultimately he arrives at the term "regeneration" as a possible English translation that encompasses the widespread social and political rebirth connoted by *ishin*. Whatever the most apt current English equivalent may be, both "*kakumei*" and "*ishin*" were ancient words imbued with new meanings beginning in the early Meiji Period. Yet like their Western counterparts, they came to describe new concepts but also retained etymological traces of synonymous roots.

The modern conception of "*kakumei*", like its Western counterpart "revolution", is linked to the translation of accounts of the events and philosophy around 1789. It is not surprising, then, that development of the term correlated with the growth of knowledge of the history of France. The French Revolution was first reported in Japan in 1794, only five years after the fall of the Bastille, and the news came into Japan in the context of the Kansei reforms in the late Tokugawa period.[10] As events progressed abroad, under both the bakufu and the early Meiji government, the official focus was upon Napoleon rather than the fall and execution of the monarch. The word "*kakumei*" was still not used to describe the events in France. Unsurprisingly, despite its officially sealed borders, knowledge of world history and the French revolution in particular continued to grow in Japan. In 1845, a Dutch Studies scholar wrote a multi-volume history of the world, and in the second volume titled *European Countries* (欧羅巴州), he wrote about the French Revolution and Napoleon. In Meiji 4 a two-volume work titled *A New History of All Countries* (万国新史), written in kanbun, introduced Honoré Gabriel Riqueti, comte de Mirabeau, Robespierre, and Danton.

It wasn't until quite late, through the work of Liberty Party members, that a comprehensive account of 1789 was disseminated, and it was finally labeled a "revolution". Nakae Chōmin wrote a history of Louis XV and XVI titled *A Record of Two Generations of the French Revolution* (革命前法朗西（フランス）二世 記事, 1886), in which he examined the causes of the revolution, with particular attention to the ideals of the Enlightenment, policies of the right of kings, analysis

50 *There is a specter haunting Communism*

of the demands of the various classes, and a consideration of the economic and idealistic backgrounds that brought about the revolution. He also wrote a series of articles beginning in February of Meiji 15 in the newspaper *Oriental Liberty Newspaper* that were titled *A Discussion of the Theory of Government*. Therein, he states that the current condition in Japan was similar to that of France before the revolution. In this series, he also translated Rousseau's *Social Contract* (民約訳解).[11]

The scholar Kuwabara Takeo points out that until there was a Japanese word to conceptually frame the event in a holistic way (which was not until rather late in this historiography), words which highlighted the effects of the event were used such as *tenpuku* (転覆 overthrow), *haretsu* (破裂 rupture), or *ōsoran* (大騒乱 mayhem, disorder). In other words, the event was seen in terms of its resulting chaos rather than its philosophical motivations. In the 1870s, Rights Movement leaders such as Chōmin helped introduce the Enlightenment philosophies behind the French Revolution, and in 1876, the first use of the word *kakumei* as a translation of revolution appeared in a Japanese newspaper.[12] Like the related word *jiyū* (liberty), it was not a new compound or a calque but rather a Chinese compound that traditionally had a related but different meaning. Specifically, the compound "*kakumei*" was an ancient Chinese word that had been used to describe dynastic change and had its roots in the cosmos like its Western counterpart. However, the change here is not in the way we currently think of revolt. According to Mencius, when rulers became corrupt and failed to rule justly, heaven would supply a new Emperor to take the throne—even if the mechanism was earthly, the agency motivating the shift was "supernatural", at least in the way and to the extent that they conceptualized the supranormal.

Mitani traces the etymology of both words even further back to the *Shijing* (Book of Songs), noting that the terms *ishin* (now "restoration") and *kakumei* (now "revolution") actually had very similar etymological roots. The term *ishin* was only rarely used in Japanese political texts of the Bakumatsu period, but beginning in Meiji 2 (1869) the term became used much more frequently, when the Chinese compound *ishin* (維新) was mapped over the more common Japanese compound (and homophone) *isshin* (一新). Its first use in the *Shijing* reads, "While we are an ancient people, the will of heaven is for a restoration [or, "by the will of heaven, all will become new"] (天命維れ新たなり)".[13]

In other words, explains Mitani, this new term "*ishin*" (restoration) carried a meaning equivalent to the classical Chinese term *kakumei*. Both carried pseudo-religious meanings that suggested a change of dynasties brought about because the heavens have become displeased with the current ruling dynasty. Neither of these terms suggests a bottom-up revolt that Mitani associates with modern "revolution", let alone carrying liberty as its motivating force as Arendt observes, and it posits a reliance upon history and continuity as justification for authority. Thus, while they were essentially synonyms from ancient times until the beginning of the Meiji Period, the term "*ishin*" has come to mean something close to the English "restoration", and the term "*kakumei*" was codified as the translation word for "revolution" in the 1870s through accounts of the French Revolution.

There is a specter haunting Communism 51

Framing 1868 as a "restoration" was particularly fraught with paradox in the case of the Meiji oligarghy, since it suggests the revival of an imperial rule that the leaders of the Meiji government insisted had never ended in the first place. It required a delicate balance, spelled out in the Charter Oath, that Japan needed to return to its ancient origins in an imperial line which was unbroken and eternal, even while the shogun held de facto control for centuries. Mitani suggests that at least linguistically this contradiction can be rationalized by looking to another source text for the meaning of *ishin*. In *Daigaku*, he cites a meaning that allows for change *within* continuity. Yet even apart from this alternate connotation of the word, he suggests that the Meiji oligarchs were not entirely averse to the notion of *kakumei* as we think of it now anyway. After all, Saigō Takamori hired the Russian anarchist Lev Mechnikov to teach at his school, and possibly saw a fellow revolutionary in his devotion to Narodnikism. Conversely, it is also true that these terms do not shift their meanings overnight, and as late as the Meiji 20s, the combined term "*ishin kakumei*" was used as a set phrase. In short, as in the case of "*jiyū*" (see Chapter 1), older terrain occupied by semantic fields does not immediately drop from words, and problems of cognitive dissonance are likely much more pronounced for us retroactively than they were for Meiji intellectuals.

In the years leading up to the overthrow of the shogunate, the theoretical problems of Western revolutions did not concern or motivate the Satsuma-Chōshu forces which brought the emperor back to power. Indeed, they were not driven at all by either a genuine or ostensible need to expand liberty to the populace, that quality which Arendt sees as a fundamental motivating force for modern revolutions. Yet as evidenced by the timeline of nomenclature used to talk about the event, and by the discussion in Chapter 1 which demonstrates the degree to which "liberty" drove political discussion in the 1870s and '80s, there was effort from a wide variety of forces to retroactively frame the events of 1868 in the terms of 1789. This created the new conundrum of rupture/dichotomy that erstwhile revolutionaries in modern instances of violent regime change face generally.

The architects and citizens of the "new" nation were thus forced to negotiate a complicated relationship with their past. While part of this negotiation took place in the realm of the written word, the process of translation and re-visiting Japan's historiography was also a performed and continually re-performed event. Performance of embodied memory of a collective history fused conflicting theorizations of revolution in a Meiji present through analogs in ancient Rome and revolutionary France.

Revolution the analog

However intellectually compelling new notions of revolution may have been, disembodied theory and histories from distant times and places are by themselves insufficient as mechanisms for driving broad-based movements such as the Freedom and People's Rights Movement or the Socialist movement. After all, in reading a historical account of Caesar or Robespierre, it could be at least as likely for a reader to feel that the ideals that motivated the actors in such a distant setting

52 *There is a specter haunting Communism*

were *not* applicable to their current situation as they were to see it as a model that could and should be adopted for Japan. One of the key ways that these new conceptualizations of "revolution" were understood and naturalized was through stories of heroic figures of foreign resistance that were transformed into explicit commentary on the current Japanese context. Performance narratives used analogies between the Meiji Restoration and a wide variety of foreign examples of revolution.

The Shakespearean translations in Chapter 1, focused as they are upon "liberty", are also instructive here in thinking through the notion of "revolution". As outlined earlier, Shakespeare's *Julius Caesar* was initially introduced to Japan through a translation published in the newspaper *Rikken seitō shinbun*. Both it and Tsubouchi Shōyō's translation one year later deal primarily with the new notion of liberty and the locus of authority as conceived by Western thinkers such as J.S. Mill. Another Roman Play, *Coriolanus*, was also translated in full just after these *Ceasars*, and as companion texts these Roman Plays carried an outsized influence in early Japanese Shakespeare translation history compared with their status in European scholarship and performance. All three of these texts unavoidably deal head-on with the texts' central theme of violent regime change, and it is clear that these authors and dramatists were struggling to reconcile new and traditional notions of revolution.

The practice of using foreign models of revolution as guidance and inspiration for local revolution is certainly not unique to the Liberty Party. Both Rome and France have been common reference points for revolutionary movements around the world. Indeed, revolutionaries almost without fail look to historical and foreign models to situate and motivate their own movements. In just one example of the appropriation of 1789, Bastin, Echeverri, and Campo note the influence translations of the French revolution had on independence movements across South America.[14]

The same practice of reading past models of change into the present existed in seventeenth-century England, although while Caesar was seen and used as a symbol of change, he was also employed as a symbol of stability and the strength of the status quo. Lisa Hopkins notes the omnipresent cultural pervasiveness of Rome in England.[15] The Roman imperial model had complex implications for religion, politics, international relations, and history. Rome was both the mythical source of the beginnings of Britain (legend credits Caesar with building the Tower of London) and contemporary authority (James I styled himself as a new Caesar). But Rome was also the seat of the Pope and a metonym for Catholicism, and thus the Roman Empire represented both stability and a threat to stability. So it is not surprising that Shakespeare was only one of many playwrights to put Julius Caesar on stage, or that the Caesars and Rome generally were read in conflicting ways by Elizabethan audiences.

While Julius Caesar was a figure who stood in the forefront of the public eye in Shakespeare's time, and while Shakespeare often grafted contemporary issues onto his scripts, the critical consensus is that characters in *Julius Caesar* are not stand-ins for real-life Elizabethan political figures. That is, the events and plays

There is a specter haunting Communism 53

are analogs. They are not ciphers taken from and read as contemporary models, nor are they morality plays meant to be read as transparent and unambiguous allegory. Shakespeare wrote and first performed *Julius Caesar* in the 1590s, before the Guy Fawkes plot and before the ascension of King James and his self-styled Roman monarchy. Thus, apt as those events may seem to be in retrospect, they could not have been his inspiration for the events in the play. However, there can be little question that current events influenced Shakespeare's productions and reception after the turn of the seventeenth century.

All of these examples demonstrate the power of analogy in framing and motivating revolutionary thought. As a literary device, analog is admittedly a blunt object, and metaphors in general are inherently overdetermined and impossible to pin down with specificity. After all, there is very little that is *actually* comparable between ancient Rome and Elizabethan England, and perhaps even less between Meiji Japan and Elizabethan perceptions of ancient Rome. Analogies recognize a relationship that in mathematical terms is not "equal" or "like" as in literary allegory, most agit-prop, or some kinds of satire, but rather it is a relationship that can be described as mathematically "similar"—sharing only some characteristics, and even those are not necessarily in equal proportions. This is in fact the same relationship that the two texts of a translation pair have with each other—not equal but similar or analogous. It is then not surprising that the most common terminology used by translation studies scholars to describe the two texts in a translation as "source" and "target" are drawn from the vocabulary, in formal logic, of two halves of an analogous pair. Yet slippery as the device can be, through their introductions and paratexts the translations examined here framed the Roman and French situations, and the European notion of revolution generally, in the context of the Meiji Restoration. As such, they served as building blocks of the stories that framed the conflicted contemporary understanding of the Restoration.

To be sure, it is not only in times of resistance, rebellion, and revolution that analogs are employed in creating group or national narratives. Yet the stories that these analogs allow resistors and activists to compose are necessary, even if they are not sufficient, elements in instigating revolution. Eric Selbin's examination (2010) of the power of story in revolution sheds light on the way these analogs are pieced together to powerful effect. He sees revolutions as drawing on four fundamental (almost archetypal, but not in a Jungian, collective unconscious sense of that term) stories that are mixed and matched. They are seen as comparable stories to whatever contemporary situation they are transplanted into, despite their temporal or spatial distance and despite the differing particulars of the events in both circumstances. One benefit to looking back is that these stories help explain why revolutions occur in one place and time but not another. To aspiring revolutionaries, for whom these stakes are that much higher, these stories allow for the possibility of the highly unlikely event of success. After all, the thinking goes, if they could do it there, we can do it here. As Selbin frames it: "The chance to reshape one's world and one's place in it is an impossible possibility. What moves a people into and, more rarely, through a revolutionary process, is the articulation of a compelling story from the past which frames the current struggles and

54 *There is a specter haunting Communism*

promises a better world to come".[16] It is these stories, then, that allow for the imaginative space to work through and motivate the notions of resistance, rebellion, and revolution.

Selbin sees these stories as grounded in four foundational archetypes which serve as ingredients for any particular revolutionary story: the civilizing and democratizing revolution, the social revolution, the freedom and liberation revolution, and revolutions of the lost and forgotten. These four stories are malleable, with parts like strands of DNA that can be rearranged and replaced or dropped completely as the circumstances dictate, and some revolutions will rely heavily upon only one or a combination of stories at any given time. This flexibility is crucial for the universal applicability of these stories, and the result is that particular iterations of these stories are similar to one another only in the way and to the extent that examples of, say, the Cinderella folktales are similar—that is, not in their particulars but in their broad strokes.

Like their folktale counterparts, these stories of resistance, rebellion, and revolution do not exist primarily on the page. They may be textual, as in the examples of French Revolution translations during the wars in South America cited earlier, but this is a secondary mode and not the form in which they function within larger movements. Selbin notes that it is only through the performative act of mimesis that revolutionary stories take myth and memory and forge a useful device through which these stories can be made real. Selbin is speaking about a mimesis that is much broader in scope than the mimesis we talk about on stage, yet it is not surprising that we see the embodiment of stories of the Restoration and revolution abound in a wide variety of performative genres in the two resistance political movements examined here.

Beginning in the Meiji Period, a plethora of embodied performative modes was employed in a wide variety of texts that grafted stories of revolution upon analogs from translated sources. One such genre was the popular songs of the Freedom and People's Rights Movement known as "People's Rights Poems" (民権詩歌). As a way to inspire the potential revolutionaries and conceptually frame their movement, new People's Rights Poems sung the praises of revolutionaries around the world. Rights Movement activist Ueki Emori's *Collection of Liberty Poems* (自由詞林) ties the notion of liberty to revolution through a long list of examples that included Caesar's assasination, the French Revolution, the Puritan Revolution, Rousseau, the Russian anarchists, William Tell, the Irish revolutionaries Parnell and Emmet, and the American Revolution.[17] Other genres included *rakugo* and *enzetsukai* as well as staged theatrical performances of the works of Dumas such as *Ange Pitou* (*The Triumphal Song of the French Revolution*, 仏国革命自由の凱歌) and Hugo's *Year 93* (*The Carnage in the Streets of the French Revolution*, 仏国革命修羅の衢), the writings of the Narodniki, as well as Shakespeare's *Julius Caesar* and *Coriolanus*.[18] Many of these translated texts, such as *Madame Terese* by Erkmann and Chatrian (which dealt with the fallout from the French Revolution), and *Julius Caesar* were initially introduced through newspapers, which as Murayama Masao has famously pointed out served as scripts for oral, communal events.[19]

There is a specter haunting Communism   55

In all of these examples, in the performative arts the models of ancient Rome and revolutionary France loomed large, so it is important to probe why these examples more than others proved so compelling. Building off of this framework of revolutionary stories, in the examples that follow I examine analogs that make up the contingent pieces of the analogies, metaphors, and ultimately the stories that constitute the performative discourse on the Restoration and revolution. This discourse plays out in a wide range of embodied performance genres, including song, lecture, stage, and film using the backdrops of ancient Rome and the French Revolution.

The Roman analog

Ancient Rome predates by millenia the modern notion of revolution, yet it surprisingly serves as the locus or referent of many examples of Japanese stories of revolution. Kawashima Keizō, Tsubouchi Shōyō, and Itakura Kōtarō were drawn to the broad historical parallels among Rome, Elizabethan England, and Meiji Japan in their translations of Shakespeare's Roman Plays discussed in the previous chapter. It is particularly interesting that they approached their stories about local issues and contemporary artistic concerns through the stories that Shakespeare used to think through the concerns of his own era. While the texts are the focus of the examination in Chapter 1 for their interest in liberty, this chapter looks to the introductory material and paratext of Shōyō's *The Amazing Story of Caesar: The Legacy of the Sharpness of Liberty's Sword* (自由太刀余波鋭鋒:該撒奇談, 1884), Itakura's *Freedom's Scourge and the Bonds of Affection: The Tale of the Greatest Hero of the Age* (豪傑一世鏡:自由の笞恩愛の繼, 1888), and Kawashima's *Rise and Fall of Rome* (羅馬盛衰鑒, 1883) for their treatment of violent regime change. These plays' introductions and paratexts highlight differing approaches in coming to grips with the problems inherent in synthesizing disparate ideals of revolution. Shōyō's introduction engages with the question of historiography versus historical fiction, while Kawashima's introduction situates Caesar within the context of Western revolutions—the French, English, American, and Russian revolutions in particular.

Of these three texts, Kawashima's translation makes the most obvious use of analog (between the conflict between Brutus and Caesar and a long list of subsequent antagonistic pairs) as the mechanism with which these three examples look to a broader European history to explain Caesar and to apply those lessons to Japan. Yet all of these texts recognize the importance of analogy in these stories of revolution. Kawashima's translation begins by listing a long heritage of revolutions, including the Bourbins and the Jacobins, the anarchists and the Czar, and the like, and this list begins with Caesar and Brutus. In other words, Brutus versus Caesar is the original revolution and presages all Western revolutions in their various iterations. In providing this list, Kawashima does not give the reader anything that marks these conflicts as distinct from the

56   *There is a specter haunting Communism*

others. On the contrary, he lists them as if they are variations on a theme that begin with Caesar and Brutus. Or, as Hannah Arendt puts it, there is only and ever one revolution.

By contrast, Yoda Gakkai's introduction to Shōyō's translation notes the very limitations of the genre of historical writing as the strength of the fictional treatment of history. He argues that in its pursuit of cold facts, history lacks the ability to convey meaning, and his analog reaches into China's literary past to favorably compare Shakespeare's *Caesar* to *The Romance of the Three Kingdoms*, which, of course, was also part of Japan's intellectual tradition. Thus it is the narrative structure, provided in the script that he is introducing, that is an essential ingredient lacking in historical writing.

Shōyō's introduction similarly looks to Japan's pre-Meiji intellectual tradition to explain the source text. In so doing, he creates a new narrative on top of Shakespeare's own variation on the Roman story which portrays a complicated view of the revolutionary nature of the conspirators. Shōyō inserts a narrative frame around the text which reaches into the Japanese intellectual tradition, and he finds a model of revolution that is decidedly un-French in nature. He highlights the narrative frame's use of a traditional understanding of revolution. The resulting text is convoluted. On the one hand, the body of the translation makes Brutus the tragic hero where the source text is deliberately ambiguous. This casts the assassination of Caesar, and revolt in general, in a sympathetic light. Yet on the other hand, Shōyō foregrounds the problematic juxtaposition of traditional notions of "kakumei" with new notions of revolution. Shōyō's narrative introduction (which is included within the text of the play) lays out a rationale for revolution that looks back to traditional connotations of kakumei:

> When there is a free government, the citizens will live in harmony. When the citizens are in harmony, the country will be pacified. If one man treats the country as his own, engages in self-dealing, and wields his power recklessly, the country will lose its footing. On the other hand, when they adhere to elevated teachings, the highborn and lowborn alike all strive together to govern. Shining like the rising sun, the country of Rome was once a golden eagle spreading its wings across the barbarian lands and the four seas, but after its system of mutual cooperation broke down, the country became arrogant and the people became crass. As frequently happens in periods of decay, evil men formed cliques, plotted only for their own gain, and vied against each other. The country faced unending strife.

> 政、自由なれば、国民和し、国民和すれば国治まる、一人国を私して、文を舞し、権を弄する時んば、国立地に乱るてふ、貴き誠をそがままに、高き賤しき押なべて、共に和らぎ政ごち、昇る朝日と輝ける、黄金の鷲は雲井做す、遠き夷乃国々の、端々までも羽をのして、四海に羽うちし羅馬国も、協和の制の弛みしより、国驕り人卑しく、廃れ行く世の慣とて、奸雄しばしば党を樹て、私利を図りて相軋る、争乱絶間なかりける。[20]

There is a specter haunting Communism   57

The right to rule is predicated on the virtues of the ruling class rather than the natural rights of the citizens, and there is nothing that suggests the existence of a social contract. The equation is simply: good rule equals a prosperous nation; corrupt rule leads to decay. There is no room in this framework for a revolution from below, and the French model of change supported by the Liberty Party is not favored or even entertained.

The notion of revolution here draws more from the traditional notion of kaku-mei than from European notions of revolution, and it is in this notion of change that the translation's referents get complicated. The obvious analog for Brutus and his conspirators are the so-called men of spirit (志士 *shishi*), or perhaps the *sōshi* of the Freedom and People's Rights Movement, who fought against the bakufu and the new Meiji government, respectively (Shōyō even uses the word *sōshi* to describe the conspirators). Yet as discussed in Chapter 1 the text is translated such that the story is primarily political and not military in nature. The difficulty in calling out the problems with the Restoration itself is tied to the oligarchy's suc-cessful use of the emperor—in other words, to communicate that everything had changed and simultaneously nothing had changed.

By turning the text into a critique of political rather than military leaders, and by portraying Caesar as just one of those political leaders, Shōyō's text neither promotes regicide nor condemns the Restoration itself, yet it simultaneously glo-rifies resistance. More importantly, it argues for increased freedom and for notions of liberty that do not necessarily make the leap to justifying revolution. In other words, Shōyō squarely places his translation on the Reform Party side of the Free-dom and People's Rights divide: it was arguing for liberty as J.S. Mill saw it, not for natural rights as Rousseau argued for, and the construction is clearly in favor of an English constitutional monarchy over the more radical French model of revolution.

The narrative frame Shōyō began in the introduction concludes in the same voice:

> The country of Rome became peaceful, and the waves rocking the nation were quelled. For laying the foundation of the empire and for the wisdom he possessed, he will be praised and his name will be remembered as part of the dawn of the age and in the history books. It must serve as a warning to all generations of the frivolous and fickle citizens of the country that this peace followed the unfortunate snapping of the sword of freedom.

> 四海波、静しずく治まる羅馬国、其帝政の基礎を、開きし君の身の内に、備はる智略末長く、朝日時代と竹帛に、ほまれを残し名を残し、憾みを残す自由の太刀、折れて治まる時勢こそ、軽佻浮薄の國人の、萬古の誠となりにけれ。[21]

There is a remarkable disconnect between this passage and the main body of the translation. Whereas Brutus is lauded throughout as the greater man as well as the hero of the translation, this conclusion seems to suggest that Caesar was

58   *There is a specter haunting Communism*

in fact the protagonist all along. It is a conflicted message that praises Caesar for founding the empire yet simultaneously regrets the failure of the revolutionaries to achieve freedom. While the closing half of the frame does logically join with the opening half of the frame in denouncing revolution from below by the "frivolous and fickle citizens" (*keichōfuka no kokumin*), it is at odds with the body of the text itself, which foregrounds Brutus as the tragic hero. In other words, the text wavers between reading traditional Chinese notions of "kakumei" and Enlightenment notions of "revolution" into Shakespeare's Elizabethan source text about ancient Rome.

Itakura's introductions to *Coriolanus* serve yet another function from that of the two *Caesars*. Itakura himself wrote two of the four introductions to his text, and both primarily give background information about Shakespeare and the play itself. Rather than construct a broad philosophical framework like Shōyō and Kawashima do, Itakura provides the lead-up to the plot of the play—a background that would not have been needed even in Meiji Japan for the much more famous figures of Caesar and Marcus Brutus. *Coriolanus* is just as much an ambiguous, open-ended meditation on governmental rule as is *Caesar*, but Junius Brutus (Coriolanus's antagonist) did not have Marcus's name recognition, and Caius Marcus Coriolanus would not have fit into predetermined constructs for the Meiji audience as would Gaius Julius Caesar. The historical background that Itakura offers not only contextualizes the play but also indicates to his audience how to respond to characters that are not otherwise clearly heroes or villains.

Specifically, unlike *Liberty's Sword* (Shōyō's *Caesar*), in *Liberty's Scourge* (Itakura's *Coriolanus*) Shakespeare puts the commoners on an equal footing at the negotiating table. Notable for Shakespeare's political plays, they actually have named characters in the persons of the tribunes Brutus and Sicinius. The right of the people to choose their leaders is a central driving mechanism of the plot, and in his introduction, Itakura situates the play in a context in which the commoners are unquestionably within their rights to resist an unjust and oppressive government. The background history that he recounts tells the story of Rome at the beginning of the Tarquin kings:

> In Rome at that time, society was divided into the aristocracy and the common people. While the common people wanted to do away with the elites, they were unable to extinguish the aristocracy's authority. Taking advantage of the cowardice of the commoners, the aristocracy plotted only for their own gain, and they didn't even consider the harm or benefit to the citizens. They held the common people down and did not let them rise. Discord arose between them, and disregarding the affairs of state, the aristocracy put all their energy into punishing the citizenry. The people finally had enough, and they took up their axes and shovels to kill the aristocrats.
>
> Then arrived in Rome a powerful leader named Tarquin. An oppressive tyrant, he planned to make himself ruler of Rome, and without discriminating against aristocrat or commoner he joined them together and raised an army. Finally there seemed to be peace. However, in his victory he relied entirely

There is a specter haunting Communism 59

upon the strength of the commoners, so in recognition for their heroic deeds in the service of their country, they expected that he would grant them some degree of freedom.[22]

Itakura goes on to describe how the commoners were disappointed in their expectations, and then were lied to in a second situation where they were called upon to defend the city. They are led out of the city to strike up on their own by Brutus, who would become the tribune in the play. In retaliation, Coriolanus cuts off their food supply so that they are forced either to starve or return to the city. The key is that Itakura sees this play, and wants his readers to see this play, not as the story of the fall of a great general (as is the case in Shakespeare's text), but rather of the struggle of commoners for liberty. Much as in the *Liberty's Sword*, *Liberty's Scourge* very consciously asks the reader to see the text in terms of class conflict.

Complementing the introductions and the translation strategies themselves, the paratextual material in these translations (described in greater detail in Chapter 1) also highlights the analogous relationship between the contemporary context of the audience/reader and the diegesis of the play. In the illustrations for *Coriolanus*, the Roman Forum is in ruins, and in Kawashima's translation, Rome is depicted as a modern, nineteenth-century city. Even more telling, some of the peasants in *Coriolanus* appear in the garb of Japanese peasants. In other words, these temporally and spatially distant models of revolution are brought into the immediate here and now.

Thus the role of Rome as an analogy is very clearly foregrounded in these translations. Yet the story that these analogs help create is not the straightforward narrative of revolution that the Roman story was so often taken to be. Rather it reflects the complicated nature that the translated term *kakumei* inevitably has in mapping a new constellation of connotations upon a preexisting word. While the Roman example may be a less problematic example of revolution than the French example, the French model was also appealing for both the Freedom and People's Rights and Socialist performers. It is situated at the beginning of European modernity and the originary narrative of modern revolutionary stories.

The French analog

Significant as the Roman story was for Meiji Japan, it is the French Revolution (per Arendt and others) that is the *sine qua non* of modern revolution stories. Rooted in the study of 1789 by Japanese intellectuals as far back as the Restoration Period, the fall of the French monarchy played a significant role in how the Japanese thought about the Restoration. It also became a key focus for Japanese leftist thinkers in the late 1920s in the crisis over how to understand Japan's stage of history. After all, if 1868 was not the Japanese Bourgeois Revolution, where did that leave the future of the movement? The way forward was murky without fundamentally re-theorizing Marxian revolution. Theorizing a story of 1868 which adhered to the fundamental narratives of 1789 served as ideological

60 *There is a specter haunting Communism*

materiel both as resistance against an oppressive regime and in the fight over the nature of the Japanese communist movement itself. The performance of Sasaki Takamaru's Restoration Plays was thus more than agit-prop or entertainment for the workers. His first play in this genre, *The Death of Danton*, represented his first theatrical argument in demonstrating the lasting impact of 1789 on Japanese stories of resistance. It crafts a story of revolution that, through translation, strips the original story of its connections to a non-modern, non-revolutionary past.

The way this play came into its Japanese performance is a bit convoluted. *Danton's Death* was published in 1930 and lists Sasaki as the translator and Aleksei Tolstoy as the author. Yet, while Sasaki knew French and had access to the historical material in the original language, he did not read Russian. There were actually more steps in the translation process than is acknowledged in the Japanese version. The original text was *Dantons Tod* by Georg Buchner, written in German in 1835. Aleksei Tolstoy then adapted the text in 1918 into Russian, making significant changes in the process. At this point, Buchner's name was removed as author. Nikolai Hohlov then translated Tolstoy's text into Esperanto in 1928 (again without Buchner's name attached), and it was this Esperanto version that Sasaki came across and translated. It isn't entirely clear why neither Buchner nor Holhov are credited in Sasaki's translation—a fact made even more curious because it was published in 1930, one year after *Danton's Tod* was translated directly from German and published in the same series, under the same title, and by the same publisher as Sasaki's translation. In any event, Sasaki's was a Japanese translation of an Esperanto translation of Tolstoy's Russian adaptation of Georg Buchner's German play.

Not surprisingly, the text underwent shifts in the course of its translations that offer insights into what Sasaki and the Leftist Troupe found compelling about the script. Buchner's play characterizes the clash between Danton and Robespierre in terms of Robespierre's austere, uncompromising moral code and Danton's ostentatious drinking and womanizing. Buchner's text is also rich with allusions to ancient Greece and Rome—Danton and Robespierre are repeatedly compared with either Caesar or Brutus. And in Buchner's text, Danton is almost lackadaisical in his defense until he reaches the court. Sasaki's text, after its several iterations from its original version, is significantly shorter. Gone is the foregrounding of the clash of moral codes, and absent also are almost all allusions to ancient Greece or Rome that bind the original to a pre-modern past which resists a Marxist revolutionary reading. Instead, a decidedly more spirited Danton faces down Robespierre in a clash that is primarily political in nature and focused in temporal scope.

Thus, by the time it had arrived in Japan, the text had already been subject to political modifications, and it was already seen in terms of a historical and political analogy. A Japanese reviewer saw in a German performance of the play a critique of Stalin by the German Socialists. The narrative became, in other words, about internal conflict within the movement in ways that would have resonated with Sasaki's current context, as is discussed later. Tolstoy made heavy changes to the text, presumably at least in part to remove such a reading (he had a history of

There is a specter haunting Communism 61

making changes at the behest of Stalin's regime). Yet even with these changes it is hardly a story to rally potential revolutionaries around. Buchner's original text ends with Lucile Desmoulins sitting on the scaffold where her husband Camille and Danton were guillotined. The final line of the play has her committing suicide by calling the mob upon herself by yelling aloud, "Long live the king". As a revolution story, it is hardly inspiring to rally to the monarchy as a final act. Rather, it is a tale of mourning of the internal collapse of the movement as a result of the clash of two powerful factions and a full-throated rejection of revolution. Sasaki's version elides this final scene, and the final lines are Danton's famous defiant words to his executioner. He says, "People of France, I leave you my influence as a gift. Executioner, show the crowd my head. It is well worth seeing". As such, Sasaki's production leaves the audience not with a rejection of revolution but with the tragic consequences of the internal disputes in the party, and he stands as a figure for what Eric Selbin would call a revolutionary story of the lost and forgotten—one that would have resonance with Sasaki's contemporary audience.

Danton was the first of Sasaki's Restoration Plays, which in each iteration more tightly and obviously imbricated the French analog into the story of 1868. In *Danton*, he wrote a "true" translation of a text co-created by Georg Buchner, Aleksei Tolstoy, and Nikolai Holhov; he followed this with *The Secret Account from Tsukuba*, which bases his story of Meiji resistance upon French literary models; Sasaki then comes into his own as a playwright with *Itagaki Taisuke* and *The Brothers of the House of Oki*, which are essentially original compositions but reference and are informed by French theorizations of revolution and liberty. This trajectory of writing his French model more seamlessly into "original" writing is mirrored in his growth from fundamentally modern Western theatrical modes of performance into theater that drew (controversially) on Japanese performance traditions. In *Danton*, Sasaki produced a traditional shingeki performance in a modern European mode; *Tsukuba*, however, utilized kabuki-trained Shōchiku actors, and *Brothers* was performed in a shinkokugeki style. Thus text type and performance genre are working in tandem to reach into spatial and temporal distance to think through revolution through embodied memories of the Restoration and French Revolution.

The specter

The Rights Movement thinkers' understanding of "revolution" centered on the promise of modernity. A key struggle for Meiji Period revolutionary ideals was the way they competed semantically and philosophically with earlier Japanese notions of violent regime change. In the late 1920s, however, the schematics of the discussion had dramatically changed from a debate that focused on which foreign revolution was the best model for the Restoration to whether *any* model of revolution was appropriate at all. Previous sections of this chapter have detailed the introduction of the word "revolution", and how this notion was embodied in performative texts that examined the Restoration through the lens of other revolutions which themselves were interpretive accounts of historical events. I now turn

62   *There is a specter haunting Communism*

to Sasaki's Avant-Garde Theater (*Zen'eiza*), the rupture of which immediately preceded his interest in the Freedom and People's Rights Movement and helps explain his theatrical experimentation in the production of *Tsukuba* with the Popular Theater (*Taishū za*).

The Proletarian movement inherited the translation word "kakumei" from the Freedom and People's Rights Movement, but the Rights Movement's conception of revolution was different from the leftists of the 1920s and 1930s. One way to think about this paradigm shift, relying on Translation Studies scholar Maria Tymoczko, is to think of it as a shift from a "cluster concept"—that is, a notion that cannot be defined with necessary and sufficient elements but rather by inclusive examples that in this case included both Ancient Rome and the French Revolution—to a fixed, monolithic ideal. In a Marxist context, and even more importantly in a post-1918 context, revolutions for Japanese socialists could no longer be analogs of one another. Each case had to fit specific qualifications and be "equal to" a platonic ideal that was nonetheless almost impossible to envision in practical, concrete terms. The definition of this platonic ideal was closely tied to the position of Japan in a Marxist progression of history. For many socialists at the time, the Bourgeois Revolution was a model which served as a key criterion for entering the capitalist stage of history, which in turn was a prerequisite for the communist stage of history. Thus, whether the Meiji Restoration qualified as a Bourgeois Revolution was of crucial importance to many in the Japanese socialist movement.

This debate over the status of the Meiji Restoration as a Bourgeois Revolution polarized leftists in the 1920s and 1930s. Marxist theory was dominated at the time, both in Japan and in key conduits through which socialist thought was imported from abroad, by what might be termed "stage-ism", or the view that temporality is unitary and that historical progression must be achieved in complete stages. For some, there was little room for the recognition that different modes of production could coexist within a system.[23] Yet as Harry Harootunian and others have explained, this kind of Marxian historical determinism had a difficult time explaining many non-European models of development.[24]

These internal conflicts reached beyond the rarefied realm of dry political theory and played out in visible ways in the Proletarian Theater world, which became an important venue for navigating these debates over historical stages and multiple temporalities. In one specific example, in 1929, Kubo Sakae posits a theater history that addresses the current stage of Japanese history while simultaneously sidestepping the thorny question of the status of the Meiji Restoration. In crafting a history of modern Japanese theater, Kubo outlined a theater history that was starkly at odds with the picture as it is usually drawn when relying upon performance conventions or genre. He divides theater after the Restoration into the three broad categories of Marxist stages of development. The first grouping (the feudal period) was dominated by kabuki in the early Meiji Period. The second classification (the capitalist period) included Sudō Sadanori and Kawakami Otojirō's *sōshi* theater, New School theater (*shinpa*), Tsubouchi Shōyō's Literary Arts Society (*Bungei kyōkai*), Osanai Kaoru's Free Theater (*Jiyū gekijo*), the Arts Theater

There is a specter haunting Communism   63

(*Geijutsu-za*), the Modern Theater Society (*Kindai geki kyōkai*), the Literature and Arts Theater (*Bungei-za*), the *Shunka-za*, the Stage Society (*Butai kyōkai*), and the Tsukiji Little Theater (*Tsukiji shogekijo*). The third category is made up simply of "Proletarian Theater". This materialist theater history is intriguing on a number of levels, particularly in the exclusion of the Tsukiji Little Theater from the Proletarian Theater Movement and the wide variety of performance genres and troupes grouped together in the second category. Yet even more significantly, Kubo's chronology insists that Japan had reached a point of performing Proletarian Theater independent of the Restoration playing a part in the historical development of Japanese theater.

Sasaki Takamaru also stood front and center in these debates over temporality and performance. Because of this, and his place in the movement generally, the degree to which he has been forgotten in the history of the Proletarian Theater Movement is surprising. He headed some of the most important leftist theater troupes in the '20s and '30s; he enjoyed a long career on stage and screen both before and after the war; he translated what was and is widely seen as the first truly Proletarian performance in Japan; he produced the Japanese translations of *Internationale* and *The Red and the Black*; he was one of the four people sent to collect the body of Kobayashi Takiji after he was murdered in police custody; and he published widely in leftist magazines. Sasaki's rise to prominence in the movement, and interest in leftist thought, differed from many of the figures who were either well educated or came from the large population centers of Tokyo or Osaka. The son of a Buddhist priest based in Shikoku, Sasaki traveled around Japan after leaving home and eventually ended up in Tokyo. Upon arriving in Tokyo, he met and befriended the famous playwright Akita Ujaku who took Sasaki under his wing. With a small group of friends from a reading group, they formed the Forerunner Theater (*Senkuza* 先駆座) as well as the leftist magazine *The Sower* (*Tanemaku hito* 種蒔く人) in 1921. He then went on to help found the Trunk Theater, part of the "moveable theater movement", and then founded and headed the Avant-Garde Theater (*Zen'eiza* 前衛座). In other words, he was centrally involved with the events and discussions which defined the prewar leftist movement.

As the head of troupes from the Forerunner Theater to the Trunk to the Avant-Garde Theater, Sasaki dedicated his dramaturgical work to the advancement of socialist theater that was both ideologically pure and artistically sophisticated. As an example of his ideological profile, Sasaki was willing to perform at the Tsukiji Little Theater, the central theater of prewar modern Japanese theater, but he never became affiliated with the troupe after which the theater was named. This troupe, led by Osanai Kaoru, was the flagship of New Theater (*shingeki*) in the 1920s, with which most proletarian performance was affiliated. At the same time, members of the Proletarian Theater Movement were frustrated by the lack of political commitment on the part of the Tsukiji Little Theater. Senda Koreya left the theater for this reason and was drawn to Sasaki's Trunk and Avante-Garde theaters as a way to reach the working class. In contrast to Tsukiji, the Avant-Garde Theater took pride in being an artistic medium through which to bring the Socialist message to the masses.

64 *There is a specter haunting Communism*

Yet the larger ideological clash in the movement that centered in large part on the role of revolution in Japanese history proved the undoing of the Avant-Garde Theater. The writings of Fukumoto Kazuo generated an enthusiastic and controversial following under his brand of Marxism, known as Fukumotoism, which had the short-term benefit of a spike in participation in the leftist political and culture movements. The Avant-Garde Theater at first experienced a surge in membership from this boom, but it quickly became clear that these new members could not get along with the existing members of the troupe in a conflict that mirrored the larger clash of the Fukumotoists with the Yamakawists. They were more ideologically rigid than Sasaki, Senda Koreya, Murayama Tomoyoshi, or any of the other established members, and according to the original members they were also less concerned with their craft and showed little interest in producing quality theater. Yet at its core, the conflict was an ideological one that rent the political organizations of the party, creating a rift that severed groups throughout the political and cultural leftist movement. The conflict between the new and old members came to a head when the troupe called a meeting in which all members heatedly argued about politics and the future of the troupe in a multi-day series of speeches. No consensus was reached, and the group agreed to split into two troupes based on their political leanings.[25] The strife at the Avant-Garde Theater, which coincided with similar ruptures such as in the proletarian writers' organization, originated in the political organizations of the movement and spread throughout both leftist cultural and political institutions.[26] The Avant-Garde Theater split into two troupes that were grounded in the conflict over the meaning of Marxist Revolution in a Japanese context.[27] One of the new factions became the Purogei (Proletarian Arts), home to those sympathetic to "Fukumotoism" (Marxism as interpreted by Fukumoto Kazuo); the other was called the Rōgei (Worker's Arts) and was affiliated with Yamakawaism.[28,29]

With the troupe taking such a hit and the break being so ideologically heated in nature, there was unsurprisingly a great deal of bad blood between the groups. Sasaki had invested himself personally and professionally in the Avant-Garde Theater, and he felt betrayed and angry that their project was undermined from within. Murayama Tomoyoshi wrote scathing critiques of the Fukumotoists and insisted they were not Marxists. This animosity even lasted into the postwar years when in Sasaki's memoir, riffing off of Marx, he wrote that Fukumotoism was the "specter that haunted Communism". Tempers ran equally hot on the other side of the breakup; in an insert included in the very first issue of *Puroretaria Geijutsu*, the Purogei blasted their former comrades and the troupe that they left behind:

> They have already made clear that they are enemies of the proletariat. We refuse to pal around with members of the Avant-Garde Theater, which has become a hive for a horrible anti-movement faction. We fully expect that it will be demolished.[30,31]

In addition to the drama around the rupture in the movement's cultural institutions, the debates over historical stages and temporality motivated the keen

There is a specter haunting Communism 65

interest in the historiography of the Restoration that manifested itself on stage as the Restoration Plays—plays in which the productions themselves as well as in published introductions, playbills, and reviews described the Restoration as either a fully Bourgeois Revolution or as the harbinger of the Communist Revolution (which essentially amounts to the same thing). Thus *Tsukuba*, produced shortly after this breakup, entered into a fraught ideological landscape in order to make the case for the possibility of a Japanese revolution.

Performing modernity and tradition

The messy rift over notions of history and revolution played out in the greenroom (with the Purōgei/Rōgei split) and on the stage itself, meaning that *Tsukuba* was ideologically controversial both in its content and in its artistic methods. Mainstream Proletarian Theater had both an appropriately socialist content and was done in the *shingeki* style associated with modern Western scripts and performance conventions. Sasaki Takamaru matches his setting in the wake of the Restoration with dramaturgy that reached into Japan's dramaturgical past and relied for its success upon the contemporary popularity of kabuki actors using kabuki performance conventions. Yet this was a bold and confrontational move on Sasaki's part: to what degree could the ends of communicating a Socialist ideology be reached using what were seen as inherently feudal artistic means? In other words, the production of *Tsukuba* confused ideological fault lines and served as a locus for a larger debate about performance genres.

Advocates and practitioners of Proletarian Theater saw it as not only different from but incompatible with other kinds of theater, particularly traditional forms of dramaturgy. In this perspective, kabuki was a product of feudal culture that was necessarily infused with feudal values at multiple performative levels. The costuming, sets, and acting styles were equally problematic, and because of this, even in plays that featured resistance to feudal authority such as *Chūshingura*, the scripts inherently inscribed anti-revolutionary values onto their audience. Many in the proletarian movement wanted every last whiff of kabuki (and every other feudal art form) scrubbed from the proletarian stage. Cartoons published in proletarian newspapers and journals foregrounded the incompatibility of kabuki with proletarian ideology. In Figure 2.2, taken from *Theater News* (演劇新聞), a hammer labeled "Proletarian Theater" smashes down on an anvil, crushing little people marked "kabuki", "shinkokugeki", and "shinpa" (genres of theatre that were generally not affiliated with progressive political values). The ideological campaign against feudalist art was thus fought on many fronts.[32] Yet it was not necessarily so simple to maintain this divide in practice.

In his analysis of the complicated relationship between kabuki and Proletarian Theater, Masaki Yoshikatsu notes that one metaphor frequently invoked in theorizing the place of theater was that of theater as a "building". Intriguingly, Sasaki was one who argued that this "building" must be torn down and an even better one put up in its place. Others argued that the old building should merely be renovated, and that to demolish it entirely was a waste.[33] This

Figure 2.2 Cartoon from *Theater News*

building metaphor was also employed by the more artistically radical fringes of the Proletarian Theater Movement as well, such as in an article by Maki Toshio published in the seventh edition of the avant-garde magazine *MAVO*. In this article, titled "Two Plans for the Theater", he advocates an approach to theater that he calls the "anti-drama and theaters" movement. The article employs the building metaphor by provocatively comparing contemporary theater buildings to hospitals, or sanatoriums, but not in the sense of a sunny place where one goes for the "rest cure" and returns refreshed and rejuvenated. Rather, theaters are dark, isolating places where you go for a short time, probably do something dirty and degrading, and then when you come out all you can say is that you are a little bit closer to the grave. His proposal is a radical rethinking of the very model of the theater experience in that he argues theater should be performed without any stage at all. That is, the building that he wishes to demolish (with no attempt at renovation) is more than just a metaphor. His model prefigures the European Situationists, where guerilla theater is performed in the street with no distinctions between actor and audience and no boundaries between stage and spectators, and it recalls Meiji sōshi performance. Like the less radical suggestions by others in the "demolition" faction, such an approach rejects inherited

There is a specter haunting Communism 67

performance conventions altogether, but in this case does not replace it with anything remotely comparable.

However, not all theater practitioners were so radical in their approach to the past. Some theater practitioners worked to salvage Japan's theatrical history. A key point of contention between the "demolition" and "renovation" factions was the extent to which form and content were separable. All of the socialists could agree that the content of traditional kabuki plays, which were written during feudal times and thus inherently supported feudal values, was ideologically soiled. The history represented in the content of the plays, by the very nature of being written under feudal circumstances, works to inculcate feudal values in the audience. Yet many socialists questioned to what extent the formal properties of kabuki were infused with feudal ideology and to what extent form and content in kabuki were interdependent. Masaki says:

> The primary resistance that Proletarian Theater practitioners had towards kabuki was their consciousness of the "feudalistic contents" of the plays. It goes without saying that this is true with the history plays (*jidaimono*) about imperial nobles and samurai. This was even true in the domestic plays (*sewamono*), for example Ono Miyakichi criticizes "feudalistic obligation vs. human emotions and love" as being "undigestible". Sano Seki attacks kabuki and says, "We are overflowing with kabuki plays that rely on the crossroads of loyalty and filial piety, or the bonds of feudalistic obligation and human emotion". Needless to say, Proletarian Theater wanted to completely do away with the feudal system, and the aesthetic and intellectual foundations that reflected the contents must also be rejected. Yet this critique was not led from a thorough analysis of the contents of individual works. We can't reject the entire genre of kabuki because of a recalled surface impression.[34]

In other words, as compelling as these arguments to "demolish the building" may have been, there were also important figures on the other side of this debate. Indeed, sometimes even the same people ended up on both sides of the argument. For example, despite his calls for abandoning professional actors (including dancing, and singing on stage) as part of his attempt to break with kabuki generally, Osanai Kaoru also worked to promote the formal properties of the art.[35] In his book *Kyūgeki to shingeki* (旧劇と新劇 *Old Theater and Shingeki*), Osanai argues for the importance of the genre in the Japanese theatrical world.[36] Similarly, Sasaki, despite proposing that the "old building" of kabuki be destroyed, went on to produce *Tsukuba* in a kabuki style with kabuki actors. Further, Masaki notes that leading socialist intellectual Kurahara Korehito argued that kabuki was an intrinsically more artistic form than more prototypical Proletarian modes of performance. In fact, Kurahara argued, Proletarian Theater could use the popularity of kabuki against itself by infusing proletarian ideology into kabuki-style performances. Proponents of the formal properties of kabuki such as Kurahara argued that Japan's stage of historical progression limited the formal possibilities

68 *There is a specter haunting Communism*

of Proletarian Theater. Since Japan was still in a bourgeois stage of development, he argued that the potential for developing appropriate proletarian modes of performance was constrained.[37]

Others shared this view, so while there was a strong argument for the inextricability of form and content, there were also those who made the case that the form of kabuki could be disaggregated from its content and turned to suit socialist ends. A primary goal of the Popular Theater (which put on *Tsukuba*) was, as Sano Seki put it, to probe how kabuki techniques could be infused with new ideology ("それは新しい思想をもった演技をやる場合、歌舞伎の技術をどの程度まで取り入れ得るものだるか").[38] Likewise, the lead actor in *Tsukuba*, Ichikawa Yaozō, argued against many of his contemporaries who promoted doing away with *kata* (codified kabuki stage movements). He said:

> It is not old kabuki *kata* that we need, but rather *kata* instilled with new meanings that are necessary. I am very grateful to the many actors of the Popular Theater who could accomplish this.[39]

Director Kagawa agreed with this move to renovate traditional dramaturgy. While he saw the message of the play and the form that it was delivered in as linked, he also saw the possibility of their production as being able to convey a message that other genres could not ("普通の新劇団ではできない歌舞伎の技術を充分発揮させたい").[40]

Thus, despite all the negative baggage associated with "feudal" kabuki, traditional modes of performance were integral to some in the Proletarian Theater world. Beyond these theoretical debates, the facts remained that kabuki was popular with the masses, and there is a powerful economic incentive in theater to fill the house. There is an equally powerful incentive for leftists to spread their message to as many ears as possible. The combination of these two factors created room and incentive for formal experimentation.

The secret account from *Tsukuba*: tradition and revolution

A key scene in *The Secret Account from Tsukuba* that comes at the end of Act II highlights two key goals of the performance (see Figure 2.1 at the beginning of this chapter). While the rebels are preparing themselves for the final battle, a representative of prominent Freedom and People's Rights figure Ōi Kentarō is sent from the city to announce that his orders are to recommend restraint and to quell the uprising. The revolutionaries react to his mission with shock:

People (*Talking to one another*):

- What did he say?
- Did he say he came to stop us?
- What kind of military leader is that?
- Get lost!

There is a specter haunting Communism   69

UGA: (*Raises his hand to restrain them.*) Hold on a second. Listen to what I have to say. (*The people quiet down.*) So, that was the reason I was sent here. However, since I got here, Kakinuma has convinced me otherwise. (*Applause.*) On top of that, upon seeing the remarkable ardor of you party members I have decided to throw in my lot with you even to the bitter end. (*Applause. "What a mensch!" "Huzzah!"*) Following the advice of the local Liberty Party leadership, if I am accepted by all of you and although I may be unworthy, I would like to fight with you to the end as your commander. (*Applause. "Of course!" "We shall rely on you!" etc.*) Well then, I shall immediately organize our military divisions and report back promptly. (*A young peasant ascends the platform.*)

A YOUTH: Everyone, we have unanimously chosen our commander. Now that we have ourselves a military leader, we must strictly follow each and every one of his orders. We must all toe the line and keep sharp. There can be no fighting within our own ranks. (*"Hear hear!" "Absolutely!" etc.*) All for one and one for all! Do you all pledge to strive to follow the command of our military and party leaders?

EVERYONE: (*In unison.*) We do!

A YOUTH: I have one more thing to discuss. Actually, this is what I really want to talk about. I want Murakami Hanko, who has struggled with us more than any man who has run day and night, east and west, I want her to protect our military flag that we are raising here. (*"Huzzah!"*)

A YOUTH: I am not well schooled, but according to our learned Kakinuma, when the crowds stormed the jail in the French revolution, there was a young woman in front of them carrying a green branch of a tree. I want everyone to agree to have our martial woman, Murakami Hanko, carry our banner! (*Applause. "We agree!" etc.*)

(Act II, Scene 3)

人々口々に：

- 何だと？
- 俺達止めさせに来たんだって？
- そんな軍師があるかい。
- 引っ込め。

宇賀：　（片手で制して）　まあ待ってください。後を聞いて頂きたい。（人々静かになる）で、そういう目的で派遣されてきたのではありますが、此処に居る柿沼君からあべこべに私の方が説き伏せられ(拍手)、さらに、党員諸君の熱誠、及びこの義軍に参加する諸君の意外に多数なのを見て、断然、諸君と生死を倶にする決心をした次第であります。

(拍手。「偉いぞお！」「そうこなくちゃいけね！」)上毛自由党委員会の勧告に従い、諸君の御許しを得るならば、不肖ならば、

70 *There is a specter haunting Communism*

軍師の任に就いて、諸君と共に最後まで戦いたいと思うのであります。(拍手。「是非やって呉んなせい！」「頼んだぞお！」等々)では直ちに各部の隊の編成を致しまして後程報告致します。

若い百姓、壇上に飛び上がる。

若者：諸君、俺達は、今満場一致で軍師を推戴することが出来た。軍師を戴いた以上、これからさきの一切の駆け引きは軍師の命令通り秩序正しくしなきゃいけねえ。各々勝手な真似をして足並みを攪したり、味方同志、仲間割れをするようなことがあっちゃならねえ。(「そうだそうだ」「その通りだ」等々)俺達は皆一心同体になって、これからさき、総司令と軍師の命令通りに働くってことを誓おうではないか。

一同：　(一斉に)誓おう。

若者：それから俺はもう一つ諸君に相談したいことがある。と云うのは外でもない、今度の旗挙げで、日夜東西奔走して男も及ばぬ程の働きをして下すった村上はん子さんに俺達の本営の旗を守って貰うことにしたいんだ。(「ヒヤヒヤ！」)

若者：俺は無学だが、柿沼先生から聞いた程に寄ると、仏蘭西の革命では、最初に牢屋を襲った民衆は、青い木の枝をもった何とか云う若い女を先頭に立てていた相だ。俺は俺達の女丈夫村上はん子さんを、俺達の旗手にすることをみんなに賛成して貰いたいんだ。(拍手。賛成賛成の声)

It is significant that these two key themes of unity and the French revolution come almost in the same breath on stage. Sasaki Takamaru uses the past as a model for unity in a fractious present split on both ideological and aesthetic grounds and then looks back to the Bastille to establish building blocks of archetypal stories of revolution in ways that Eric Selbin has noted is a universal revolutionary practice.

The actors of the Popular Theater were primarily disaffected Shōchiku kabuki actors who had quit in protest of salary cuts (in fact, this was not long before the large strikes by *benshi* and other Shōchiku employees, so their socialist leanings came in the context of a greater dissatisfaction with their capitalist bosses).[41] At least one of the actors in the show, the lead Ichikawa Yaozō, was still performing at Kabuki-za in the evening while he attended rehearsals for *Tsukuba* during the day. The production was paired with a dramatization of Upton Sinclair's *The Spy* (1920), which was said to borrow the aesthetic of *rensa-geki* (live performances in front of a film projected on a backdrop, discussed in greater detail in Chapter 4) but without using actual filmed projections. While *The Spy* did not enjoy the critical success of *Tsukuba*, both productions allowed actors to draw upon their kabuki training, to the point that some critics came down on them for relying too much on the kabuki technique of *tachimawari* (stage combat). Further, in *Tsukuba*, the stage directions are written for a kabuki stage, such as calling for entrances on a hanamichi (the runway entrance in kabuki stages). On many levels, the Popular Theater's project was a very deliberate attempt to resituate kabuki production conventions within a modern context.

There is a specter haunting Communism 71

As such, the production engages with the debate on the ideology of form, and in so doing Sasaki's play represents an about-face on his stand on the question of content versus dramaturgical conventions. Whereas he had previously come out in favor of demolishing the "old building" of kabuki, he says that this production was an attempt to reach members of the public who might not otherwise be drawn in simply by the political ideology of the play. Likewise, his director, Kagawa Susumu asks, "To what degree can kabuki techniques be absorbed into new performances? It is my firm conviction that they [new performances] can be revitalized by the techniques that we have accumulated".[42]

The first act of the play is set in and around Mount Tsukuba and centers on Hansaku the hunter and his young son Inosuke. Inosuke is tasked with bringing food to a People's Rights partisan friend of Hansaku's who is in hiding, but the child is accosted by government sōshi and manipulated into revealing his location. Hansaku threatens to shoot his son when he finds out he has failed in his mission, but Inosuke falls off a cliff and is rescued (although Hansaku thinks he has died) by a pair of People's Rights bomb makers. Act II takes place in Chichibu, mostly in the house of Murakami Hanko, the widow of a People's Rights fighter who has taken her late husband's place as a leader of the fight at Chichibu. The act focuses mostly upon the writing of a declaration of purpose for their fight, based on Rousseau, Meiji Rights Movement leader Ueki Emori, and the American Declaration of Independence. As we have seen earlier, the plot is driven by the arrival of a representative of Ōi Kentarō named Uga Naokuni who has been sent to dissuade the members of the group from resorting to violence to achieve their aims. However, it turns out that Uga is moved by the fighters' steadfastness into supporting their cause (the end of this scene appears in the aforementioned excerpt). Act III consists mainly of the final battle and defeat of the Rights Movement fighters.

The play inscribes the French Revolution into multiple layers of the performance. The three acts sandwich an Act II, based on *Les Miserables*, between an Act I and III based on *Mateo Falcone*. This structure houses People's Rights fighters in the play, who draw revolutionary inspiration from the same intellectual sources as their historical counterparts. For example, they sing a song from the 1880s that refers to the American and French revolutions. The song sung on stage (and written in the text in kanbun) bears a striking resemblance to the poems of Ueki Emori and is probably authentic. It reads:

> Remembering the old United States
> Waving the humble flag of independence
> If blood did not fall like rain
> The foundations of freedom could not be laid.
> To envy the flowers of liberty
> Is to be a coward
> Give me liberty or give me death, the thirteen colonies stained with blood
> If you are envious, the flowers ought to bloom.[43]

72 *There is a specter haunting Communism*

This transparent translation of foreign revolutionary thought and action continues in the reading of the rebels' manifesto. In the following lines, Kakinuma introduces his draft to the group:

KAKINUMA: Finally, done!

KIKUCHI: Oh, you're finished? (*Everyone crowds around Kakinuma.*)

KAKINUMA: At first I worked in parts of Rousseau's "Social Contract" and essays by Professor Ueki. I explained the origin of natural rights, but when I tried to bring in examples of the French revolution and the Russian anarchists it started getting really long, and on top of that for a piece of convincing oratory it was a little complicated. So I threw all that out, and I made it really simple.

ARAI: Just go ahead and read it.

KAKINUMA: Alright. I'll just read through it really slowly, and afterwards you can tell me what you think. (*Begins to read.*) "Manifesto: The fundamental key for building a nation . . ."

YOUTH: (*To Kakinuma.*) Sensei, a man named Uga Naokuni has come from Tokyo to see you.[44]

柿沼：やっと出来た。

菊池：おお出来たか。
　　　一同熱心に柿沼の周囲に集まる。

柿沼：初めは、ルウソオの「民約論」と植木枝盛先生の論文とを参酌して、先ず自由の原理から説き起こし、フランス革命とロシヤの虚無党との例に引いて書きかけて見たんだが、それではあんまり長くなるし、第一、檄文としては少し難しくなり過ぎると思ったので、そんなことは一切省いて、極く簡単なものにした。

新井：兎に角読んで貫おう。

柿沼：じゃあ一応ゆっくり読むから、後で諸君の意見を聞かして呉れ給え。（読みかける）　檄抑々（そもそも）建国の要は。。。

若者：（柿沼に）先生、東京から宇賀直邦という方が尋ねて来られました。

So after his big lead-in, Kakinuma is denied the chance to show off his work by the arrival of Uga. Happily, Kakinuma has a chance to present it in full later, and it closely follows the model of the American Declaration of Independence.

In basing his play largely off of historically accurate events, Sasaki is able to bolster his case that Rights Movement fighters were true revolutionaries. Unlike many of his contemporary socialists, Sasaki considered the historical figures in the history in his work to be closely connected to the contemporary Socialist movement. He says:

Basically *Tsukuba* follows the source material, but as for my free adaptation of the historical facts and the time and place of the violent incidents, it wasn't for that old writer's dodge of "poetic license". Even the few

There is a specter haunting Communism 73

places where the historical facts were adjusted, I simply did my best to make appealing theater and at the same time to accurately portray the Narodnikism of the leftist Liberty Party at that time. Further, I simply wanted to reignite in the common people of today this admirable [censored] consciousness that they had. I have many more things to say about the early Meiji leftist Freedom Party movement.[45]

大体「筑波秘録」のネタは以上の通りだが、史実を勝手に変改した
り、事件の時と所を勝手に変えたりしたのは、作者が昔から云い古
るされていえる所謂「詩人の特権」を振り廻はしたかったからでは
決してなく、多少史実にそぐはないところが出来て来ても、出来る
だけ劇的興味を深めながら、当時の自由党左翼のナロードニキ的運
動を、全体として描き出したかったからに過ぎない。そして、彼等
のもっていた比類なきXX的精神を再現せしめることによって、今日
の大衆に強い刺戟を与えようと欲したが為に外ならない。明治初年
の自由党左翼の運動に就いては、私にも相当云いたいことがある。

In a discussion published in the same issue of *Gekisen*, director Kagawa Susumu expresses similar sentiments:

The script is about the Liberty Party members in Meiji 16 and 17 [tr. note: 1883–4], however it goes without saying that it would be insufficient for the writer to simply write the history of Liberty Party members as is. Writing in an historical mode, it would be very clear to what extent the leftist Liberty Party movement was [censored], however even though he wrote it as a history, his writing also highlighted events in such a way as to influence contemporary society, and to simultaneously teach the masses and give them what they want. For example, the riots and disruptions that flourished at the time such as the so-called Saitama Incident, Iida Incident, and Chichibu Incident, all have many points in common with the desires of the contemporary common people. For example, it was not simply the small numbers of a clique of the Liberty Party involved in the "discontented movement", but rather the theater that inspired both the general uninformed population of farmers and townsmen is very close to that of the contemporary common people. Also, with respect to the leaders of the Freedom Party, while Ōi Kentarō, Itagaki Taisuke—Kawano Hironaka was in jail at the time—and the rest do not appear on stage, their weak-willed compromises are rejected, and the way that those leaders did not stand in the vanguard is remarkably similar to the situation in the contemporary Communist Party movement. Those are points that we wanted to bring to the audience members' attention, and on top of that to focus on those facts while also maintaining the audience's interest. Our ambition was to do all this and also to adequately convey these thoughts using kabuki techniques that cannot be performed on a normal shingeki stage. Happily, we were able to adequately express this.[46]

74 *There is a specter haunting Communism*

それであの脚本は明治十六七年頃の自由党員の運動を書いたもので
すが、勿論作者は単に其自由党員の運動史実を其儘書いて、それだ
けで事足りとしたのではないと思う、歴史的に見せると同時に自由
党左翼の運動が如何に○○的であったかということは史実上明らか
な事実であるが、史実其儘を決まり取って書いても現在の社会に大
きな刺戟を与え、或は教える所がある、就中最も現在大衆が要求し
ているところと一致している様な所を引ツ抜いて来て書いてある様
に思う、例えば当時盛にあった所の一揆とか騒動、所謂埼玉事件、
飯田事件、秩父事件、の内容というものは現在大衆が要求している
所と一致している点が可成りある、例えば自由党員の一部少数の者
の不平運動のみでなく寧ろ一般の何も知らない農民とか町民とかい
うものが共鳴している劇などは現在の大衆と可なり近いものがあ
る、同時に又自由党の首領連中、舞台の表面には現れてこないが、
大井憲太郎とか、板垣退助とか――河野廣中は当時獄中に居たが―
―そういう首領連中の弱さ妥協性を排撃して首領連中が尖端に立た
なかったという風な事も現在の無産党の運動などと非常に似た点が
ある、そういう点を観客に訴えかけるという所を眠目として演出し
たのであるが、そういう事実を中心として而もそれに興味を持たせ
て観客を倦かせずに見せたいということを考えた、而も普通の新劇
団ではできない歌舞伎の技術を充分発揮させたいという野心、それ
が幸い充分表現し得た。

In other words, the members of the Liberty Party who fought in uprisings such as Chichibu and Kabasan were just as revolutionary as the contemporary audience of the play, and they could actually serve as role models for the contemporary socialist community. Yet it is also the intra-party conflict that serves as a particular warning to contemporary socialists. Indeed, the conflict between the passive city intellectuals and the Liberty Party activists in the countryside is in many respects even more important for driving the plot than the ultimate conflict with the government's forces, since defeat is essentially a foregone conclusion.

In this context, Uga's first entrance does more than just rain on Kakinuma's personal parade by cutting off his chance to share his writing with his comrades. Uga's interruption of the reading of their manifesto foreshadows his mission of quelling the rebellion. In his arguments for withdrawing from the fight, he disparages the peasants' cause by arguing that they have no clear plan with which to go forward. This accusation of rash action from the intellectual leaders of the movement incites a strong rebuttal, and Kakinuma accuses Uga, Ōi Kentarō and the intellectuals in Tokyo by extension, of "gradualism" (*zenshinshugi*). His fiery response concludes with:

Kakinuma: You out there in the city don't understand the lives of the peasants. After the Restoration, we were continually told that the government would improve, but at the same time the land taxes kept increasing. One new tax after another kept being added. Our only sons were drafted into the army during their best working years. All of the peasants boiled inside whether

There is a specter haunting Communism 75

they showed it or not. And on top of all this, we have now been rounded up and arrested. . . . (*Stares at Uga.*) Hey, Uga. Do you still not get it?[47]

柿沼：君は都会にいて、百姓の生活を詳しくは知るまい。維新後、政府は善政を施くと云いながら、地租はどんどん上がる一方だ。次から次へと新税は課せられる。徴兵令が施かれて働き盛りの一人息子がとられる。百姓はみんな顔色に出そうと出すまいと、腸の煮えくり返えるような思いをしているんだ。そこへ持って来て今度の大検挙だ。。。（じっと宇賀を見据えて）おい宇賀、これでもまだ分からない？

(Sasaki, 519)

Singling out this select group of historical radicals from among the broad swath of people affiliated with the Rights Movement allows Sasaki to confront the argument popular among many socialists and anarchists that members of the Liberty Party were at best dupes who were co-opted by the victors of the Restoration, which itself was simply a failed Bourgeois Revolution. Rather, Sasaki re-frames these "failed revolutionaries" as the precursors of future revolutions, thereby embracing the 1880s partisans as ideological brothers. When rallying his troops for the coming showdown with the government-sponsored (or "Imperial forces") sōshi, Kakinuma says:

This is the chance we've all been shooting for. I have no idea whether this time we will succeed or fail. Nobody here knows. Yet I can declare with certainty that this plan will be an invaluable cornerstone on the path towards securing the rights and liberty of the people. Can you call that a rash deed? If you call this a rash deed, you can rip off the label of revolutionary. As I said before, if that is the case then you can leave.[48]

今日の機会を狙っていたのだ。今度のことが、どの程度に成功するか失敗するか、それは俺にも分からん。此処にいる誰にも分からん。ただこの企てが、人民の権利と自由を獲得する道程の上で貴重な土台石の一つになるだろうってことだけは確信を以て断言することが出来る。それでも君は、猶この企てを無謀の挙というか？これをもし無謀の挙というなら、君は君の額から革命家のレッテルを取り去って了い給え。そしてさっき云ったように、此処を立ち去って呉れ給え。

(Sasaki, 520)

Kakinuma then goes on to finally read the proposed declaration for the Chichibu insurgents. It begins:

The fundamental key for building a nation is to make clear a belief in the equality of the citizenry [衆庶平等の理]—that they are each endowed with an innate [天与] right to happiness. The purpose of government is to protect

76 *There is a specter haunting Communism*

the people's innate [天賦] liberty and happiness, and it goes without saying that government should not allow evil laws, tyranny, or oppression.

However, in observing the state of the current government, it is clear that it does not do a single thing for the people's liberty and happiness. They raise taxes without cause and oppress the rights of the people, and yet they still declare themselves honest leaders. They are a terrible insult and scourge upon the people.[49]

抑々建国の要は、衆庶平等の理を明かにし人民各自天与の福利を均しく享くるにあり。而して政府を置くの趣旨は、人民天賦の自由と幸福を保護するにあり。ほしいままに悪法を設け、暴政を施し、虐圧を事にすべきにあらざるや言を俟たざるなり。
　然るに現在、我国の形勢を観察すれば、政府の為すところ一として人民の自由と福利にそうものなく、みだりに租税を増し、民権を抑圧し、而も自ら公明なる政治の行使者なりと称す。人民を侮り詐ること何ぞ其甚だしきや。

(Sasaki, 520)

Kakinuma frames their fight as rising above particular ideology and as foreshadowing the revolution that Sasaki's audience members looked forward to.

Conclusions

The questions that these Restoration Plays probed through the medium of Japan's past are still unsettled today. Both academic and non-academic writers in Japan still argue as to whether the Restoration was a revolution, and if so what kind. From a certain perspective, it can certainly appear that the Restoration Plays were part of a larger failure by the Communist movement to provoke a violent rejection of the oppressive capitalistic government. This unfulfilled goal is indeed retroactively foregrounded in the Restoration Plays.

Yet Sasaki Takamaru's plays reach into history and attempt to recover both a political and artistic past for his contemporary socialist audience. By drawing a picture of the Rights Movement as a proto-revolutionary group that laid the foundation for the Proletarian class, Sasaki created stories of revolution that resonated in the present. Combined with the analogies to foreign revolutions, Sasaki is making the claim that the Restoration Period was indeed Japan's bourgeois revolution. After all, if 1789 was a bourgeois revolution, and the Rights Movement shared their ideological underpinnings, then surely Japan had achieved its revolution and was ready to move into the next stage of history with their international brothers.

The story is also fundamentally about rupture and healing within the movement itself as a way to move forward into that socialist future. Looking back at Figure 2.1, the scene is blocked with the cast spanning the entire proscenium arch downstage and facing the audience in defiant unity in preparation for their final battle with the government forces. This blocking of the

There is a specter haunting Communism 77

climactic preparation for their final battle communicates a unified front of brothers devoid of internal struggle and prepared to fight together to the end.

This staging comes as a resolution to the scene quoted earlier in the chapter when Uga is convinced by the ardor of the fighters into joining their fight. In the context of the plot, this is a greater victory than they could reasonably hope for on the battlefield against the government forces. Further, the subplot based on source material from *Mateo Falcone* is driven by personal rift and reconciliation that is melodramatic to an almost absurd extreme. Hansaku believed he had killed his own son at the beginning of the play; the end of the play sees father and son reunited on the battle field after Hansaku has been mortally wounded. The play closes with Hansaku's final words telling his son to spread the news of their revolt after his death, and oh-by-the-way, that the gun he had brandished at him had not actually been loaded. As absurd as the subplot may seem, this story of personal reconciliation mirrors the desire for reconciliation within the party at large and even trumps the theme of resistance and revolution. It is not hard to imagine, coming from the dramatist involved in the Rōgei/Purōgei split, why this call for unity was so compelling. Sasaki writes in his memoir about the time as one when friendships were broken by the breakup of the party. He despaired at the dysfunction within the movement at large.

The goal of *Tsukuba* was thus twofold. The most urgent aim in the contemporary context was to look back to the past for models of reconciliation in the present. At the same time, the play looks to the past to lay the conceptual groundwork for a future revolution. This reading helps to contextualize what otherwise might be viewed as the complete failure of the Proletarian Theater Movement to inspire revolution. As a means to explore the representation of the past as present, modernity versus tradition, and ideological unity, *Tsukuba* is a bold experiment in melding difference.

Notes

1 The period and events covered in these plays extend beyond 1868 and are not limited to the efforts to topple the shogunate. While denoting the endpoint of revolutionary movements is never a clear-cut exercise, I follow Kyu Hyun Kim's lead and consider the "Restoration Period" as the time from the collapse of the bakufu in 1868 to the unveiling of the Meiji constitution in 1890. See Kyu Hyun Kim, *The Age of Visions and Arguments: Parliamentarianism and the National Public Sphere in Early Meiji Japan* (Cambridge, MA: Harvard University Asia Center, 2007).
2 Writing as Azuma Kenkichi.
3 Harry Harootunian, "'Memories of Underdevelopment' after Area Studies," *Positions: East Asia Cultures Critique* 20, no. 1 (Winter 2012), 7–35.
4 In his memoirs, Sasaki describes his four Restoration plays as existing on a spectrum from full translation at the beginning (*The Death of Danton*) to fully original creation (*Itagaki Taisuke* and *The Brothers from the House of Oki*) at the end. In the middle of this continuum sits *Tsukuba*, which is based on the two French works *Mateo Falcone* and *Les Miserables*. *Tsukuba* is thus an adaptation that sits temporally and conceptually in the middle on a continuum of translation and original writing. Takamaru Sasaki, *Fūsetsu shingekishi: Waga hansei no ki* (Tōkyō: Gendaisha, 1959).

78 *There is a specter haunting Communism*

5 Eric Selbin. *Revolution, Rebellion, Resistance: The Power of Story* (London: Zed Books, 2010).

6 Ogasawara Mikio, "Minken kōshaku kara sōshi shibai he," *Studies on Theater Arts* 31 (1990), 215–224.

7 Hannah Arendt, *On Revolution*, (Penguin, 1973).

8 James W. White, *Ikki: Social Conflict and Political Protest in Early Modern Japan* (Ithaca, NY: Cornell University Press, 1995).

9 Kuwabara Takeo, *Furansu kakumei no kenkyū* (Tōkyō: Iwanami Shoten, 1959), 601.

10 Ibid., 59.

11 Ibid., 216.

12 Ibid., 602.

13 Hiroshi Mitani, *Meiji Ishin wo kangaeru* (Tokyo: Iwanamishoten, 2012), 2.

14 George L. Bastin, Alvaro Echeverri, and Angela Campo, "Translation and the Emancipation of Hispanic America," in *Translation, Resistance, Activism* (Amherst, MA: University of Massachusetts, 2010).

15 Lisa Hopkins, *The Cultural Uses of the Caesars on the English Renaissance Stage*, Studies in Performance and Early Modern Drama (Aldershot, England: Ashgate, 2008).

16 Selbin, *Revolution, Rebellion, Resistance*, 72.

17 Nakabayashi Yoshio, *Meiji zenki no seiyogeki no juyo ni tsuite: "Jiyū tachi nagori no kireaji" wo chushin ni* (Machida: Tamagawa Daigaku, 2009), 22.

18 Mikio, "Minken kōshaku kara sōshi shibai he," 216–217.

19 Ibid., 220.

20 William Shakespeare and Tsubouchi Shōyō, *Jiyū No Tachi Nagori No Kireaji: Shiizaru Kidan* (Tōkyō: Yūshōdō Shoten), 1.

21 Ibid., 304.

22 William Shakespeare and Kōtarō Itakura, *Jiyū no shimoto On'ai no kizuna Gōketsu isse kagami: Itakura Kōtarō yaku* (Tōkyō: Ōzorasha 2000).

23 In contrast to the view that each stage replaces prior stages completely and uniformly, some Marxist scholars such as Rosa Luxemburg insisted that capitalism *must* coexist with non-capitalist modes of production (see Luxemburg Rosa, *The Accumulation of Capital*, Chapter 27, trans. Agnes Schwarzschild [London: Routledge and Kegan Paul Ltd, 1951]).Yet the notion that dominated many conversations in Japan over the Restoration held that transitions between stages of history (i.e. between modes of production) must be complete.

24 While writing about a very different context (Cold War and post-Cold War area studies), Harry Harootunian outlines these concepts of "stage-ism" and "multiple temporalities" in a way that is very closely related to my concerns here. He explains, "This 'end of temporality' excludes time's agency (although not chronology) and spatializes world regions, transubstantiating multiple temporalities (with their different histories and modes of production) into a single temporality that marks the distance between developed and underdeveloped. This spatial privileging converts a purely quantitative measure of time—chronology—into a qualitative yardstick, whereby a different temporality becomes a symptom of backwardness". See Harootunian, "Memories of Underdevelopment," 8.

25 Biographical material of Sasaki and accounts of the troupe are taken from Murayama Tomoyoshi's and Sasaki Takamaru's memoirs of their time in the Proletarian Theater Movement. See Murayama Tomoyoshi, *Engekiteki jijoden 3* (Tokyo: Toho, 1974); and Sasaki Takamaru, *Fūsetsu shingekishi: Waga hansei no ki* (Tokyo: Gendaisha, 1959).

26 Iwamoto Yoshio, "Aspects of the Proletarian Literary Movement in Japan," *Japan in Crisis: Essays on Taishō Democracy*, eds. Bernard S. Silberman and H.D. Harootunian (Princeton: University of Princeton Press, 1974), 163.

27 Revolution was a central (but not the only) conflict between these two factions. For a more detailed account of the ideological conflicts between Fukumotoism and Yamakawaism, see Chapter 2 of Gavin Walker's, *The Sublime Perversion of Capital: Marxist*

There is a specter haunting Communism 79

Theory and the Politics of History in Modern Japan (Durham, NC: Duke University Press, 2016).

28 Sasaki was unwilling to part with *Bungei sensen*, the institutional journal that had originally been *The Sower* before the Kantō earthquake, and where Sasaki had gotten his start in writing and in the proletarian movement. So the Rōgei kept *Bungei sensen* as their institutional journal, and the Purogei created the *Puroretaria geijutsu* journal and also took control of and renamed the Trunk Theater.

29 The rest of the company formed the Rōgei troupe (Workers Arts), made up of Senda, Murayama, Aono Suekichi, Komaki Oumi, Hayama Yoshiki, Maedakō Hiroichirō, Kaneko Yōbun, Kobori Jinji, Satomura Kinzō, Kuroshima Denji, Imano Kenzō, Sano Kesami, Taguchi Kenichi, Ogawa Shin'ichi, Tsuji Kōsan, Akagi Kensuke, Fujimori Seikichi, Kurahara Korehito, Hayashi Fusao, Yamada Seizōrō, and Sasaki Takamaru.

30 Insert in July 1927 issue of *Puroretaria Geijutsu*.

31 This declaration was signed by "former colleagues" Hisamatsu Eijirō, Murakumo Kiichi, Ono Miyakichi, Ōtake Kazuo, Sano Seki, Seki Ranko, and Yashiro Kō.

32 Uncredited cartoon on page 2 in *Theater News*, November 1, 1931.

33 Masaki Yoshikatsu, "Puroretaria engeki ga mita kabuki," *Engeki ronshū* 47 (2008), 43.

34 Ibid., 44–45.

35 Ibid., 46.

36 Osanai Kaoru, *Kyūgeki to shingeki* (Tokyo: Genbunsha, 1919).

37 Masaki, "Puroretaria engeki ga mita kabuki," 49.

38 "Taishūza dai ikkai kōen gappyō kai," *Gekisen*, March 1930, 44.

39 Ibid., 43.

40 Ibid., 45.

41 Shōchiku is an entertainment conglomerate that produced many large kabuki and film productions, including those at Kabuki-za.

42 "Meeting of Response," *Gekisen*, March 1930, 46.

43 Sasaki Takamaru, *Tsukuba hiroku*," *Puroretaria gikyokushū* 2 (Tokyo: Shin Nihon Shuppansha, 1988), 517.

44 Ibid.

45 Sasaki Takamaru (writing under the pseudonym Ochiai Saburō), "Tsukuba hiroku no shijitsu ni tsuite," *Gekisen*, March 1930, 41.

46 "Taishūza dai ikkai kōen gappyō kai," 45.

47 Sasaki, "*Tsukuba hiroku*," 519.

48 Ibid., 520.

49 Ibid., 521.

3 Democracy dies in Gifu

In a trip that would end in a violent attempt on his life, at 8 a.m. on March 10, 1882 (Meiji 15), Itagaki Taisuke (1837–1919) boarded a train from Shinbashi Station in Tokyo to begin a lecture tour along the Tōkaidō highway. Itagaki was the leader of the Liberty Party (*Jiyūtō*), which in 1882 was just reaching the height of its political and cultural influence. In the beginning of April, he arrived in Gifu Prefecture and attended a gathering on April 6 at 1 p.m. at the Chūkyōin hall near the town castle in Gifu City. Itagaki left the event early, and as he was leaving the event at around 6:30, he was approached by 27-year-old school teacher Aihara Naobumi who yelled, "You are the enemy of the future!" (*shōrai no zoku* 将来の賊). Aihara stabbed Itagaki multiple times as he walked down the front steps of the meeting hall (Figure 3.1). Before being rushed to the hospital, Itagaki reportedly declared, "Itagaki may die, but liberty will never die!" (*Itagaki wa shisu tomo jiyū wa shisezu* 板垣は死すとも自由は死せず).

This dramatic incident sparked a flurry of performances in the immediate aftermath of the event, and Itagaki's story remained a popular theatrical subject for decades after. One such early story was Kawakami Otojirō's play, which was informed by pseudo-news reports, fiction, and visual representations, including woodblock prints and nishikie about the so-called Gifu Incident. Growing out of this generic medley, news stories provided rich fodder for performers in a wide variety of formats, including the speech-meeting (*enzetsukai* 演説会) itself (where Itagaki was attacked), which was a vibrant performative genre in the mid-Meiji Period. These Gifu Incident plays, prominent in early Itagaki plays but supplanted by other topics in later years, function as remediations in two senses of that term: first, in the sense used by Linda Hutcheon of the story being simply placed into new media;[1] and second, in the sense that these plays remediate the genre of the speech-meeting into new media that included kabuki performance, sōshi theater, and modern shingeki productions.[2] By taking the popular form of the speech meeting and resituating it as an object of performance itself in a related performative mode, these Itagaki performances trade on the popularity of one genre in order to meta-theatrically enhance another mode of performance. By commenting upon their theatricality in this way, these layered performances highlight the degree to which they themselves existed in a rich performative world that included traditional stages and kabuki performances but also

Democracy dies in Gifu 81

Figure 3.1 Nishikie of the Kawakami Ichiza troupe's production of *Itagaki Taisuke sōnan jikki*, with Aoyagi Sutesaburō (left) as Itagaki and Kawakami Otojirō (right) as his would-be assassin, Aihara Naobumi

Source: Reproduced with permission from The National Theater of Japan.

utilized non-traditional performance spaces and genres. It is in this engagement with a wider performative context, in translating narrative across generic bounds, that the Itagaki plays are uniquely situated to foreground the degree to which genres that are and were treated as dramaturgically isolated were in fact engaged in extended dialog.

The Itagaki plays, of which the Gifu Incident narrative plays a significant part, are performatively unique in the way that they manifested in a range of genres throughout three distinct periods. Performances came initially in the immediate aftermath of the assassination attempt, staged primarily for sympathizers of Itagaki and members of the Liberty Party and in an "old theater" (*kyūgeki*) style. The assassination narrative was revived nine years later, coinciding with the promulgation of the Meiji Constitution and performed on the sōshi stage. The last plays were produced over a half century after the event itself and occurred on the shingeki stage. As performance history, these plays sit at important transitions in performance conventions in modern Japanese theater and are uniquely situated to highlight the inter-relationship of these seemingly disparate performance modes. And while performance is ontologically rooted in immediacy, this performance history records a process of a story with an appeal grounded in current events that then transforms into historical drama. In other words, the content becomes less

82 *Democracy dies in Gifu*

immediate. Early stories were about the present through the lens of the future, highlighted in Figure 3.1 by the contrast between Itagaki in a Western suit, the anathema that drives Aihara to deride him as the "enemy of the future!". Yet the narrative becomes one where the present is seen through the lens of historical events.

The historical figure Itagaki had an outsized impact on the Japanese modern political world. Born in Tosa (now Kōchi prefecture), he allied with Saigō Takamori in the Boshin War and led troops in toppling the Tokugawa Shogunate. He then served as a counselor in the new government until resigning in protest in 1873 over the *Seikanron* debates (a dispute over the proper time line and course of action for invading Korea), and in 1881 he founded the Liberty Party. As one of the founders of the modern Japanese state and an early leader of the opposition to that same government, he held a unique dual role in relation to the Japanese authorities. Ultimately, his legacy was embraced by the state, as evidenced by his likeness being placed on the 50-yen coin and the 100-yen note. Yet he is also a symbol of resistance to the power of the government he helped form, as evidenced by the prominence that his famous line about liberty retains in his legacy. In fact, Itagaki's credibility as a true reformer is highlighted by the fact that the Itagaki plays are perhaps the only instance of shared subject matter between the stages of the Freedom and People's Rights Movement and the Proletarian Theater Movement. As the present represented in these performances turned into the past, and while the pregnant future transitioned into a quotidian present and then unfulfilled promise, Itagaki remained a figure who embodied that promised future.

Situating the dramaturgy

The Itagaki plays appear in a historiography of modern Japanese theater which is saddled with the same challenge that much of the study of modern Japan has in untangling the question of rupture versus continuity from Edo to Meiji. Even the most thorough studies of modern Japanese theater, including the monumental tomes written by leading theater historians Akiba Tarō, Matsumoto Shinko, and Matsumoto Kappei follow era divisions that begin in the Meiji Period (1868–1912), suggesting an artistic rupture that negates any inherited tradition. They include little contextualization to situate the threads of modern theater in relation to where the performative world in modern Japan leaves off at the end of the Edo period (1603–1868). This approach makes it difficult to appreciate the innovative developments in modern theater and to distinguish that which is inherited from the past. In principle, kabuki is "old" theater (*kyūgeki*), and genres that developed after 1868 are "new". Yet in practice kabuki remained a site of vital and novel performance innovations into the twentieth century, and "new" theater modes borrowed heavily from traditional performance practices. Indeed, Japanese theater historiography could benefit from a "long nineteenth-century" approach like the one adapted by Jonathan Zwicker in the context of Japanese literature.[3]

In conjunction with this temporal break that coincides with era divisions, contemporary and historical theater scholarship and official policy split the Japanese

Democracy dies in Gifu   83

performance world between productions on formal stages, usually the "large theaters" in Tokyo or Osaka, and those staged in less formal spaces. Performances on minor stages are sparsely covered in theater histories and were also treated differently in official censorship and regulatory policies. In 1869, for example, the new government enacted regulations that banned the use of costumes in *yose* (the omnipresent small and local performance spaces low on the pecking order in the performance world), ensuring that performances on these stages would not be confused with "real" theater.

Matsumoto Shinko's influential theater history of the early Meiji Period explains the policy history for this formal distinction. In this telling, the Meiji Restoration had offered the Japanese theater world a temporary reprieve from the regulations of the Edo bakufu.[4] While implementation of performance regulations had been uneven at best throughout the Edo period, one of the most well-known regulations officially proscribed performances of current events and members of (well-known) clans with living descendants. Of course, these rules were often skirted through unsubtle changes in character names and the like. For the first few years after the Restoration, the new government had its hands full with more pressing matters than policing the entertainment world, and popular productions of current events were allowed to pass scrutiny by the local officials who were responsible for both interpreting and enforcing regulations of Meiji performance.

This lack of clear regulation allowed for performances such as one in Yokohama in Meiji 7 (1874) titled *The Forerunners of the Recent Port Openings* (*Chikagoro minato no sakigake* 近世開港魁), a play set in contemporary times that parodied the late bakufu, featured female actors on stage, and had characters in Western clothing with modern props such as cameras—all of which stood out as provocative dramaturgical choices. In a series of events that were not without precedent and occurred for conflicting reasons reported in the press, the audience of the production erupted into a riot that spread outside the theater itself and into the neighboring streets. This production highlights the place of theater at the intersection of translation, politics, and modernity, and at the time it alerted the Meiji authorities to a perceived risk from the lack of oversight that theater had received since the Restoration seven years earlier.

The newly returned Iwakura diplomatic mission that toured Europe and the United States for lessons in developing Japan into a modern nation took the incident around this play as motivation to bring performance into its policy of "civilization and enlightenment". In policy conveyed through meetings with Morita Kan'ya, Kawatake Mokuami, and Sakurada Naosuke (leading contemporary producer, playwright, and actor, respectively), the new government attempted to co-opt the theater for political ends and build a Japanese theater on a model with those they had seen in the West—one that they could use to display their cultural sophistication to foreign emissaries.[5] The resulting top-down policy dictated that theater could not be performed about figures who were alive or who were members of families who had living descendants (a policy almost identical to bakufu regulations). It also reformed the traditional relationship between kabuki and history by mandating a policy of "fidelity to truth" (真実に忠実).

84 *Democracy dies in Gifu*

Lastly, these new policies envisioned a theater that was primarily for edification and learning that both women and children could attend, learn from, and enjoy.[6]

These policies were supported by powerful members of the intellectual and political worlds. Yet the Itagaki plays in the Meiji Period flouted all the tenets of "reformed theater", in part because many of these performances fell below the status threshold for these performance regulations.[7] The humble *yose*, the streets, and other public areas provided varied and vibrant settings for performance which flouted rules enforced in more formal performance settings. Genres that did not occupy larger theater spaces existed throughout all the major cities and even the countryside.[8] This divide between performance on a formal stage and the slippery distinctions among these genres was tacitly recognized at the official level as well, as government restrictions often dealt with all genres of street theater as a monolithic unit and in separate legislation from formal theatrical venues.[9]

The generic distinctions of these less formal performance modes are difficult to assign to specific works with certainty for a number of reasons: the nomenclature was used at least somewhat idiosyncratically; performers shared and borrowed techniques and subject matter freely with one another, and unlike more formal, established schools, performers were not bound to one genre (even in cases in which performers were registered with the government as one kind of performer, they could and did switch their classification with ease);[10] for many of these arts, performers did not necessarily undergo formalized training or mentorship; and perhaps most importantly, these were ephemeral arts that were not canonized or privileged, despite many of these genres' origins dating back to early Edo and some even as far as medieval times. All of this makes differentiating the genres challenging, especially now that these arts have largely died out.[11] It is also possible that these difficulties help explain why these popular performance genres have been largely excluded from Japanese theater histories. Yet these biases have artistic and status basis as well which manifested before the performance genres had died out and became more difficult to access. Akiba Tarō in 1937 asserted that early sōshi theater (which was closely connected to *kōdan* and *enzetsu*, both genres of speech making) was "un-artistic" (非芸術的).[12] He explains the popularity of these forms with commoners in the merchant town of Osaka by positing that theater goers there did not have refined aesthetic taste, so they would watch any old kind of theater.[13] While not as explicitly derogatory, Matsumoto Shinko, Matsumoto Kappei, and Ihara Toshirō, all of whom focus almost solely upon theater on a conventional stage, also give scant attention to these performances in their extensive theater histories.

The regulatory distinctions between performances above and below this cut-off between mainstream large productions and informal performances extended back before Meiji, and these performance genres were mostly extensions of prior practice dating back centuries.[14] Government licensing of yomiuri dates back to at least the beginning of the eighteenth century, and, in 1722, authorities enacted an ordinance specifically banning yomiuri performance of love suicide stories. In 1841, Tokugawa Nariaki severely restricted the number of *yose* in a given

Democracy dies in Gifu 85

community and restricted the material they were allowed to perform. There was thus a solid precedent for the regulations that were enacted in the Meiji Period. Yet, while these restrictions began almost immediately following the Restoration, theater censorship at all levels took nearly a decade to formulate and put into full effect. In 1869, only one year after the Restoration, the aforementioned restrictions were re-enacted upon performances at *yose*, limiting their content to war tales, *jōruri*, and edifying ancient tales (*mukashi banashi*). Yet it was not until July of 1879 (Meiji 11) that the government passed the first laws targeted directly at *enzetsu*, enabling the police to shut down *enzetsu* meetings. The law was strengthened in December of that year, and the first arrest at an *enzetsu* meeting was made in that month.[15] In April of 1880, the government passed the Ordinance on Public Meetings, which granted the police wide authority to prohibit public gatherings and regulate political parties. The dual-level censorship practice of seating a police officer on stage with the performer and vesting him with the authority to close down a performance for deviating from the authorized script may date from this set of regulations. In other words, these policies treated these performances with the same regulations as those on political speech and assembly and not the same as standard theater.

In short, even though there was a great deal of cross-fertilization in performances both laterally across genre and horizontally across status levels of performance, the performance world in Meiji Japan is one that was bifurcated legally, artistically, and, of course, economically, between street art and lower-level performance and performance on the larger stages. This segmentation is reflected in both current and past scholarship. Yet the Itagaki plays bridged these divides, blurring temporal divisions between Meiji and early Showa and demonstrating how in practice performers paid scant heed to the boxes in which genre attempted to confine them.

1882: the early Itagaki plays

Because of their widespread appeal, the Itagaki plays are ideal for demonstrating the fluidity both laterally and horizontally on this matrix of Japanese performance. The scholar Tsuchiya Momoko has identified two groups of Meiji Period Itagaki plays which help to demonstrate this fluidity.[16] The first period came immediately after the Gifu Incident in 1882, in a variety of play known as *ichiyazuke*, or "one night pickles". The one-night pickles were plays about current events that were written, rehearsed, and staged within a very short time of the event actually taking place, thus bridging the gap between staged theater and other performance genres that represented current events in public venues. The one-night pickles were not new: prominent examples include Chikamatsu's famous love suicide plays from the Edo period which were based on sensationalized current events, and the term was also used for plays commissioned by theaters to fill in holes in productions schedules when unpopular performances were dropped before the scheduled end of the run.[17] Nor were they rare in the modern period: as James Brandon comments in his monograph on war-time kabuki, "Like TV docudramas

86 *Democracy dies in Gifu*

today, *ichiyazuke* plays exerted a powerful emotional hold on audiences because the wartime stories were well known to audiences and emotionally affecting".[18] This emotional appeal came despite the fact that these vegetables did not have sufficient time to "properly pickle". Importantly, these pickles flew in the face of the official stance on the relationship between performative and lived temporality. That is, they ran counter to the official Meiji oligarchy position that privileged the performance of the ("true") past as the past over the performance of the present as the present.

Several Itagaki performances were produced in the weeks and months after the attempted assassination of Itagaki took place. One titled *The Dawn of Liberty in the East* (*Azuma nada jiyū no akebono*) was performed in Itagaki's hometown and political base of Kōchi in June and July of 1882 at the Horizume Theater; another titled *Falling Cherry Blossoms at Inaba in the Twilight* (*Hana fubuki inaba no tasogare*), with the alternate title of *The Evening Storm at Gifu*, was performed in Gifu and Nagoya at the Suehiro and Hōshō Theaters, respectively, in July and August; and there are records of two productions at the Kadoza Theater in Osaka, one in September (title unclear) and another titled *The Decorated Scabbard of Liberty* (production date unclear). Very little archival material remains of any of these productions, but we can easily guess that political concerns contributed just as much to their popularity as did their performative qualities. *Falling Cherry Blossoms*, for example, was almost certainly performed for the sudden influx of Liberal Party activists who flocked to Gifu in the wake of the assassination attempt.

All of these adaptations of the story conform to contemporary theatrical conventions and expectations. For example, love interests appear in the story—and in *The Dawn of Liberty in the East*, Aihara even has two lovers. They all follow the actions of Aihara rather than Itagaki in the run-up to the event, thus casting him in the mold of a kabuki-style hero-villain. This is not surprising, since the actors who performed these roles were members of local kabuki troupes.[19] Yet many elements were also drawn straight from the news. In both of these productions, Aihara stays at the Tamai-ya guest house, and while at the guest house he attempts but fails to gain an audience with Itagaki. The Tamai-ya was the actual name of the place where he stayed (although in a twist that is not represented in these stage versions, he was kicked out for suspicious behavior and had to suffer the disgrace of sleeping outside the night before his assassination attempt). The plays also all include Itagaki's famous line, if in different variations: in *Dawn of Liberty*, Aihara yells out "Traitor to the nation—wait!" (*Kuni-zoku matte*) and stabs Itagaki. Itagaki responds with "Even if you kill me, liberty will not die, you fool" (*Ware o korosu mo, jiyu wa horobinuzo, urotaemonome*); in *Falling Cherry Blossoms* Itagaki's famous line is rendered "People, do not fear. Even if Itagaki dies, the Liberty Party of greater Japan will not die".

These stories are grounded in the present, looking to the future, in the way that the stories were timely and informed by newsgathering efforts both on stage and in print. In performance, the aforementioned productions highlight the timely

Democracy dies in Gifu   87

nature of the plot by prominently featuring newspapers and newsgathering in the productions. This manifests in the props and in plot devices. In *Dawn of Liberty*, for example, the stage directions for Aihara's initial entrance call for him specifically to be carrying the *Nichi-nichi shinbun* newspaper, and it is made clear that it was through information gleaned in this paper that he was driven to his crime.[20] All of this highlights the immediacy of the material that was put on stage just weeks after the event took place. Thus, at the same time newspapers provided content, they also served as source material for these stage adaptations. Original newsgathering efforts informed more than just these productions on stage. They also informed short (and cheap) bound accounts of the event and its aftermath, which were essentially news aggregators that were undoubtedly sold via *yomiuri*-style performances. One pamphlet is titled *The Record of Itagaki's Tragedy* (*Itagaki Taisuke sōnan tenmatsu jikki* 板垣退助遭難顛末実記), written by Fujii Reisuke and published in Tokyo only eight days after the event in Gifu. The bulk of the 40-page pamphlet is devoted to the facts of the case and draws attention to conflicting accounts. Yet the introduction begins not with the factual account but with Ueki Emori's poetic line, "Unless blood falls like rain, we will never achieve liberty" (曰く血雨を降らさざれば真の自由を得がたし).[21] This is followed by a discussion in the vein of a radical political tract about how to measure the efficacy of assassinations. Specifically, it offers up the examples of the assassination of President Garfield and Okubo Toshimichi and argues that the attacks should be judged by their results rather than their morality. While Garfield was successfully killed, Fujii points out that the governmental system continued unchanged. As a result, he says, "Setting aside the right or wrong of the act, just as [Garfield's assassination] should be considered futile and useless [*mukō mueki*], if we don't call the assassin stupid for the anger that drove him to his crime, then we have to call him insane". In other words, Fujii suggests that rather than judge the motivations behind the attempt, we should view it as a case of the ends justifying the means.

By this logic, the attempted assassination of Itagaki is already *mukō mueki* at the outset. Common to each version of Itagaki's declaration that liberty will not die is the fundamental point that, since liberty will not perish, the future has already been written and the spread of liberty will not be stunted by Aihara's act. Thus, Fujii's examples of past assassinations are not raised in order to ask his readers to wait and let history judge Aihara's actions. There is no "history will be his judge" because history has already spoken: liberty will not die, and thus the future looks bright for the Japanese people. Moreover, Fujii does not condemn assassinations as inherently cowardly or immoral acts. Fujii's pamphlet, after all, begins with Ueki's claim that blood must fall like rain to achieve liberty. He tacitly leaves the door open for Liberty Party partisans to employ the technique if it would prove effective even as he condemns this specific act. The narrative of the assassination attempt is grounded in a temporality of the present through the lens of the future. Like the title of a recent political tract in the contemporary United States, Itagaki as a symbol gives his followers a way towards "winning the future".

88 *Democracy dies in Gifu*

Sōshi theater: translating the Gifu Incident for the youth

About nine years after the Gifu Incident, Itagaki once again became a popular subject on stage, this time by rowdy sōshi in their political performances around the time of the unveiling of the Meiji constitution. Their performances in many ways represent a novel development in the theatrical world, a fact reflected in the words they used to describe their work. As described in earlier chapters, sōshi theater (*sōshi shibai*) was alternately referred to as student theater (*shosei engeki*), new theater (*shingeki/shin'engeki*, not to be confused with the shingeki that emerged in the first decade of the twentieth century under figures such as Osanai Kaoru), "reformed theater" (*kairyō engeki*, not to be confused with the theater reform movement led by Ichikawa Danjūrō, Yoda Gakkai, and others working to model kabuki on internationally acceptable theatrical norms), and later, "new school theater" (*shinpa*). Contemporary theater histories generally use *shinpa* as the standard term encompassing the theater that ranged from the 1880s to the early twentieth century. Yet, while earlier sōshi theater and the later shinpa share many features in common, not least a large number of the later shinpa actors were earlier sōshi performers, the differences between the two make using a blanket term for them misleading. In 1902 (Meiji 35), the prominent shinpa actor Ii Yōhō argued in *Kabuki* magazine that in fact sōshi theater and shinpa were not the same, saying, "There are some new actors (新俳優) who are annoyed that *shin'engeki* is thought of as simply sōshi theater . . . this theater was not born from the so-called sōshi theater" (この新演劇というものを、単に壮士芝居と思われると、大変に迷惑をする新俳優一派がある . . . 所謂壮士芝居というものから生まれて来たのではない).[22] Similarly, Akiba Tarō says that, "It is widely said that the theater that Sudō and Kawakami first established is shinpa; however, I think that it is rather more accurate to call it sōshi theater. Of course, speaking broadly, compared to contemporary kabuki, sōshi theater is closer to shinpa, but it is not fully shinpa".[23] Yet, while there was a great deal of variety across these theaters that spanned several decades, it is also true that theater historians and critics both at the time and today generally use these terms interchangeably. This extends beyond the bounds of the academy. As one non-scholarly example, Shochiku's "Shinpa gekidan" website's page entitled "The Birth of Shinpa" (新派の誕生) refers to Sudō Sadanori's Japanese Reform Theater in 1888 as the first shinpa theater. Throughout the careers of the two most prominent sōshi performers, Sudō Sadanori and Kawakami Otojirō, these terms were all used interchangeably.

Implicit in these terms used to describe these theatrical traditions is the self-styled stance that something about this theater is fresh and novel (new school theater, new theater, reform theater). Indeed, this nomenclature intentionally helped to differentiate this form from "old" theater (*kyūgeki*, i.e. kabuki). Clearly these practitioners wanted to be viewed as effecting change. Ayako Kano, in addressing this question from the perspective of performed gender on stage in her groundbreaking monograph *Acting Like a Woman in Modern Japan*, locates the "new" in "new school" in performative practice that manifests in the performance of

Democracy dies in Gifu 89

gender.[24] Focusing on the Sino-Japanese war plays of Kawakami and contrasting them with those of Ichikawa Danjurō IX, she draws a distinction between relative "direct action" in Kawakami's theater and relative "indirect action" in Danjurō's. At its heart, it is an explanation of the fact that embodiment in kabuki is based on *kata*, whereas shinpa is an initial move towards modern theater's model of acting that is internally motivated and more ostensibly spontaneous. Yet a closer examination of the theater of Sudō and Kawakami troubles this common distinction, because performative practices at this time were widely shared across genre. Sōshi theater and later shinpa all drew on performance traditions which were rooted in their own past.

The *enzetsukai* (speech meeting) is one strong early performative influence upon the development of modern Japanese theater. It played a central role in bringing members of the Freedom and People's Rights Movement together in one space; it was an essential early way for disseminating the newly translated Western philosophy and literature that informed the movement; and it was a path by which Sudō Sadanori and Kawakami Otojirō found their way into the performance world. The word "*enzetsu*" itself was a translation word coined by Fukuzawa Yūkichi (福沢諭吉 1835–1901) in the 1889 (Meiji 22) edition of *Kōjun zasshi* as reported by Miyatake Gaikotsu in his "History of the Meiji *Enzetsu*".[25] It was a word that he used to translate the English words "debate" and "speech". It defined a genre of knowledge dissemination that involved "performance" (演) which required a location dedicated to training and practice. The first example of this new genre cited by Gaikotsu is in 1874 (Meiji 7) (incidentally, the same year of the performance in Yokohama that sparked changes in policy for large stage performances, mentioned previously). In other words, much about the *enzetsu* was indeed new. Fukuzawa himself certainly thought of this as a new form. He says that he thought about translating the English words as "*danron*" (談論, argument), "*kōdan*" (講談, lecture), or "*benzetsu*" (弁舌, speech), all previously existing words, but he settled on "*enzetsu*", clearly feeling that the practice of "speech" and "debate" was sufficiently different from these established terms that they warranted a new word in Japanese.[26] In coining this neologism, Fukuzawa took a word that he had heard once (*enzetsu*) and changed the second character to one that he thought was more elegant. However, in a translation event that mirrors the introduction of the form itself into Japan, it turns out that the word had actually been in circulation for many years before Fukuzawa's "coining". Gaikotsu makes it clear that the *enzetsu* has deep roots in Japanese history. He says that like the newspaper, which seemed like a new adoption from the West in the Meiji period but was in fact based on the *yomiuri*, so too the *enzetsu* was based in Japanese modes of lecture and performance. "The origin of the *enzetsu* was in premodern times when the warrior-leader gave orders to his troops during wartime. However, if these pronouncements are the origin of *enzetsu*, then they have been loudly recited in the west of our country in the fields of Hyūga in Kyūshū as far back as 2,600 years". (演説の起源は未開時代に頻々行われた戦国の際、大将が兵員に対する軍令の下如であるというが、その下如が演説の起源であるとすれば、我国でも二千六百年の昔、西は九州日向あた

90 *Democracy dies in Gifu*

りで、野外演説が朗々の大音声で行われたであろう).[27] Thus, as performative practice, the *enzetsu* was firmly rooted in Japanese performance traditions, even if there were cosmetic nods to newness such as the occasional adoption of Western clothing or seemingly Western mannerisms. In this way, it resembles the sōshi theater which it helped to foster, in that it appeared to be new and point to Western modernity even while it drew on past performative practice.

Growing out of this tradition of performance that is not, strictly speaking, "theater", sōshi performance is a particularly clear example of the fluid nature of Meiji performance genres. *Enka* (political songs) singers shared much in common with the *yomiuri* (singers of current events). Both consisted of singers in the streets who used their performance to sell printed material that could then be performed by the purchasers with friends, for example at parties in the pleasure quarters. And both consisted largely of performance scripts that were temporally immediate and perishable: sensationalized current events and satire of contemporary figures. Likewise, *sōshi kōdan* (lecturing/storytelling) shared visual elements with both of these storytelling arts as well as *rakugo* and *naniwabushi*—performers in each style often sat behind a low table, had a teapot and glass on stage with them, and often dressed in very similar ways.

The genres below the demarcation of the mainstream, large theaters shared skills, subject matter, and stagecraft between them—and the *enzetsu* was part of this milieu. Some of these performance arts utilized song, some of them relied upon speech, and some employed a mix of both, yet all were at some level storytelling arts. In addition to telling current news, their shared content included retellings of war tales and translations of Western history and literature.[28] Further, instruments and performance conventions were shared across genres. In short, the generic labels of these street performance artists and storytellers did mark distinctions, but the boundaries between them were also fluid, and their visual representations are often difficult to distinguish without contextual explanation.[29]

In addition to lateral cross-fertilization between genres of street theater (外演芸), Hyodo and Smith make the equally important observation that these performance arts are also part of a vertical hierarchy.[30] There is a distinction between *haiyū* (actors) and other performers in theater scholarship, based upon both the quality of the narrative and the level of formal training involved. This sets up a hierarchy which focuses on the *haiyū* to the exclusion of other kinds of performers, a status framework that is at the center of the divide in scholarly attention to formal and informal performance. While Kawakami's Itagaki play is widely cited as a key moment in the founding of modern Japanese theater, very little of his career prior to this production appears in most theater histories. This bias is particularly pronounced in the work of the prolific Japanese theater historian Akiba Tarō, who draws a very deliberate distinction between the political partisan Kawakami, who performed "political criticism" (政治批判), and the "actor" (俳優) Kawakami when he switched to "social satire" (社会風刺). He is not precise in defining when this transition occurred, and since the term "sōshi theater" is used freely to describe Kawakami's theater throughout his career (even into the twentieth century and the end of the Meiji period), it is not exactly clear when he was to have made this transition. Yet most theater historians in Japanese and English cite Kawakami's Itagaki play along with his hit song *Oppekepe bushi* (treated in detail in Chapter 1), and very few mention his career before these breakthrough productions. For this reason, it seems reasonable to surmise that Akiba also sees this as Kawakami's point of transition into an "actor".

Despite these scholarly divisions, in actual practice material, techniques, and performers moved both horizontally and vertically on this performative matrix. The enormously popular actor Soganoya Gorō (1877–1948) began his own theater troupe by performing on the smallest stages and working his way up to the largest stages in Japan as a star managed by the Shōchiku entertainment conglomerate. Likewise, Kawakami went from guerilla street performances to performing at the Nakamuraza theater in 1891 (Meiji 24). In other words, access to the top of the theater world wasn't only afforded to famous kabuki families, even though they did have a powerful position in the theater world. Texts were also shared, and the Itagaki plays appeared both in the lowliest street performances and in the largest formal theaters. Publications such as *The Details of the Itagaki Tragedy* (*Itagaki sōnan tenmatsu* 板垣遭難顛末) in 1882 (Meiji 15) were almost certainly performed and sold by lowly *yomiuri* players. At the other end of the spectrum, in addition to the above-mentioned Nakamuraza production, the Gifu Incident appeared on stage at the Kadoza in Osaka in Meiji 15 (1882), and also in Meiji 27 (1894).[31]

Sudō Sadanori (角藤定憲 1867–1907) was born in what is now Okayama City. In his youth, he worked delivering mail in Okayama before moving to Kyoto and becoming a police officer.[32] While in Kyoto, he became involved in the Freedom and People's Rights Movement, and he quit his job with the police when he decided not to follow orders to prosecute members of the movement. He began his performance career on the street performing *bukkyō enzetsu* (literally "Buddhist speeches", among the most humble of all performance genres according to Hyodo and Smith). When the authorities banished hundreds of members of the Rights Movement from Tokyo on December 26, 1887, with the Regulation for Preserving Public Order, Nakae Chōmin moved to Kansai, along with Kōtoku Shusui and others. Chōmin started the institutional newspaper *Daybreak News* (東雲新聞), and the young Sadanori met Chōmin when he began writing for the paper. Both Chōmin and Sudō were interested in utilizing theater to further the ideals of the movement, and Chōmin encouraged Sudō to form a theater troupe.

The "Japan Reform Theater Association" (日本改良劇会) included Yokota Kinba, Kanbara Seizōrō, Iwao Hajime, Ikeda Kichinosuke, Kasai Eijirō, Arima Tatsuji, Hosoi Minoru, and Satō Toshizō, and it was established in August 1888 with Sudō as head (座長) of the troupe. Nakae Chōmin supported the show, going even so far as to pen an endorsing editorial in *Daybreak News*, and Chōmin's name received prominent billing on the advertisements for Sudō's debut production at the end of December 1888. Sudō traveled around the country performing scripts about current events. One of

92 *Democracy dies in Gifu*

these scripts included Kōtoku Shusui's "Kunino Minpei in Prison" (*Kunino Minpei Gokusha no ba*), one scene in the larger production "Beautiful Tales of Loyalty to the Emperor: The Dawn at Ueno" (*Kinnō bidan: ueno no akebono*). Kunino tells the tale of the Osaka Incident in 1888, but in order to evade censorship, it was reset in the context of the fall of the bakufu.[33]

In contrast to Sudō, Kawakami Otojirō (1864–1911) was less politically connected, but he achieved a greater level of fame and a much longer career. Yet much of his early career shares key features with Sudō. Kawakami was born in Hakata and spent his early life doing a wide variety of different jobs. Like Sudō, he was employed as a police officer when he became interested in the Freedom and People's Rights Movement. He took on work at the *Rikken seitō shinbun* in 1882, where he served as the newspaper's *hakkōmeiginin* (発行名義人), essentially a position that made him legally responsible for the paper so that he could serve as the scapegoat who went to jail when the censors cracked down on the paper. During this time, he became active in Liberty Party speech meetings (*enzetsukai*) and met and began performing with Aoyagi Sutesaburō.[34] Just as Sudō began as a street performer of Buddhist lectures, Kawakami engaged in a wide variety of performance genres in the years leading up to his breakout hit with the Itagaki play and his ballad *Oppekepe bushi*. In addition to *seiji enzetsu* (political speech making), he performed as a *benshi* (narrator) at Liberty Party speech meetings, a *kōdanshi* (lecturer/storyteller), *rakugoka* (storyteller of *rakugo* tales), and *enka* (political songs) singer. In addition, he auditioned for established kabuki houses in Osaka and with Ichikawa Danjūrō IX in Tokyo.[35] While Kawakami's ultimate success was noteworthy, his versatility was not unique. Performers changed genres at will, often (as was the case with Kawakami) to avoid government censorship, while not substantially changing their performance content or conventions in any meaningful way.

This versatility also served purposes other than artistic exploration. Prompted by the need to evade the authorities, Kawakami regularly exploited the fluid nature of the genres he performed. He consistently tested the limits of legality, and he claimed to have been arrested more than 170 times during his career. In 1885, he was banned from political performance for one year, which pushed him to find creative ways to evade the letter of the law. His troupe advertised their services as "English lessons", even though Kawakami did not speak English (presumably he simply continued performing the same speechifying that got him banned). Another time, because he was banned from performing "Political Orations" (*seiji enzetsu* 政治演説), he participated in an event advertised as "Ridiculous Orations" (*kokkei enzetsu* 滑稽演説). Along with generic shifts, when he was officially banned from performance of any kind for an entire year, he performed under different newly assumed names—once as Kawakami Otokichi (this ruse was uncovered by a particularly motivated Kobe police officer) and then under the name Jiyūtei Setsubai (自由亭雪梅).[36] While this latter name sounded like a *rakugo* performer or a *kōshakushi* (professional lecturer), his ruse was uncovered in March during a performance at the *Senbon-za* theater in Kyoto, and he was sentenced to seven months in jail.

Democracy dies in Gifu   93

In other words, while Sudō's and Kawakami's primary genre is considered to be sōshi theater, their careers are examples of the degree to which generic boundaries were permeable. In lieu of formal actor training, these influences informed their versions of Gifu Incident plays during their tours around the country. Sudō's troupe's production was titled *The True Account of the Tragedy at Gifu of Liberty Party Leader Itagaki Taisuke* (*Jiyūtō sōri Itagaki Taisuke shi sōnan Gifu jikki*). One production of this play took place in Nagoya at the Shinmoriza Theater on July 17, 1891, and as part of their repertory Sudō's troupe undoubtedly restaged it elsewhere. Kawakami performed his play under varying titles, one of them being *The True Account of Itagaki's Tragedy at Gifu* (*Itagakikun Gifu sōnan jikki*), one early recorded production coming in Osaka on February 5, 1891.[37]

Sōshi Gifu Incident plays

Sudō's and Kawakami's Gifu Incident plays represent a revival of the topic after the boom of pickle plays immediately after the event. Both Sudō's and Kawakami's performances retell the story with important differences to those that came in the wake of the incident. The titles indicate a turn away from the kabuki-style names discussed in the previous section to ones that highlight the accuracy of the events portrayed on stage. Further, Kawakami's version of Itagaki's response to Aihara's attack is less reverent than its predecessors when he says, "Liberty may die, but Itagaki will never die".[38] Yet in both plays, the narrative focus is upon Aihara in the run-up to the event, with a remediation of the *enzetsukai* providing the scene for the climax of the play (incidentally, just like the previous period of Itagaki plays).[39]

Thus both Sudō and Kawakami innovated on the story but also drew from stage versions that came before them. Just as importantly, these performances reach up the performative hierarchy to genres with higher status than they have on their own. Ihara Seisen's account of Kawakami's play speaks to the extent to which they borrowed freely from kabuki and bunraku choreography:

> The scene at the Gifu Chūkyōin Hall was a story based around *tachimawari* [translator's note: staged swordplay commonly used in kabuki and bunraku productions] when Aihara (Kawakami) attempts to assassinate Itagaki (Aoyagi) and is saved by Naitō Kamiichi (Iwada). However, the fight choreographer was the ex-kabuki actor Mori Sankichi, so he simply used the style of Nikki [Danjō] in his Ninjō scene. Yet since the actors were amateurs, they did not perform as choreographed and simply fought naturally. The script was also done in a kabuki style, with *chobo* [narrations] used in acts one and two on a daily basis. It utilized *chobo* from common *jōruri* that resonated with the production. The fact that there was *chobo* means that obviously there was also a musical accompaniment. Yet since the actors were amateurs, they followed the lead of the musicians and did not make requests or demands.

94　*Democracy dies in Gifu*

岐阜の中教院の場は、例の板垣（青柳）を相原尚褧（あいはらなおふみ）（川上）が暗殺しかける、内藤魯一（岩田）が駈けつけて大立ち回りとなる筋だが、立ち回りの格好をつけたは旧役者あがりの森三吉だから、仁木（につき）の刄傷（にんじょう）をそのままつかった。しかし素人だから格好がつかないので、自然に擲りあいをする。セリフも旧役者の風で、一日の狂言にチョボを?一幕も二幕も入れた。そのチョボは特に新作したも?のは稀で、大かた在り来たりの浄瑠璃で、その場面?に縁あるものをつかった。チョボがあるくらゐだか?ら、無論囃子もはいって居たが、囃子方まかせで、素人だから、役者が注文をするとか、ダメを出すとかいふ事は無かった。[40]

    This description is enlightening in that it presents a paradigm that is very different from the one under which sōshi theater and modern Japanese theater generally is often understood to operate. Contrary to the notion of sōshi theater being direct action, a performance without the constraints of *kata*, this production is actually *less* actor-centric and more constrained than kabuki, because the actors are taking their cues from the musicians. Actors are not performing in an unrehearsed, internally motivated way, and thus it presents a picture of the theater that does not eschew *kata*, choreography, and "indirect action".[41]

Violence and Itagaki: *A Record of the Saga Disturbance*

The *enzetsukai* and theater of the sōshi stood out particularly for the violence which was intrinsic to their performance. Physicality and a brash machismo were part of the culture of the sōshi, but the degree to which real, spontaneous violence occurred at these events required that the performers be strong enough to physically defend themselves. Itō Chiyū says that "Sudō was a well-built, thick-boned, strong man, about 5 *shaku* and 5 or 6 *sun* (about 5' 6–7") tall . . . the audiences in Osaka were a foulmouthed lot who jeered at him, so he would end up fighting with the audience" (角藤もその有力な一人であったが骨の太い、丈は五尺五六寸、厳丈造りの偉丈夫であった . . . 大阪だって見物には口の悪いやつがあるから，散々の半量を飛ばすので、元気の好い角藤は、とうとう見物と喧嘩をしてしまった).[42] For his part, Kawakami speaks about casting an actor in a villain role not for his acting chops but simply because he was large enough to fight off the crowd.[43] Images of *enzetsu* meetings from the Meiji Period attest to the brawls and violence that could and did break out at any time.

    Violence occurred not only among the audience and between the actors and the audience, but also with the police monitors of the shows. Censorship laws required a script to be pre-approved by local authorities and for police to monitor the performances to make sure the troupe adhered to the approved script. Police could shut down a production at any point and for any reason, and the actors received a great deal of credibility from goading the police and pushing the limits that would be deemed acceptable. Just one instance of Sūdō doing exactly this is recounted by Ihara Toshio:

    The crowd loved it when the actors argued with or defied the police, so their performance strategy was to work this in as much as possible. After returning from Kyushu, he [Sūdō] performed a play about Oi Kentarō at the Shinmoriza Theater in Nagoya. Sūdō changed Oi's name to Shakai Kin'ichirō, and in the play he was tied up, gagged, and pretended to be dead. An officer left to fetch help, and the remaining officer bent down to fix the thong of his footwear. Seeing his chance, Sūdō's character cut his ropes and strangled the officer to death. However, on opening night, the actor who played that police officer faced the observing police officer's seat from the stage, stuck his tongue out at him, made faces at him, and mocked him. The police officer angrily ordered the show to stop immediately. When the crowd got raucus in response, Sūdō came out and gave a rousing speech to the audience before leaving for the station to argue with the police. As a result, the officer agreed to allow them to amend their script and continue the performance. But the changes made the script unperformable, so the next day they changed the play. When he did this, the audience said that Sūdō had lost to the police, and his popularity plummeted. Because of this, his performance in Nagoya ended in failure. Originally they had planned to continue on to Tokyo, but their plans changed and they went back to Osaka via Ise.

また臨監の巡査と議論をしたり、警察に反抗したりすると、見物が喝采?するので、興行政策として何処でも其ういふ態度を?執った。九州から帰って、名古屋の新盛座で、例の?大井憲太郎の劇を演じた。角藤は大井を変名した社会均一郎といふ役で、捕縛されて舌を噛んで死んだまねをする。役人は手当てをするため引っ込んで、見張りのため一人だけ残った巡査が草鞋の紐を締めようとする、その隙を見て、角藤の役が取?り縄を切って巡査を絞め殺すといふ筋であるが、初?日にその巡査になった俳優が、舞台から警官席へ對?って（むかって）、舌を出したり、滑稽な顔をした?りして愚弄した。警官は怒って即座に興行中止を命じた。そのために見物が昂奮したところへ、角藤?が現れて、引き続いて興行するといふことを演説し、すぐに警察へ出かけて議論した。結局脚本の一?部を訂正して興行を許される事となっただけど、その訂正のために筋がこはれて芝居に出来なくなったので、翌日から脚本を替えた。すると見物の方では、角藤が警官に負けたといふので、そのために人気が落ちて急に入りがなくなった。名古屋の興行はこれで失敗に帰して、最初はそれから東京へ乗り込むつもりであったが、急に予定を変更して、伊勢へ廻って大阪へ逆戻りした。[44]

Kawakami, for his part, could not be accused of backing down to the authorities, and he made the most of his 170 arrests to burnish his sōshi bona fides. As punishing as jail sentences in Meiji Japan were (Kawakami recounts suffering from serious illness as a result of one stint in jail that at the time he was not expected to recover from), he seemed to relish conflict with the police and imagined innovative ways to flout their authority. It even served him creatively, as one of his early popular performances was a biographical account of his time in jail.

96 Democracy dies in Gifu

Extra-theatrical violence was a key element of sōshi theater and part of the appeal for those who attended. The dramaturgical practice of the performers reflected this perspective. In other words, there was very little interest in creating an immersive narrative with a fourth wall that called upon the audience to suspend disbelief. This is after all not surprising, as other contemporaneous genres did not generally employ these techniques either.

This real-life violence was a fundamental base upon which layers of performative violence were built in sōshi productions. The staged violence (*tachimawari*) of the Gifu Incident plays is clearly a key appeal of the material, but it was not the only story associated with Itagaki Taisuke that was staged during this time. Kawakami once again made Itagaki a theatrical subject in his play titled *A Record of the Saga Disturbance* (*Saga bodōki* 佐賀暴動記) (production dates for this show are unclear).[45] The play is set in the wake of the actual Seikanron debates in 1873 in the cabinet over whether to instigate a military invasion of Korea. Itagaki and Saigō Takamori were serving in the cabinet provisionally while much of the cabinet was abroad on the Iwakura Mission, and the planned itinerary of the mission was cut short to handle the crisis at home generated by these debates. Ultimately, Itagaki resigned from his position over the failure of the cabinet to support invasion. Based on historical events, *Saga* follows the story of Arai, who is incensed at the failure of the government to act, and joins a small group of sōshi in a farcical attempt at forcing the Japanese government to launch an attack on the Korean navy and ultimately the Korean peninsula (Figure 3.2).

The opening scene speaks to the intertwining of violent content, stage violence, and a presumed antagonistic relationship between the actors and audience that

Figure 3.2 Nishikie of the dramatic final scene from Kawakami Otojirō's *A Record of the Saga Disturbance*

Source: Reproduced with permission from the Tsubouchi Memorial Theater Museum.

Democracy dies in Gifu   97

could erupt in real violence at any time. Here, Arai has been explaining Japanese history to his friend Kunino and continues:

(ARAI) If that is the case, as you know recently the heroes of the Restoration Saigō, Etō, Itagaki, and Soejima have caused a stir in the cabinet and have left the government. Because of this, I worry that the country will face another disturbance. Have you heard about this incident?

(KUNINO) I've heard a little, but I don't know any of the details. Tell me about it.

Both are deeply engaged in the discussion, and Kunino edges forward.

(ARAI) Hmm. I'll tell you all about it.

ACCOMPANYING MUSIC PLAYS.

(ARAI) This all started in the tenth month of last year when the Minister of the Right Iwakura Tomomi was sent to Europe and America as Ambassador Extraordinary and Plenipotentiary with Councilor Kido Kōin, Minister of Finance Ōkubo Toshimichi, Minister of Works Itō Hakubun [translator's note: Hirobumi], and Junior Assistant Foreign Minister Yamaguchi Shōhō (these latter serving as vice ambassadors to the special diplomatic mission). They were there for three years and returned last month. While they were gone, our government sent Foreign Minister Soejima Taneomi serving as Minister Plenipotentiary to our neighboring countries in order to build stronger bonds of friendship and also sent a letter to Korea. However, not only did they treat our diplomats extremely rudely, their reply lacked appropriate humility. Because of this, Councilor Gotō Shōjirō, Councilor Itagaki Taisuke, and Soejima Taneomi wrote a proposal arguing whether Korea must be punished. This discussion over the need for war with Korea has come to be called *Seikanron* [translator's note: "arguments in favor of the invasion of Korea"]. However, an influential ambassador returned and made this option impossible. Those who had remained and those who had gone overseas on the Iwakura Mission were unable to come to an agreement. In the end, the court denied the possibility of invading Korea. The cabinet became gridlocked with discord because they were unable to express their opinions and they nobly and bravely resigned together from the government, resigned office, and left the cabinet. I've heard that Saigō returned to his former home in Kagoshima. What do you think of this major incident?

(KUNINO) Now I understand the details, but in my opinion it is as Iwakura says. We should not invade Korea.

(ARAI) How dare you spout such crap. Our Imperial government tried to the last to spread peace. Those scumbags who arrogantly returned our gesture with rudeness and sullied the holiness of our Japanese Empire are a bane on the international community. I will promote *Seikanron* as forcefully as I can and raise up our country's rights.

98　*Democracy dies in Gifu*

(KUNINO) Well, the reason I oppose the invasion of Korea is only that the disturbance from our country's Restoration has only recently settled down. We are not ready for international relations, and our military is not yet prepared for international campaigns. The most important focus for the country now is the living standards of the people. If we shift to foreign conquest, how will we pay for military preparations?

(ARAI) Tha-that's no no no no that's the perspective of a frog in a well who can't see the big picture. There are plenty of places to get the money. It is the responsibility of a country's citizens, so we can raise taxes.

(KUNINO) Really, even if we act as impetuously as you say, it is a much higher priority to reform the administration of government. Raising taxes and increasing the suffering of the people is a particularly ineffective policy. That trouble is the cause of our complaint that the invasion of Korea should be put off to the future.

(ARAI) No. You are biased because you understand one thing but not another. Even if our military is unprepared and granaries are depleted, what is the problem with attacking nearby small countries like Korea? If we wait for our military to be prepared and our coffers to be fully stocked we will lose our chance, and various foreign countries will mock us. The honor of our Japan will be sullied, and from this we may well end up losing our independence. Therefore, in light of the nature of Korea's offenses, isn't it the most pressing priority for those possessing the spirit of Japan to conquer them?

(KUNINO) No no no. We shouldn't be gabbing this kind of thoughtless and empty theory. It is not just you, many sōshi have shallow and ignorant notions, and they spout off tough talk without understanding the governments of Western countries, the honoring of international law, and the foundation of national sovereignty. Recently, those guys have been making me laugh.

Arai bristles at this.

(ARAI) What?! Thoughtless and empty theory?!! Now, for even a minimally vibrant society, what would flip floppers like you have the government do? You must know that India now is under the rule of masses of English people. If all of the Japanese citizens were like you people, in the future someone like Clive Hasting will show up here and we'll end up just like India. At that time your shame and regret after the cart has overturned will mean nothing. I have more and more respect for this stand, and us sōshi are throwing ourselves in to the task of waking up the authorities for the sake of the national polity.

He speaks all this angrily.

(KUNINO) It would be a real bummer if a police officer heard you shouting in a crowded place like this.

(ARAI) I ain't afraid of the cops.

Kunino sneers at Arai over this.

Democracy dies in Gifu 99

(KUNINO) Well, if that's the case, do whatever the hell you want. But I call that kind of foolhardiness irresponsible. I can't agree with *Seikanron*. It is a tragedy to think about the unhappy people in a future Japan with lots of people like you punks.

At this, Arai rolls up his sleeves and steps forward.

(ARAI) You gotta learn some manners. You can't insult me like that!

(KUNINO) I have no idea if I need to learn some manners or not, but this is the customary way to talk smack. You wouldn't dare point fingers.

(ARAI) Oh I wouldn't, would I? I will not lose my courage till the end in support of *Seikanron*!

(KUNINO) Right. That kind of courage is what is known as ignorant courage.

(ARAI) You dis me again? Let's decide if this is ignorant courage or not right now. Bring it on.

(KUNINO) Come on with it, bitch.

(ARAI) Punk!

Arai swings at Kunino, and Kunino blocks him with his dagger-walking stick.

Both of them fight, but before they really get into it, Shosei Michida Naomasa enters from kamite *wearing a* chappeau *and* haori. *He steps in between them and breaks up the fight.*

(MICHIDA) Wait a minute! Wait a minute! Both of you!

(新井)
　　サレバさ別の義でもない既に君が知っての通り此頃廟堂に紛議が起って維新の功臣たる彼の西?郷江藤板垣副島の人々が不平をいだき官をやめたゆ?へ又も天下の紛乱になりはせぬかと思うが君は是の?事件を知っているのか

(国野)　イヤ少しは我輩も聞いてはいたが委しき訳は知らぬ聞かして呉れぬい
　　ト　此の談話両人とも熱心なる仕打あるべし此時にいたりて益々国野は前に進む

(新井)　ムヽ然らば其由を御話しやさふの
　　ト　合方に成り

(新井)　抑も今回の事の起りは一昨年十月右大臣岩倉具視君を特命全権大使参議木戸孝允大蔵卿大久保?利通工部大輔伊藤博文外務少輔山口尚芳の諸氏を特命左権副使として欧米諸国へ派遣され三年を経て先月中帰朝されし處其の留守にては又我が政府より隣国の好誼を結ばん為参議外務卿副島種臣氏を全権?公使として諸国に遣し又書を朝鮮に送られしに彼の国にては我が使節に対して無礼亡状を極めしのみか朝鮮の答書不遜なれば参議後藤象次郎参議板垣退助副島種臣の諸氏建言して朝鮮打たざるべからざ?るを論じ問罪の師を起すべしと主張す世に是を征韓論と云う然るに名ある大使の帰朝ありてより其の事を不可として洋行し来りたる人々と残り留りし人々と自から議論協はず是に於て朝廷終に征韓を不可

100　*Democracy dies in Gifu*

とて廟議俄に変す意見の行はれざるを憤りて一同高踏勇退官を辞し冠を掛け朝を退き?西郷氏には郷土鹿児島へ立ち帰りしと聞及しが君は是等の大事変を何んと思はるゝや

(国野)　夫れにて詳細解たが我輩の思う處では岩倉氏の云はるゝ通り征韓は止めた方が宜しかろうと思う

(新井)　イヤ是は怪しからぬ事を云はるゝ者哉あくまで我が帝国政府に於ては平和なる好誼を求めんと努其図に乗じ無礼極りなき彼れ賤奴斯る奴等は我が日本帝国の神聖を汚すものである国際上の大害物拙者は飽く迄征韓論を主張なし我が国権を振起なす所存で御座る

(国野)　イヤ僕の其征韓を不可とする訳けは我が国今日維新の騒乱ようやく鎮定成したるのみにして未だ外国とも交際の道もとゝのはず海陸の軍備も充分?ならず人民生計の度は極めて国要にとぼしき處ある萬一外征の変起らば其軍備は何んによりてしべんすべきや

(新井)　サゝ夫れはゝゝゝゝイヤソリヤ所謂井蛙の議論で其の支弁すべき金の出處はいくらもあらふ夫れは国民の義務だから諸税を重くしても宜ろしい何?でもやッつけるがよろしい

(国野)　サゝ君の様に短兵急に事をせいでも随分征韓より目下に施政の改良を計るべき急務がある特に?此上重税に人民を苦しむるは得策ではない斯る患ひ?のあるゆへに我れらは征韓論は後年にすべしと是れ?其の不平となる所以の原因で在る

(新井)　イヤ夫れは君が一を知って二を知らず偏論と申すもの今軍備は乏しく穀用は足らずとも何んぞ接近の一小国朝鮮如きを伐つべきに何の難き事のあ?らんや若し軍備国庫の充分なるを待つに於ひては恐?らく時期を失ふて諸外国の慢悔を受け我日本の体面?を汚し独立の国権は是れによりて終に失ふにいたる?ならん夫れゆへにこそ宜しく朝鮮の罪状を問ふて是れを征討するこそ目下の急務日本魂を持ちし者のゝ成す處ではないか

(国野)　イヤイヤ夫れ等の論は軽躁者流の空論と云へるものにして到底見るべき處はなし君のみならず当時の壮士多くは浅見無智にして欧米諸国の政府は勿論国際法や建国の基礎の如何は豪も知らずに漫に?暴論を吐荒弁を振ふ輩のみ多くして近頃片腹痛き事で御坐る

　　ト　是にて新井立腹の体にて

(新井)　ヤア軽躁者流の空論とは何ぞや今いやしくも今活発なる社会に於て君らの如く優柔不断に在るときは国の政治は如何にすべきや今印度を億兆英人の軌範羈絆に属したる其理を存知なきや今日本の人民の皆君等の如きものゝみ在らば前途必ずしもクライブ、フースチング等の如き者の顕はれ終には印度の覆轍を踏むにいたらん其時にいたり慚愧後?悔なすも坂より落ちし小車の其詮なかるべし僕はますますこの議論を重んじ当路の人の目を醒させる?こそ国家のために身を擲つが我々壮士の本分かと存?ずる

　　ト　よろけて云う

Democracy dies in Gifu 101

（国野）　イヤ此の群集の中で其の様な大声を発し若し警察の官吏が聞
　　かれたらつまらんぜ
（新井）　イヤ拘留くらいは少しも恐れぬ
　　ト　是れにて国野は苦が笑ひして新井に向ひ
（国野）　然らば何ふとも勝手にするがよひが我等は暴虎馮河主義所謂
　　無責任の論ともいふべきである右等の如き征韓論は甚だ不賛成
　　だイヤ君の様なやつらが多き　我日本の前途も思ひやられて人
　　民の不幸はさこそと思はるゝ遺憾遺憾
　　ト　是にて新井は腕まくりして前へ出る
（新井）　イヤ是れは失敬だ甚だ今の論は僕を侮辱した感があるぞ
（国野）　イヤイヤ失敬の語が在つたか知らぬが此れは俗に云う売詞に
　　買詞だから敢えて君が咎がむる権はない
（新井）　イヽヤ権があらふが無からふが飽くまで征韓論に賛成の勇気
　　は砕けぬ
（国野）　ハテ其勇気が所謂匹夫の勇だ
（新井）　イヤ是は失敬だそれでは匹夫の勇か勇でなひか此処で果しあ
　　いをいたそふ腕力を以ってやるぞ
（国野）　ヤレヤレ僕も相手にならふ
（新井）　エヽしやらくさい
　　ト　国野に打って掛るを国野は洋杖をもつて是れを支へ
　　ト　両人立廻りになる此以前より上手にシャッポ羽織着流し書
　　生道田直正出で居りて此時両人の中へ這入り左右へ引き分け
（道田）コレコレ両君とも待ち玉へ待ち玉へ[46]

As Ayako Kano has observed in other New School theater, there are at least three levels of violence going on in this production. There is a performed violence on stage which reflects and reifies the violent milieu in which the sōshi actually operated in the real world. It also points to the threat inherent to any discussion of the *Seikanron* debates—that an invasion of Korea would involve violence that would dwarf anything that these *sōshi* could muster among themselves. The trajectory of this discussion speaks to the nationalism that was integral to the Freedom and People's Rights Movement: the argument quickly devolves into physical violence not over whether Korea should be invaded—that was a given—but whether Japan should build itself up internally first and then attack, or build itself up internally *by* mobilizing for war. These early performative representations of Itagaki, both in the Gifu Incident and the *Seikanron* debates, latch onto the entertainment value of Itagaki's life and the immediacy of the events on stage, and they play to the audience's political sympathies.

Yet in retrospect, as popular as his firm stance on invading Korea made him with many in the Freedom and People's Rights Movement, it complicates our picture of Itagaki as a liberal reformer who faced death and said, "Itagaki may die, but liberty will never die". Much of this complication comes, of course, from the fact that the metrics that determined the progressive and conservative dichotomy at the time do not map onto our contemporary notions. Yet even while ideological and political dynamics shifted, the Itagaki story remained a touchstone for

102 *Democracy dies in Gifu*

resistance politics and a key component of the memory landscape of the Restoration Period as reimagined for nearly a century.

Sasaki's Itagaki: the Proletarian stage

The practice of performing resistance political theater in a paratheatrical mode did not end with the Freedom and People's Rights Movement in the Meiji Period. Borrowing from a similar tradition in avant-garde circles in Europe, the Japanese Proletarian Theater Movement relied on performance outside the traditional theatrical space both as an aggressive style of outreach and to support sympathetic workers. Jennifer Weisenfeld, in her book on the avant-garde group MAVO, reproduces a photo of a sculpture that is a theater stage in the shape of a boat—a work which articulates the theatrical philosophy held by many in the Proletarian Theater Movement that performance at its most ideal is not anchored to an unmovable building. The Trunk Theater, formed in 1926, was founded on the notion of a portable theater, and this troupe traveled to the scene of strikes to put on performances in support of workers. Thespian Murayama Tomoyoshi wrote in *Theater News* (*Engeki shinbun*), giving detailed instructions and encouraging readers to produce theater in improvised spaces with improvised seats. Perhaps most radically, Maki Toshio writes in the seventh issue of the avant-garde magazine *MAVO* about how theater buildings themselves are soul-crushing spaces where spectators are little more than voyeurs who have little to show for their time when leaving a performance except that they are a little closer to death. He promotes the "anti-theatrical theater movement", where theater is impromptu and there is no distinction between spectator and performer.

Yet in the 1920s and '30s, some socialists also sought to harness the cultural capital of traditional theater spaces for their own ends. The proletarian playwright Sasaki Takamaru employs just such a strategy in the staging of his Itagaki play. He had been and remained actively involved with the Trunk Theater. However over drinks with a friend, Sasaki proposed forming the Avant-Garde Theater, and in their founding document they articulated an approach to socialist theater that used the Bourgeois Theater to subvert the ideology of Bourgeois Theater itself. It is a choice that is echoed by many others in the Proletarian Theater world, including Sano Seki, and it allows for a modern stagecraft in the next Itagaki production I discuss here that, for both technical and economic reasons, would not have been possible in performances by Sudō or Kawakami.

Despite the complicated implications of the Freedom and People's Rights Movement for subsequent liberal resistance movements, Itagaki still had appeal as a source of resistance. Of all of the topics from the Restoration Period to which the Japanese Marxists of the early twentieth century might look back for inspiration, Itagaki generally and the Gifu Incident in particular are perhaps obvious choices. Both had many ingredients that the socialists could rally around: Itagaki took a principled stand for the cause of nominal equality and widespread representation of (nominally) the working class; he faced stiff resistance from the government; and best of all, he steadfastly faced down death without bending his principles.

On a larger conceptual level, Marx noted that capitalist literature is about the present while communism is about the future. The assassination story is an event that is fundamentally about the future. Itagaki's famous line is structured around the notion that what happens in the present, even his own death, is insignificant in the grand scheme of things (a valence that is carried in each staged iteration of the story, except for Kawakami's declaration that Itagaki will never die). All that matters in his locution is that there will be liberty in Japan in the future. This stance is highlighted by Aihara's charge that Itagaki represents a threat to *his* vision of the future with his call of "You are the enemy of the future!" In short, all of the ingredients are easily at hand to craft a story of Itagaki as a proletarian hero, or even better, a proletarian martyr. And indeed, the socialist playwright, translator, director, and political activist Sasaki Takamaru wrote one of his four Restoration Plays about Itagaki. Fittingly titled *Itagaki Taisuke* and published in the journal *Nihon hyōron* in 1935, it was produced by the Shin Tsukiji Gekijō in June 1937 starring Usuda Kenji as Itagaki and Shimada Keiichi as Ueki Emori (Figure 3.3).[47]

Yet Sasaki's play does not make use of any of these juicy features of the story that prior dramatizations of it do. The play diverges in significant ways from plays about him produced during the Restoration Period. Most notably, the two aspects of Itagaki's story that were most compelling to the People's Rights audiences—the Gifu Incident and the *Seikanron* debates—are remarkable for their absence from Sasaki's play. The play is a relatively simple one. In contrast to those early

Figure 3.3 Scene from Sasaki Takamaru's play *Itagaki Taisuke*
Source: Reprinted with permission from the Tsubouchi Memorial Museum.

plays, Sasaki begins in 1873 in the wake of the *Seikanron* debates and covers the years between then and the assassination in 1882. Sasaki's Itagaki is a hero for the working class and a peacemaker above all. In this version, Itagaki is not actually in favor of occupying Korea, and he only reaches out to Saigō Takamori just before the Seinan War in order to peacefully harness his political opposition. Itagaki's role in the push for an invasion of Korea is thus whitewashed. In fact, this is likely a conscious revision given the contemporary conflict on the Asian mainland that was unpopular with many Japanese leftists. Coincidentally, within a month of the staging of this play, full-scale war broke out in China with the Marco Polo bridge incident.

The play has an episodic plot structure that captures snapshots in Itagaki's life between 1873 and 1881. Highlighting his role as peacemaker, nearly every scene begins with a conflict, either on stage or reported, that Itagaki resolves. Often this resolution comes even when the conflict represents a direct threat to himself. In the opening act, a drunk man named Yokoyama nearly gets himself arrested for wandering around the street waving his sword and threatening to go find Itagaki and kill him. When Itagaki happens by chance to pass by, he stops, has the man released, brings him to his home, and eventually helps him start a Rights Movement–affiliated newspaper. Later, students at his home in Kōchi discover a government spy in their midst (Figure 3.4). Yet when Itagaki finds his students preparing to administer brutal justice on the interloper, Itagaki tells them to let him go and uses the opportunity to teach them a Confucian lesson about

Figure 3.4 Sōshi confronting a traitor in their midst in a scene from Sasaki Takamaru's play *Itagaki Taisuke*

Source: Reprinted with permission from the Tsubouchi Memorial Museum.

maintaining impeccable personal morals in order to protect themselves against a bad reputation with the authorities. When a student asks him, "Didn't all of us come here now because it is a time to take up weapons and stand up for ourselves?", Itagaki replies, "What a stupid thing to say! That is not a thing to be said lightly. Our weapon is argument; the discussion of human rights. Go read more books!"[48]

Each scene is a snapshot in time, and together they create a scrapbook that tells a story of the movement over nine years. The most significant result of structuring the play in this way is that the focus is not on the days and hours in the run-up to the assassination attempt. Unlike the aforementioned Gifu Incident examples, that event is downplayed, and the focus is on the history of the Rights Movement up until the assassination attempt. The absence of the scene at Gifu is striking. Simply from a dramaturgical perspective, including it would have been an easy way to structure the narrative and give it a climactic ending. The opening scene described earlier seems to foreshadow a closing scene that will depict the Gifu Incident, yet the play does not end in this expectedly satisfying way. The remarkable rejection of the kind of violence that grounded the sōshi versions of the Itagaki plays highlights the degree to which Sasaki is doing something very different. It is important to note that as history this is a consciously constructed image rather than an outright fabrication. The scene with his students in Kōchi, for example, resonates with the historical Itagaki's split with Saigō Takamori when he said, "'Saigō fights the government with arms . . . but we will fight it with people's rights'".[49] Yet this picture of Itagaki is selective, and it is a deliberately crafted portrait by Sasaki.

Contrasting with earlier versions of this story, by Sasaki's time the contents of this play were no longer temporally immediate as was the case when it was in the news in 1882, or still relatively recent news as in Kawakami and Sudō's productions. Sasaki's drama is a Restoration Play. Yet, despite the historical nature of the content of the play, the production values embrace the modern theater in its stagecraft. Design elements draw from *rensa-geki* (a hybrid performance genre made up of film and live theater) aesthetics and practice, such as the image on the proscenium in Figure 3.3.[50]

Couched in this modern theatrical mode, the fact that the content of this play is a historical drama has important implications for the impact and production of the play. Sasaki's view of historiography on stage is unapologetically revisionist. In talking about his other Restoration Plays, he is open about taking poetic license to get to the larger truths that he feels history teaches. These truths are invariably lessons to be learned about the present in which he is writing. In the promotional materials for the *Itagaki* production put out by the New Tsukiji Theater, Hatori Yukisato gave the context of the play in an article titled "Establishment of the Diet and the Birth of the Left Wing Liberty Party":

> In Meiji 14, the Liberty Party and the Reform Party overlooked their main differences, and for a while they united for the cause of liberty. The Emperor declared that there would be a national diet. "In order to prepare for the

106 *Democracy dies in Gifu*

coming diet," the united political parties seemed to achieve unprecedented progress. In fact, they were in the process of achieving this progress. The Fukushima Incident was the first success by the Liberty Party to get past the "aristocracy and powerful farmers and merchants" and become directly involved with the peasants. Whether or not he knew that this was an essential turning point, Itagaki went on a speaking tour of the entire country and suffered tragedy in Gifu. While Itagaki did not succumb to his wounds, liberty— his Liberty Party—had already begun to wither.

In other words, the years before the assassination attempt represented a special time of unity and camaraderie by competing factions in the Freedom and People's Rights Movement.[51] After the assassination attempt, Itagaki was embroiled in scandal from traveling abroad for the government, and the Rights Movement began to cannibalize itself. It is this story that Sasaki chooses to tell when he puts Itagaki on stage. All of the narrative hooks that made the story so compelling in its earlier iterations are absent from Sasaki's version, and the story is no longer frontloaded with hopeful promise. While the earlier plays are about the future—the liberty that will never die and the fearless leader who will lead them to the promised land—Sasaki's play is decidedly about the past. That is, the assassination attempt does not mark a beginning but rather an end to the best days of the party.

The context in which Sasaki was writing helps to make sense of this take on the Itagaki story. Sasaki recalls in his memoir that when he was writing the play, the Proletarian movement was falling apart in front of his eyes. Mass arrests, censorship, and intimidation were not new tactics used by the government in the 1930s, yet by the middle of the decade he says that the authorities took their measures to new levels and targeted the theater world with much more vigor than it had in the past. Productions were frequently stopped mid-performance for real or spurious reasons, and audience members were subjected to intrusive searches by *kenpeitai* (military police) officers before they were allowed into theaters suspected of harboring leftist leanings. Sasaki describes the results of these tactics as devastating to the camaraderie that marked his time in the movement in the 1920s, in contrast to similar tactics of oppressing sōshi theater. Friends turned on one another, and when Sasaki was released from by-then familiar stints in jail, there were no longer crowds of party members welcoming him and accompanying him home. In one instance that he speaks of with particular bitterness, he was sent by the party to give a lecture denouncing religion—a difficult task for the son of a Buddhist priest. He felt personally betrayed, and it is not hard to see why Sasaki would look to a parallel time in Japan's not-so-distant past for examples of opposition movements that also lost their unifying vision and fell apart. Indeed, while Itagaki's famous line is left out, perhaps Kawakami's farcical rewording of it in 1889 ("Liberty may die, but Itagaki will never die") would have been an appropriate articulation of the current state of affairs. After all, Itagaki did not in fact die in the assassination attempt, but the freedom of Japanese socialists was at the very least on its deathbed in 1937.

Sasaki's take on Itagaki's story stands in stark contrast to the one-night pickle plays that emerged immediately after the incident and the Freedom and People's

Democracy dies in Gifu 107

Rights plays from nine years later in a number of ways. While those earlier plots were temporally immediate and future oriented, they made use of dramaturgy that was rooted in the past. By contrast, Sasaki's production is a historical drama, yet it used modern staging and acting and even the cutting-edge technology associated with *rensa-geki*. This commitment to a sophisticated and complex theater infrastructure represents a turn from the kind of minimalistic paratheatrical performance that grounded the theater surrounding the early Rights Movement performances. Indeed, this performance was not an aberration, as other Restoration Plays examined in this study relied on established theatrical infrastructure and made use of advanced theatrical technology like *rensa-geki* techniques and aesthetics. Thus, Sasaki's *Itagaki Taisuke* turns much of the earlier productions on their heads, and it becomes an example of the not-often acknowledged fact that the Japanese Proletarian Theater Movement was not only, as Marx would have it, a theater of the future. It was also a theater of the past. Specifically, the Itagaki plays transition from narratives of a future to ones of their own past of the Meiji Restoration to which Japanese socialists looked to understand and make sense of their own political and performative present.

Unlike the Restoration Plays examined in Chapter 2, this Restoration Play about Itagaki can trace a performance history back to the Restoration Period itself. These appearances appear across a broad range of performance modes throughout this long performance history to a degree that is unique in early modern Japanese theater. Yet, while few narratives spanned generic divides quite like Itagaki's story did, this case study demonstrates the sometimes overlooked degree to which prewar performance modes readily cross fertilized. Chapter 4 continues to explore examples of the translation of narrative across genre and media. Yet unlike Itagaki, who represented some ideological leanings that were in concert with twentieth-century Marxists, Chapter 4 examines a set of Restoration Plays valorizing the Shinsengumi, whose embrace of a xenophobic feudalism (crystallized in the slogan "Revere the Emperor, expel the barbarians!") ostensibly flies in the face of the Marxist vision of a global proletariat. These plays represent an intriguing translation of ideology in new and innovative performative modes.

Notes

1 Linda Hutcheon and Siobhan O'Flynn, *A Theory of Adaptation*, 2nd ed. (London: Routledge, 2013).
2 This notion of "remediating" a live event—one that is ostensibly unmediated—calls into question the very notion of liveness. Leaving aside a more detailed unpacking of this concept to a later chapter, what is salient here is that one form of performance (mediated through the human body) is represented within the conventions of another performative genre. This question will be taken up in more detail in Chapters 4 and 5.
3 Jonathan E. Zwicker, *Practices of the Sentimental Imagination: Melodrama, the Novel, and the Social Imaginary in Nineteenth-Century Japan* (Cambridge, MA: Harvard University Press, 2006). In the case of modern kabuki, recent works in English have begun to make important strides in understanding the transition from pre-modern to modern. For two particularly notable examples, see: James R. Brandon, *Kabuki's Forgotten War: 1931–1945* (Honolulu: University of Hawai'i Press, 2009); and Satoko

108 *Democracy dies in Gifu*

Shimazaki, *Edo Kabuki in Transition: From the Worlds of the Samurai to the Vengeful Female Ghost* (New York: Columbia University Press, 2016).

4 Matsumoto Shinko, *Meiji engekiron shi* (Tokyo: Engeki Shuppansha, 1980), 30.

5 Ibid., 33–36.

6 Ibid., 108.

7 The "reformed theater" (*kairyō engeki*) is not to be mistaken with the "reformed theater" of the *sōshi* Sudō Sadanori, who put on one of the Itagaki plays.

8 Just some of these varied genres included goze (songs by traveling female singers), yomiuri (singing of news stories), rakugo (storytelling), saimon (singers of religious tales), naniwabushi (storytellers, often accompanied by a musician), chobokure-chongare (a storytelling-musical genre), sekkyōbushi (storytellers of tales that had Buddhist moralistic lessons), jōruri (a musical storytelling genre), utai (singers of ballads), onkyoku, tejina (performers of sleight-of-hand tricks), kuriningyo (puppetry), and kōdan (lectures, but often indistinguishable visually and in content from the other storytelling genres listed here).

9 Kurata Yoshihiro, *Kindaigeki no akebono: Kawakami Otojirō to Sono Shūhen* (Tokyo: Mainichi Shinbunsha, 1981), 16.

10 Hyōdō Hiromi and Henry DeWitt and Smith, "Singing Tales of the Gishi: Naniwabushi and the Forty-Seven Rōnin in Late Meiji Japan," *Monumenta Nipponica* 61, no. 4 (2006), 476.

11 Ibid., 461.

12 Akiba Tarō, *Tōto Meiji engeki shi* (Tōkyō: Chūsei Shobō, 1937), 632.

13 Ibid., 233.

14 The *sōshi* make a brief appearance in *Shochiku kyodai monogatari*, a historical novel by Muramatsu Shōfū from 1955 about the brothers who founded the modern entertainment conglomerate Shochiku. It describes the street performances of the *sōshi* as a modern version of the blind itinerant monks who performed the *Tales of the Heike* in the medieval period.

15 Miyatake Gaikotsu, *Meiji enzetsu shi* (Tokyo: Seikōkan Shuppanbu, 1929), 24.

16 Tsuchiya Momoko, "Itagaki Taisuke Gifu sōnan no shibai: Meiji jūgonen no sakuhin wo chūshin ni," *Gifu Daigaku Kokugo Kokubungaku* no. 3 (2012), 11–27.

17 Shimazaki, *Edo Kabuki in Transition*, 80.

18 James R. Brandon, *Kabuki's Forgotten War, 1931–1945* (Honolulu: University of Hawai'i Press, 2009), 4.

19 Tsuchiya Momoko, "Itagaki Taisuke Gifu sōnan no shibai," 16.

20 Ibid., 17.

21 Fujii Reisuke, *Itagaki kun sōnan tenmatsu: Gifu kyōhō* (Tokyo: Gangandō, 1882).

22 Ii Yōno, "Shingeki no rekishi," *Kabuki*, December 1902, 29, 56.

23 Akiba Tarō, *Tōto Meiji engeki shi* (Tokyo: Ōtori Shuppan, 1975), 232.

24 Ayako Kano, *Acting Like a Woman in Modern Japan: Theater, Gender, and Nationalism* (New York: Palgrave, 2001).

25 Miyatake Gaikotsu, *Meiji enzetsu shi* (Tokyo: Seikōkan Shuppanbu, 1929).

26 Ibid., 3–9.

27 Ibid., 3.

28 Ian McArthur describes how a British man, Henry Black, succeeded in becoming a successful Meiji-era *rakugoka* in part through his performance of Western stories in translation. See Ian McArthur, *Henry Black: On Stage In Meiji Japan* (Clayton, Victoria, Australia: Monash University Pub., 2013).

29 In fact, their very lack of canonical status was crucial for allowing this flexibility of form. "In the case of the more respectable and hierarchically organized forms of singing and storytelling such as *nagauta* 長唄 and *gidayū* 義太夫, it seems safe to assume that the first modern recordings, made shortly after 1900, were not that different from what might have been heard a century earlier. The same cannot be said of the humbler

Democracy dies in Gifu   109

forms of performance, which tended to be more fluid and unstable, particularly during the Meiji period when the old feudal class restrictions were abolished and performers had new freedom to interact and compete in the marketplace of popular entertainment" Hiromi, Hyōdō and Henry D. Smith. "Singing Tales of the Gishi: 'Naniwabushi' and the Forty-Seven Rōnin in Late Meiji Japan," *Monumenta Nipponica* 61, no. 4 (2006), 461.

30 Ibid., 462.

31 Tsuchiya Momoko, "Itagaki Taisuke Gifu sōnan no shibai," 12.

32 Ihara Seiseien, *Kinsei Nihon Engekishi* (Tōkyō: Waseda Daigaku Shuppanbu, 1913), 648.

33 Shioda Shōbei, "Kōtoku Shusui to sōshi shibai," *Higeki kigeki* 48, no. 4 (1975), 534.

34 Matsunaga Goichi. *Kawakami Otojirō: kindaigeki, hatenkō na yoake*. Asahi Sensho (Tōkyō: Asahi Shinbunsha, 1988) 29.

35 Kawakami Otojirō, et al, *Jiden Otojirō Sadayakko*, 24.

36 Matsunaga Goichi, *Kawakami Otojirō: kindaigeki, hatenkō na yoake*, Asahi Sensho (Tōkyō: Asahi Shinbunsha, 1988), 44–45.

37 Tsuchiya Momoko, "Itagaki Taisuke Gifu sōnan no shibai," 13.

38 Ameroku Sei, Jūgonen mae no sōshi shibai, in *Engei gahō*, May (1907), 48.

39 Yet there are also several points of contact in the stage versions in this second period of Itagaki plays. Indeed, while Sudō's 1891 title is very different than the plays of 1882, the script was likely drawn from a text published in 1882. (Its listed production title is the same as that of the text from nine years earlier, although titles for these productions are notably fluid and not necessarily reliable for connecting text to performance.)

40 Seiseien, *Kinsei Nihon Engekishi*, 656.

41 It is also germane to note that genres like *enzetsu*, while perhaps not subject to the level of training in presentation that formal stage actors were, also relied to some degree upon *kata*-like training. The 1891 publication *Jiyū enzetsu genron* features detailed diagrams with descriptions of how to convey specified emotions that essentially serve as *kata*.

42 Itō Chiyū, "Sōshi shibai no omoide", *Chiyū zasshi* 4, no. 2 (1936), 60.

43 Kawakami Otojirō et al., *Jiden Otojirō Sadayakko*, 29.

44 Seiseien, *Kinsei Nihon Engekishi*, 650–651.

45 Unlike Kawakami's more famous Itagaki play, there is at least one extant copy of *A Record of the Saga Disturbance* held at the archives of the National Theater in Tokyo.

46 *Saga bōdōki: Genpon saga no yoarashi* (Tōkyō: Okayasu Heikurō, 1891).

47 This production follows a cancelled production in 1926 of *Jiyūtō ihen*, a Gifu Incident play written by Itagaki Morimasa, Itagaki Taisuke's grandson. The play was scheduled for production and had even gone as far along in the process as to have a photo shoot for publicity stills. In the introduction to the published version of the play, he makes an oblique reference to "trouble" (紛擾) around the cancellation of the play and that he wants to set the record straight. Yet, rather than facing cancellation from the police or the censors, as was so commonly the case in the 1880s, this production was closed at the demand of Morimasa's own family. In a move that made front page headlines, the Itagaki family disowned Morimasa, and he temporarily was adopted into another household. The play generally adheres to patterns set forth in the earlier Gifu Incident plays: it follows the actions of Aihara and focuses the climax of the plot on the assassination attempt. It pegs his motivations in his antipathy for imported philosophy—specifically a newly translated volume of Rousseau. Yet the family felt that the play portrayed both Itagaki and Aihara in equally humanizing terms (*futari to mo ningen-teki*). Morimasa was eventually able to get back into the good graces of his family, however. He was brought back into the family, and he edited the collected works of his grandfather. See Itagaki Morimasa, *Jiyūto ihen* (Tokyo: Hobunkan, 1926).

48 Incidentally, this scene is indicative of the way that the very term *sōshi* had fallen out of favor. The spy is referred to in the stage directions as *sōshi-fū* (*sōshi*-like), while his

110 *Democracy dies in Gifu*

erstwhile colleagues are referred to as "students". Similarly, in *Tsukuba hiroku*, which is treated in detail in Chapter 2, the enemy forces are referred to as sōshi, while the protagonists are called "men of purpose of the Liberty Party's suicide squad" (*Jiyūtō kesshitai no shishi*).

49 Marius B. Jansen and Gilbert Rozman, *Japan in Transition, from Tokugawa to Meiji* (Princeton, NJ: Princeton University Press, 1986), 377.

50 This is most likely a projection as opposed to scene painting, a suspicion strengthened by the fact that at other times in the play different images appear on the proscenium. This would be a difficult change to make in any other way than a projection with a gobo stencil or a photographic slide. In other words, this production uses the technology of a modern stage.

51 Also, this passage is a good example of the view that saw the People's Rights Movement as a predecessor to the Marxist movement of the 1920s and '30s, a view which was not universally shared.

4 Shinsengumi live!

The previous two chapters examine Meiji Restoration Plays which probe the meaning of the Japanese proletarian revolution through performances about the Freedom and People's Rights Movement. While surprising in content (the Proletarian Theater Movement is not typically associated with historical dramas), the analysis re-discovers in these stories notions of revolution and resistance that resonate with commonly held depictions of socialist ideals in the early twentieth century. Sasaki Takamaru's work translates into a Japanese setting the historical revolutions that Marx saw as key examples of transition into the capitalist stage of history.

These stories in turn situate Japan within the framework of the socialist revolution, and they assume (albeit controversially) a notion of revolution based on Western constructs of socialism. The theaters that produced these productions, the Avant-Garde Theater, the Leftist Theater, and other related troupes, were conscious of the ideology not only of their scripts but also of their performance conventions and the organizational structure of the troupes themselves. In other words, ideology was central to both content and form in the most prototypical prewar Proletarian Theater troupes. Yet, while this ideological representation resonates with the standard picture drawn by contemporary theater scholarship on 1920s and '30s Proletarian Theater, movement practitioners actually worked in a broader range of genres and took more nuanced views of the socialist revolution than they are often given credit for.

Here I turn to Restoration Plays produced by the Zenshinza troupe about the Shinsengumi, a corps of deputized swordsmen made up of castoffs and criminals who fought on the side of the shogunate during its final collapse. The plays examined here by Murayama Tomoyoshi and Kubo Sakae juxtapose liveness with mediation in ways that challenge the dramaturgical assumptions of resistance theater examined in preceding chapters. As such, this chapter examines very different variations on the Restoration Play, ones that take as a starting point none of the orthodox ideological models of revolution seen in previous chapters. Far from the aspirations of the Avant-Garde Theater to avoid even the remotest "stench" of feudal ideology, the subject matter and performance conventions examined in this chapter pushed boundaries that proletarian troupes, as they are more typically remembered, could or did not. They trouble standard narratives of the dramaturgy and content of Japanese Proletarian Theater. These performances

112 *Shinsengumi live!*

put into play the very notion of the Communist revolution and the performance of resistance in the prewar period. In representing the Shinsengumi story multiple times throughout the 1930s, the Zenshinza was capitalizing on the recent boom in popularity of the group. Kondō Isami, the leader of the group, for all his faults displayed resolute determination to the end in the face of overwhelming odds. This no doubt helps account for the broad-based popularity of the Shinsengumi beginning in the late twenties and continuing unabated today. Thus it is not surprising that a relatively apolitical troupe like the Zenshinza would perform this story. Yet the fact that the authors of these works were Murayama and Kubo, the two most politically radical members of the troupe—indeed two of the most prominent figures of the Proletarian Theater Movement as a whole—stands out and is in stark contrast to the performances that they are known for today.

The four Shinsengumi productions by the Zenshinza span a range of performance techniques. The first of these is Kubo Sakae's 1933 *Blood Oath at Goryokaku* (五稜郭血書). It tells the story of the last days of the remnants of the anti-imperialist forces as they flee to Hokkaido with Hijikata Toshizō, the last of the Shinsengumi leadership. This is followed by his 1934 script, ultimately unperformed, titled *Shinsengumi: A Talkie Rensa-geki* (トーキー連鎖劇「新撰組」), a *rensa-geki* which utilized the new feature of recorded sound in film.[1] Murayama Tomoyoshi in 1937 then wrote his own *rensa-geki* script, film (produced by the Zenshinza's film production company), and 1940 novel, all titled *Shinsengumi* (新撰組). The interest in the Shinsengumi was thus not a one-off project for either Kubo or Murayama.

In addition to innovating with content, these Shinsengumi scripts highlight an artistic experiment in which Kubo and Murayama, along with the Zenshinza generally, wrestle with the relationship between liveness and mediation in an increasingly mediated world. These artistic experiments question the role of live action in the face of the existential crisis for live performance posed by political pressure on the one hand and an increasingly mediatized environment on the other. Liveness and spontaneity are central characteristics of the theaters of resistance throughout this book. Thus, the Shinsengumi Restoration Plays of the Zenshinza are dramaturgical counterparts to the approach to live action that drove the performances explored in earlier chapters in the way that they place performance in juxtaposition with the old media of texts and the new media of film in order to formally innovate new places for liveness in Proletarian Theater.

Further, these productions highlight the ideological role that the Zenshinza played in contrast to the two other major poles in the shingeki tent, the Tsukiji Little Theater and the Avant-Garde Theater. In doing so, they also help to illustrate the great degree of personnel movement between the troupes that allowed for figures like Murayama and Kubo produce the wide variety of work that they did. It is only through the ideological variety at play in these very different kinds of proletarian performance troupes that these scripts ever saw production. Even for playwrights Murayama and Kubo, major figures in the Proletarian Theater Movement, their scripts would have been very unlikely to be staged in the other troupes they frequently worked with. The leftist Avant-Garde Theater, for example, would

Shinsengumi live!   113

not have found the subject matter ideologically compelling, and the Tsukiji Little Theater did not typically stage period dramas.

The Zenshinza was at best nominally part of the Proletarian Theater Movement, yet they offered creative outlets for members who were very much politically motivated to present work that they otherwise would not likely have had. This variety within the Proletarian Theater umbrella allowed for the experimentation with both liveness and content involved in these Shinsengumi stories and helped to imagine the Japanese revolution.

Mapping the Proletarian Theater Movement

The performers, theaters, and key performances from the 1920s until the late 1930s which make up the Japanese Proletarian Theater Movement were anything but a unified group. As Chapter 2 recounts, there were fierce internal differences even by those who shared leftist political ideals, and not all of the theaters loosely labeled under this group even held political motivations as their key artistic aim. In this section, I identify three separate lineages of troupes which account for the majority of performances that are considered Proletarian Theater: the Tsukiji Little Theater, the Avant-Garde Theater, and the Zenshinza. It is true that there is much overlap between the labels of shingeki theater and Proletarian Theater in the 1920s and '30s. It is also true that people with overt socialist agendas participated in all three of the theater groups here. Yet shingeki is primarily a description of the dramaturgical approach of a performance, and Proletarian Theater primarily defines the ideological approach. The two categories did not overlap completely in prewar Japan. Despite advances in scholarship in the intervening years, the picture of the shingeki world in the 1920s and '30s as being locked in the grip of the proletarian movement has not substantially evolved since Donald Keene posited that prewar shingeki was dominated by leftists.[2] Yet not all of these troupes espoused the dramaturgy of modern Western theater that is associated with shingeki, and not all of these troupes were motivated by the socialist ideologies of the Proletarian Theater Movement.

The beginning of the Proletarian Theater Movement in Japan has been dated by some as starting in 1926. While there was certainly a socialist theater of resistance before this time, that year saw several seminal performances, the founding of the Trunk Theater and the Kokoroza Theater, and the publication of new journals that shaped the Proletarian Theater Movement and gave it a more substantial footprint throughout the next decade. While any beginning date for the movement is arbitrary, 1926 features prominently in all three of the theater lineages noted here.

The Tsukiji Little Theater

The Tsukiji Little Theater was founded after the Kanto earthquake by Osanai Kaoru and became the central pillar in the shingeki world. Osanai was dedicated to developing modern Japanese theater and opposed to using Tsukiji for ideological ends. Yet in 1926, a significant number of members of the Tsukiji troupe took a sharp turn to the

114   *Shinsengumi live!*

left. As a part of this shift, November of 1926 saw the Tsukiji Little Theater's production of Sasaki Takamaru's translation of Marcel Martinet's *La Nuit* (夜), which was hailed at the time as the first instance of Japanese "revolutionary theater" (革命劇). Preceding this production, Kubo Sakae, Sasaki Takamaru, and other members of the so-called Tsukiji Youth Faction (青年築地派) formed a secret Marxist study group known as the Marxist Arts Study Society (マルクス主義芸術研究会) (Maru-gei (マル芸) for short) in February of the same year.[3] This marked an ideological turn in the Tsukiji Little Theater, as noted by Hijikata Umeko:

> The new wave of the Socialist Movement inevitably swamped the Tsukiji Little Theater. This wave created a vortex of excitement generated by Martinet's *La Nuit*. Those within Tsukiji who had developed political consciousness formed a secret group, a study group in conjunction with members of the Avant-Garde Theater, and attempted to build a "new world view" [tr. note: "new world view" (新しい世界観) was a common euphemism for "socialism"]. These people who actively started the vortex from within Tsukiji felt that those in Tsukiji up until then did not measure up (Hijikata Umeko)." It is from this point that those in Tsukiji of the "new world view" standpoint, who could not be satisfied with the current repertory, began the study group activity to bring in new theater.

> 「これらの社会運動のうねりは、築地小劇場へも新しい波となって おしよせてき ざるをえませんでした。マルチネの「夜」にまきおこ った興奮の渦は、一連のつ ながりをもった波の動きであったと思い ます。築地内部ではこの波を、 ...(中略) 意識的に受けとめた人た ちは、ひそかにグループをつくって、前衛座の人たちと 研究会を開 き、新しい世界観に立とうとしました。従来の築地のありかたに、も の足りなさを感じるようになったこれらの人たちの積極的な動きが 築地の内部で も渦を巻きはじめました(土方梅子)」 ここから、築地 内部に〈新しい世界観〉に立つものたちが出現したこと、そして彼 らはもはや従来のレパートリーに満足できなくなり、新しい演劇を 受け入れるための研究会活動をはじめたことがわかる。[4]

The Tsukiji Little Theater did not openly engage in propaganda, whatever the personal ideological leanings of their members might have been. Because of this, they were required to hold their meetings in secret, and it is a tribute to Osanai Kaoru's leadership and the force of his personality that he was able to hold together a troupe of actors from widely differing artistic and political inclinations. After his death in 1928, the Tsukiji Youth Faction played a significant role in the fracturing of the group along ideological and artistic lines. As Inoue points out:

> Looking at the result, Kubo and his friends' study group can be seen as the precursor to the rupture of Tsukiji that came after Osanai's death, and it was a clear omen of the internal collapse of the group. The democratization of

Shinsengumi live! 115

Tsukiji was quelled before it saw the light of day, but the rupture-related activity went straight to the young actors. Mizushina and Umeko say that after *La Nuit*, this triggered a fierce fight within the troupe.

結果的にみると、久保たちの研究会活動は小山内死後の、あの分裂にむかって動きだした胎動と見做すことができ、この頃から築地は明らかに内部崩壊の兆を呈していたといえよう。かくて築地民主化方策は日の目を見ずに終るが、しかし分裂活動は確実に築地の若手に影を落し、水品や梅子の語る「夜」以降の激しい内部抗争を生む火つけ役となったのである[5]

Inoue's comment suggests that even during his lifetime, Osanai was not able to maintain total unity in his company. As the central troupe for what was considered shingeki in the 1920s and '30s, Tsukiji represented a broad range of personalities, as well as political and artistic ideals. Osanai's group defined what it meant to be shingeki and represented a middle ground between views espousing different political ideologies and means of formal experimentation. This theater unquestionably occupied a place at the center of the shingeki movement, yet there were other troupes that aligned with the movement, and Tsukiji did not speak for all of them with a unified voice.

The Avant-Garde Theater

The Avant-Garde Theater was a second important institution in the movement (its story is told in more detail in Chapter 2). It traced its genealogy from the Forerunner Theater (先駆座) in the early 1920s to the Trunk Theater in 1926, and all were led by Sasaki Takamaru. The actors in this theatrical genealogy were overtly political. In fact, the actor, director, and translator Senda Koreya left the more prominent Tsukiji Little Theater to join the Trunk Theater because of its political activism. While Tsukiji was moderately successful from a business perspective (i.e. it ran in the red, but less so than other shingeki troupes), this commercial success resulted from what Senda saw as a compromise in the audience that it targeted. Its location and subscription model of ticket sales catered primarily to students and intellectuals rather than workers. By contrast, Senda saw the Trunk Theater as an opportunity to bring theater to the working class. The Avant-Garde Theater inherited politically motivated performers such as Senda Koreya, and it was dedicated to creating leftist political theater.

The Zenshinza

1926 also represented an important year for the Zenshinza, a third and very different ideological, institutional, and artistic model of shingeki troupe. Kawasaki Chōjūrō IV, a student of Ichikawa Danjūrō and a founding member of the Zenshinza, had from the beginning been interested in the shingeki work of the Tsukiji

116 *Shinsengumi live!*

Little Theater. However, he remained with Shochiku because switching to the smaller troupe would have resulted in a significant pay cut. Despite remaining with his employer, he broke with Shochiku's political views when he became acquainted with Murayama Tomoyoshi, and in 1925 he formed a study group with Murayama (newly returned from Germany) and other prominent actors and thinkers.[6] The members of this group formed a troupe named Kokoroza and put on their first performance in January 1926 at the Hōgakuza in Ginza. Early performances included modern dance by Murayama Tomoyoshi, original scripts by Iketani Shinzaburō and Eguchi Kan, as well as translations of Georg Kaiser by Murayama and Kubo Sakae.[7] The group was marked by sharp artistic and political divisions, and it was soon divided into an "art faction" (芸術派) and a "socialist movement faction" (社会運動派). This division led the group to be called "a two horse carriage" (二頭だての馬車である).[8] Unlike the divisions in the Avant-Garde discussed in Chapter 2, and unlike those in the Tsukiji Little Theater outlined earlier, the Zenshinza did not break up over these artistic and political differences. Nonetheless, after production of Murayama's *Nero in Skirts*, the art faction was able to push Murayama out of the group for his political radicalism.

Thus, while remaining a shingeki troupe, many in the company resisted moves to become a truly proletarian theater. However, since Murayama was not alone in his desire for a politically motivated theater, removing him was hardly sufficient to settle the internal divisions. In July of 1928, Chōjūrō toured with Sadanji in the Soviet Union, where he was introduced to socialist thought that would inform his work at some level throughout his career. When he returned from Moscow, Chōjūrō worked with the Leftist Theater (左翼劇場) and Murayama Tomoyoshi, who had newly returned to the Zenshinza, to produce a performance of Vsevolod Ivanov's *Armored Train 14–69*.[9] While he was never as radical as Murayama, Chōjūrō's political affinity was most certainly on the left, and after the war he officially joined the Communist Party. Thus, removing Murayama weakened the political wing of the company and helped solidify the art faction's control, but it did not entirely purge the troupe of members with left-wing political sympathies.

Indicative of this split, the politically motivated Kubo Sakae remained active in the Zenshinza throughout the 1930s, despite his Marxist leanings and lack of the formal theatrical training credentials sported by other members of the troupe. At the same time, while there remained some political tension between Sadanji on the right and Chōjūrō on the left throughout the 1930s, of all the shingeki troupes that were shuttered with the so-called Shingeki Incident in 1940, the Zenshinza was considered politically docile enough by the authorities that it was allowed to remain open.

Yet forces beyond the confines of the troupe also bolstered the political faction within the Zenshinza. During the 1920s and '30s, the kabuki industry as a whole began to institute pay cuts that threatened the livelihood of lower-level actors. This spurred actors to organize, including the benshi- and onnagata-organized labor strikes against Shochiku and Nikkatsu. Prominent Shochiku actor Ennosuke responded to these moves by his employer by distancing himself from Shochiku. Nakamura Kan'emon and Nakamura Kamematsu (later Tsuruzō) founded

Shinsengumi live! 117

the leftist theater journal *Gekisen*, which Shochiku actively attempted to shut down by leaning on its financial backers. At the same time, Ichikawa Yaozō and Ichikawa Kodayū, students of Ennosuke, joined with Kan'emon, Kamematsu, and Ichikawa Emiya (later Kunitarō) to form the Taishūza Theater. Their first production, in January of 1930 at the Hongōza Theater, presented Sasaki Takamaru's *Tsukuba hiroku* (discussed in Chapter 2) and a translation of Upton Sinclair's *The Spy*. The creation of the Taishūza Theater was followed quickly by the disbanding of the Kokoroza on March 2, 1930. While Ennosuke returned to Shochiku after the Taishuza was disbanded that same year, his mentor Sadanji considered his initial departure from Shochiku a personal betrayal and held a grudge until his death. In short, even in the conservative world of kabuki theater, economic pressures led actors to organize and participate actively in the labor movement and explore leftist ideologies.

The pay cuts at Shochiku continued to drive actors away from the company, and again Ennosuke, along with Ichikawa Sashō and Ichikawa Arajirō left, this time to join the Shunjūza. In December of 1930, Ennosuke officially and permanently quit from Shochiku, and on May 22, 1931, he joined Chōjūrō and a contingent of 30 actors who formed the Zenshinza. These actors included Murayama Tomoyoshi, Ono Miyakichi, and Shochiku actors who were students of Sadanji such as Chōjūrō and Nakamura Utaemon. Given the background and personnel of this group, it is not surprising that their founding document differed significantly from that of the Avant-Garde Theater troupe. Whereas the Avant-Garde Theater focused on creating theater with a "new world view" (i.e. communism/socialism), the Zenshinza's founding document outlined an institution that was mostly limited to reforming the profession of acting by doing away with many of the feudal elements of kabuki that dated back to the Edo Period. Even low-level actors in the new troupe would now be included in governing decisions, and pay was made transparent and open. Their founding document declared that in the Zenshinza: 1) management will be transparent, and there will be no secrets (including salaries); 2) the kabuki class system will be abolished; and 3) everyone will be treated as human beings with the same rights.[10] The impetus for the founding of the group led them to articulate ideals that were practical, quotidian, and largely removed from charged ideological jargon.

If the Tsukiji Little Theater represented the political and artistic center of the shingeki world, and the family of theater troupes from the Forerunner Theater to the Trunk Theater to the Avant-Garde Theater represented the overtly political column of the shingeki community, the genealogy that continued from the Kokoroza to Taishūza to Bunkaza to Zenshinza represented a third theater lineage that was more closely tied to kabuki theater but still fell under the broad tent of the shingeki world. While actors and scripts flowed freely across these lines, the Zenshinza consisted primarily of professionally trained actors, mostly from Shochiku. Many of them retained ties to Shochiku and their mentors such as Sadanji (who, it is important to note, despite his involvement in the shingeki world was seen by Shochiku president Otani Takejirō as having political views that were safely "not red"). Not surprisingly, they often performed traditional scripts in a

118 *Shinsengumi live!*

kabuki style. In other words, shingeki was artistically more varied than the translated Western scripts of the Tsukiji Little Theater and also politically more varied than the single ideological motivations of the Avant-Garde Theater.

Kubo and Murayama

The shingeki community was a relatively small world, and it is hard to imagine any two people being removed by more than one or two degrees of separation. This is certainly true for Kubo Sakae and Murayama Tomoyoshi who met in school, long before they started theater, and had a number of common interests. Both were fluent in and translated German, both shared an interest in the German expressionists, and both were founding members of the Zenshinza and found themselves ideologically at odds with the non-leftist members of the troupe.

Yet they also had very different life experiences that led up to their involvement in the Proletarian Theater Movement. Kubo Sakae (久保栄 1900–1958) was born in Sapporo to a wealthy family who owned a brickmaking factory. In 1903, Sakae was sent to Tokyo as the adopted son of his uncle (father Hyōtarō's youngest brother, Kumazō). However, Kumazō later faced financial difficulties, and Sakae returned to his father's family registry in 1915. Despite this change of circumstances, he decided to remain in Tokyo to finish his schooling, living a much more spartan lifestyle than he would have if he had returned to his wealthy family home in Sapporo.[11] Murayama Tomoyoshi (村山知義 1901–1977), by contrast, grew up in the Tohoku region. His father died when he was 10 years old, and his mother converted to Christianity and raised Tomoyoshi in the pacifist Japanese Christian community which mingled with the early Japanese Communist community.

Despite these very different family situations, chance had it that they crossed paths with each other early in life when they happened to share the same dorm at the First Higher School (一高等学校).[12] Both went on to attend Tokyo Imperial University, but while Kubo remained in Japan for the duration of his studies, Murayama dropped out after one year to study abroad in Germany. While Kubo completed his studies, Murayama began his artistic career in the visual arts, gaining early attention for paintings in oil and water color as well as for his illustrations in children's books and magazine covers. While in Germany, he became involved with the European avant-garde, and Futurist and Constructivist art theories would continue to inform his work long after he returned to Japan. After his return, he was influential in introducing Futurism and Constructivism to Japan as co-founder of the avant-garde group MAVO, and through his wide variety of performance art.[13] Both Murayama's and Kubo's writing careers were heavily dependent upon and influenced by translation, and they jockeyed for the privilege of producing translations of the Zenshinza's German-sourced performances. Unlike Sasaki Takamaru (discussed in previous chapters), who characterized his playwriting development as moving from translation to original scripts, Kubo's and Murayama's writing careers paralleled their translation careers, with their translation work informing their original writing and vice versa. Working from German, with a particular

Shinsengumi live! 119

interest in expressionist playwrights like Georg Kaiser, as well as with original texts such as *The Blood Oath at Goryokaku*, Kubo made his writing debut in 1926 with a translation of *Die Hose* by Carl Sternheim.[14] Thus, despite sharing a great deal in common in their personal biographies and political sympathies, they also competed as rivals in their capacities as theater professionals.

A Shinsengumi with political consciousness?

The interest in the Shinsengumi story for Murayama and Kubo was anything but idiosyncratic to them or the Zenshinza. The Shinsengumi has enjoyed enormous popular appeal ever since the early decades of the twentieth century. Yet if interest in the story is not unique to them, it is surprising given Murayama's and Kubo's leftist political leanings that the Shinsengumi would find a place at the center of four of their productions (not to mention be the subject of an entire novel by Murayama). After all, the Shinsengumi were on the losing side of a civil war for the feudal bakufu, and they were ultimately militarily defeated and disgraced. To recount their story briefly, as the shogunate collapsed in the 1860s, it took the unprecedented move of enlisting *rōnin* (masterless samurai, also called *rōshi*) to police the streets of Kyoto and to protect the shogunate's interests. It even emptied prisons in a desperate attempt to defend against the rising threat of anti-shogunate forces. The motley corps of skilled swordsmen made up of peasants, samurai, and ex-felons that answered the bakufu's call for a police force in Kyoto would eventually become the group known as the Shinsengumi.

The group was initially led by two figures: Serizawa Kamo (1830–1863), a samurai by birth who had been released from death row during an amnesty deal issued by the bakufu, and Kondō Isami (1834–1868), the head of a dōjō in Tama to the west of Edo. When Kondō closed his dōjō and traveled to Kyoto to join the bakufu's defense corps, he brought with him six students who would make up the core of the Shinsengumi and who have since become famous through creative retellings of the group's history. They included Okita Sōji, a sword-fighting prodigy who died at a young age of tuberculosis (often portrayed as a romantic hero), and Hijikata Toshizō, the so-called "Demon vice commander" (鬼の副長). With the official sanction of the bakufu and the financial backing of the Aizu clan, the Shinsengumi was a widely feared brute squad who extorted protection money from local merchants and fought against other *rōshi* deemed enemies of the bakufu. Just before their defeat at Kofu Castle in 1868, Kondō was given official rank by the Shogun, and he had a triumphal homecoming in Hino on the journey west from Edo to his final defeat. He was captured alive in the battle and publicly beheaded in Itabashi—not even granted the honor of committing seppuku. The last of the Shinsengumi's leadership was defeated in Hokkaido in the final battle of the Boshin War the following summer.

In contrast to this short existence and ignominius defeat, the group has had a long and flourishing afterlife in creative output and historiography since at least the end of the Meiji period (i.e. the early 1910s). In 1928, two early important historical accounts of the group were produced by Hirao Michio and Shimosawa

120 *Shinsengumi live!*

Kan. Creative representations of the group are far too numerous for a comprehensive listing, but they include the 1932 stage and film productions titled *The Shinsengumi Who Survived* (生き残った新撰組); Shiba Ryōtarō's 1962 novel *The Battle Records of the Shinsengumi* (新撰組血風録); the 1969 film *Shinsengumi* starring Mifune Toshiro, directed by Sawashima Tadashi, and produced by Inagaki Hiroshi; the 1996 manga *Rurouni kenshin* (るろうに剣心), which also was adapted into anime, film, and video games; the 1999 film *Taboo* (御法度) directed by Oshima Nagisa; the 2004 NHK taiga drama *Shinsengumi!* written by Mitani Kōki and starring Katori Shingo as Kondō, with a follow-up titled *Shinsengumi!!* (note the two exclamation marks for the sequel), a two-hour New Year's special that ran the following year; the video game, manga, and anime franchise *Hakuōki* (薄桜鬼) which began releasing titles in 2008; and the 2015 zombie comedy *Shinsengumi of the Dead* (新撰組オブザデッド) directed by Watanabe Kazushi. Thus, unlike the Restoration Plays in Chapters 2 and 3, the works examined in this chapter are part of a large and popular corpus of creative output outside of the limited confines of prewar Proletarian Theater. The story is unquestionably one of the most popular stories in Japanese history, with new tellings appearing consistently across the decades and across written, performance, and digital genres.

Ideologically this subject matter would seem to require a delicate dance for the political sensibilities of Murayama and Kubo. Yet the historical record and the narrative history of the Shinsengumi diverge a great deal. While most of the aforementioned narratives feature some of the major historical events of the group, such as the attack at the Ikedaya and the assassination of Serizawa Kamo, the narratives have coalesced around interpretations of those events that are independent of the academic historiography of the group.[15] Thus, this group that might otherwise be remembered as ruthless thugs, or forgotten completely, have had their stories recovered in narrative in a way that have made them popular heroes even for the leftist theater of Kubo and Murayama. Kubo's and Murayama's scripts inscribe motivations to their ruthless actions that present them as flawed actors but with noble intentions. In the case of Kubo's Kondō Isami, for example, his motivation for leaving Tama was to become a crusader for the peasant farmers in his hometown of Hino:

> HIJIKATA: Commander, even at this point, what can be said? You took up your sword to fight for the noble cause of the union of the court and shogunate and to expel the foreign barbarians in order to help the impoverished farmers. Commander, is that just a passing whim? Are those just empty, vain words? Even now there are people at court who are bending the knee to foreigners, and we have no hope to expel the barbarians. Can you quietly return to your dojo in Edo? Commander, when you face the people of our home region in the twenty villages in Tama County, how will they see you?
>
> KONDŌ: Hijikata. How long do you want to be the laughing stock of the world?

Shinsengumi live! 121

土方：隊長、今さらとなって、何を言われるのだ。公武御一和、上に攘夷の大命を戴き、人心を定め農の疲弊を救おうために、剣をとって非常に処すると　いわれたは、隊長、あれはただ一時の気まぐれにすぎなかったのか。口か　ら出まかせの大言壮語にすぎなかったのか。すでに京都方も諸外国に、膝を屈したこの上は攘夷も望みなしと言って、ただ恬然と江戸の道場に帰れますか、隊長、何の面せあって多摩郡二十ヶ村の郷党に見えることができ　るのです。

近藤：土方。貴公は、いつまで世間の物笑いになりたいのか。[16]

KONDŌ: Just as I guessed. Hijikata, recently I have begun to hate myself. It has already been a year and a half since we joined up with the Shinchō Rōshi Corps and came to the capital. It isn't like I dreamed it would be. Although the shogun has come to the capital twice, he did not issue any edicts or make any decisions about expelling the barbarians. My hopes are fading to achieve my life aspirations of unifying the populace, helping the oppressed peasants, curbing the domination of trade by foreigners, and bringing peace to the land. I bravely volunteered myself to charge ahead and attack the foreign ships, but we are simply killing the other *rōshi* that are in the small world of the capital. On top of this, whenever we kill a single person, people whisper slandering gossip about the Shinsengumi, and Kondō Isami's name is feared both in and out of Kyoto. This is not what I wanted at all.

近藤：推量のとおりだ。土方、拙者はこのごろ、われながら自分というものに愛　憎がついた。新徴浪士隊に加わって京へのぼってよりすでに一年有半、事志と違って、将軍家には二度の御上洛にもかかわらず、勅命を奉じて攘夷決行の御英断もなく、国論合一によって人心を定め、農の疲弊を救い、外　国通商の跋扈をおさえて、天下を安きにつかしめる近藤畢生の志願も今は　望みが薄い。身を挺して異国船打払いの魁けともなろうとしたものが、た　だ京洛の小天地にあって人別外の浪士どもを斬って廻る。――しかも、人　ひとりを斬るたびに、新撰組の虚名は天下に轟き、近藤勇の名は、洛中洛　外を恐れしめる。たが、近藤は決してこのような出世を望んだのではない。[17]

In other words, Kondō has his heart in the right place with helping the struggling peasants, but systemic forces are too much for him. The script frames the story within the context of the political struggles of the common people in ways that may diverge from the historical record but would have resonated with the audience of the production.

Murayama was likewise sympathetic to the dilemma faced by Kondō as a commoner in late nineteenth-century Japan. Murayama saw him as a farmer whose frustration with the feudal system was simply misdirected at foreigners rather than at the bakufu and the ruling class.[18] These scripts differed in profound ways

122 *Shinsengumi live!*

from the subject matter of other performances by Kubo and Murayama and from the Proletarian Theater Movement generally. For example, Kubo's *Fascist Doll* and Murayama's *Record of a Gang of Thugs* are both contemporary narratives which tell their story from the perspective of the oppressed working class. These Shinsengumi performances worked through the transition from feudal Japan to nominally capitalist Japan in a very different way from the approach towards re-thinking the relationship between the Restoration and Bourgeois Revolution discussed in Chapter 2. These productions also collectively represent a reckoning with the relationship between political goals and modes of performance at an ontological level.

The Blood Oath at Goryokaku

In a testament to the fluidity of personnel and content between the varying shingeki troupes, Kubo wrote *The Blood Oath at Goryokaku* (*Goryōkaku kessho* 五稜郭血書) for the Zenshinza, but the debut production run was at the Tsukiji Little Theater from June 25 to July 5, 1933, before it was restaged by the Zenshinza in 1934. It was then restaged at least twice after World War II: in 1952 by the Gekidan Mingei troupe at the Shinbashi Enbujō (with nearly identical scenic designs as the prewar stagings), and in 1969 at the National Theater of Japan by the Bungakuza. These stagings in the postwar period set *Goryokaku* apart from other Restoration Plays, most of which did not receive critical or dramaturgical attention after 1945.

The play recounts the final collapse of the forces of the Shogun who fought on even after the shogunate conceded defeat and turned over Edo Castle to the Satsuma-Choshu armies. It tells of the shogunal army's flight from Aizu to Hakodate in Hokkaido, their establishment of a short-lived government, and their defeat at the hands of the Imperial forces. The final battle features the death of Hijikata Toshizō, the former second in command of the Shinsengumi (Figure 4.1). This conflict takes place within the context of competition by European powers over colonial expansion between France (which supports the shogunate with military advisors and trade) and England (which supports the Imperial army with military advisors and materiel). The play resonates with Kubo's most successful production *The Land of Volcanic Ash* (火山灰地) both in its setting in Kubo's native Hokkaido as well as with his attention to the economic forces that oppress the commoners in the new Japanese colony. In *Goryokaku*, this is particularly highlighted by the role of the merchant Kobayashi in monopolizing *konbu* (a variety of edible kelp) harvesting rights and using this market share advantage to force down prices to the disadvantage of small-scale harvesters.

Kubo states that a primary goal of the play was to explore the economic underpinnings of the Meiji Restoration. It is also seen as being prompted by the 1932 theses issued by the Comintern which reiterated its doubts about the status of the Meiji Restoration as a bourgeois revolution.[19,20] Kubo was very conscious of this international political context as well as the increasing repression that the movement faced in the mid-1930s, and this context informed his artistic vision for proletarian historical drama.

Figure 4.1 A scene from *The Blood Oath at Goryokaku*, by Kubo Sakae; the play tells the story of the fall of the final holdouts for the Shogun even after his abdication, including Hijikata Toshizō and the other remnants of the Shinsengumi

Source: Reproduced by permission of the Tsubouchi Memorial Museum.

Figure 4.2 Kubo Sakae's *The Blood Oath at Goryokaku*

Source: Reproduced with permission by the Tsubouchi Memorial Museum.

124 *Shinsengumi live!*

At its most simple, *Goryokaku* is a *jidaigeki*—a historical drama. Yet Kubo is attempting to use history in a very different way than did, for example, Sasaki Takamaru in *A Secret Account from Tsukuba*. In writing about the debut performance of *Goryokaku*, Kubo lays out his philosophy for the role of politically motivated historical drama:

> Taking into account our current environment, we have to represent historical truth in our plays with more innovative formal properties than our current historical drama. Our historical drama should not select out arbitrary instances of class conflict, but rather focus on specific times that are instructive to the contemporary proletariat and the wider oppressed masses which demonstrate one part of humanity's historical legal development. Our works should have direct meanings and effects that do not overlook contemporary themes. If these two points are taken as one suggestion, my work as a writer can largely be said to be successful. Then we as a community can take this work as one concrete source for consideration, and using this strict critique we can solve the question of the new genre of historical drama. On top of this, these solutions will be put into actual practice.

> ただ吾々が当面の必要から、従来の吾々の歴史劇よりも、はるかに飛躍した発展　的形態に於いて、史実を描けなければならないという事、吾々の歴史劇とは、任意の時代の階級闘争の姿を、あれこれと取り上げるべきでなく、現代のプロレタ　リアートおよび一般被圧迫大衆にとって最も教訓を含んだ一時期を、全人類史の　合法則的発展の一環として描き出す時、決して現代的テーマを描いた作品に劣ら　ない直接的な意義と効果を持つものであるという事の、一つの示唆たり得れば、作者の労力の大半は酬いられたと言っていい。吾々の同志達は、この作品を一つ　の具体的な参考資料として、その厳正な批判の上に、吾々の新しいジャンルとしての歴史劇の問題を解決し、さらに実践に於いてそれを推し進めて呉れるだろう。[21]

Kubo mirrors Lukács here in pointing out that historical drama is not about the past but about the present.[22] History for Kubo finds its utility in the present in its imbrication with innovative form (発展的形態). While he does not spell out what this means exactly, *Goryokaku* is not the kind of paratheatrical performance that we have seen elsewhere in the Proletarian Theater Movement with the Trunk Theater and the performance theories of MAVO. Besides the fact that this production was in a fixed location in an established theatrical venue, the scenic design of *Goryokaku* resonates with a very different dramaturgical tradition than do those other productions. The design renderings show elements which are generally weighted stage left with a visual break approximately two thirds of the way across the stage. There are strong anchoring elements stage right and, at the bottom of the hanamichi, most of the scenes are designed with a clear open space free of visual distractions which directors can use for character movement and for its strong

Shinsengumi live! 125

blocking position. All of these design elements are commonplace, even standard practice, in kabuki stagecraft. In other words, innovative form for Kubo was not in breaking from the design practices of traditional theater. Instead, the scripts of *Goryokaku* and *Shinsengumi: A Talkie Rensa-geki*, written immediately after, both indicate that Kubo located his vision of innovation in the tension between liveness and mediation. It is a tension that played itself out with old media in *Goryokaku*, and then with new media in *Shinsengumi*. In the case of *Goryokaku*, the play defers authority from the live performance to the written word.

The written word, as opposed to live orality, serves as the foundation of the production. Each act in the script of *Goryokaku* is introduced by quoted material from various historical documents in a written style that is more appropriate for the page than live, oral recitation. In fact, the script does not indicate that this text should be read or communicated to the live audience; it is part of the reading experience of the published script. While the script ends with a statement that the text is "not necessarily based on authorized history" (*seishi* 正史), *Goryokaku* is a performance grounded in documented textual artifacts. Kubo's formal approach in this historical drama sets up a paradigm in which the live performance is explicitly grounded on, and is thus dependent upon, the written word. Because the script itself clocks in at 260 pages, time limitations alone dictate that the play is only able to be approached in its entirety as a mediated text rather than a live experience. It is thus a curious paradox that the live experience is the raison d'etre of the script, yet it represents only a portion of the narrative.

The interaction between liveness and mediation stands out at the structural level of the play and in the way this conceit of textual authority is picked up in the narrative. A key character in the plot, Admiral Enomoto, espouses a strong internationalist stance, and unlike Hijikata Toshizō (former second in command of the Shinsengumi), he welcomes the French military advisors who are supporting the bakufu. He values their guidance, even though the respect is not mutual, and his worldview comes across as enlightened and principled, particularly in contrast to members of the "expel the foreign barbarians faction". At one point he argues with Hijikata that their prisoners should be treated humanely, including being fed and medically cared for just as well as their own casualties—a position which infuriates Hijikata. Yet his enlightened knowledge is dependent upon the possession of a translated book of European law that he received during his time in Holland. In one comic scene, after he has misplaced the book, he is shown looking for it in a panic while the two people who have found his book enjoy watching him sweat and revel in having discovered his secret. Like Kubo's play itself, Enomoto's status and value to the bakufu army is primarily grounded in textual authority that is scripted through this translated text. In concert with the structural elements of the play, this provokes the audience to think about the place of mediated information on stage. In other words, where exactly does the "real" *Goryokaku* reside: in the text, or on the stage?

126 *Shinsengumi live!*

Merging forms in *rensa-geki*: hybrid ontologies

The Zenshinza's two Shinsengumi *rensa-geki* productions were formally innovative, but the genre of the *rensa-geki* itself was well established. The first pairings of film and performance in Japan go back at least to the early twentieth century, although what constitutes the first iteration of the *rensa-geki* genre is up for debate. One of the first productions that combined film and live performance in Japan was called *The Incursion of the Imperial Forces into Russia* (征露の皇軍), put on in 1904 at the Shinmyōza theater in Tokyo.[23] *Rensa-geki* as a genre had its heyday in the 1910s, and it is essentially a prewar genre.[24] Another iteration of the Zenshinza's new variation on *rensa-geki*, the talkie *rensa-geki*, which emerged after the advent of recorded sound films, came out in the same year as Murayama's *Shinsengumi*. It was titled *The Laughing Letter* (*Warai no tegami* 笑いの手紙) and drew a great deal of critical attention.

Contemporary with prewar *rensa-geki*, performers in Europe and the United States also experimented with film and live performance on stage, so it is hardly a form unique to Japan. Yet there are a number of conventions that unified the genre in the minds of Japanese audiences and critics, such that there was a unique Japanese style of performance that could be characterized as "*rensa-geki*–esque". While the term *rensa-geki* has essentially disappeared from the Japanese language, blending live and filmed content in multi-media performance is more common than ever, with increasingly fuzzy borders between the two.[25]

How to think about this hybrid genre in critical terms was and is an open question. Scholarship on *rensa-geki* is generally relegated to film history, and any mention that it receives in theater histories tends to be brief—mostly as an aside. Even within film scholarship, Japanese cinema histories tend to treat the form simply as a bridge between silent and sound films. Yet this kind of production, one that is both live and mediated, sits at a crucial juncture in competing understandings of the ontology of performance. It represents a theoretical fissure that has yet to be bridged more than a century after the first experiments in fusing stage and film.[26] Iterations of the film-stage combination speak to this schism in thinking about liveness in the context of *rensa-geki*. Fundamentally, the question is whether film and live performance are separated at the ontological level. This was a question that theorists wrestled with throughout the 1930s, with a particular flurry of scholarship in 1937 surrounding the two productions of *The Laughing Letter* produced by Senda Koreya and the Zenshinza's *Shinsengumi*. Influential and critically acclaimed, Senda's production falls into a critical tradition that treats its live and filmed sections as different elements that operated in parallel—as essentially unbridgeable elements.

Yoshie Takamatsu argues in 1937 in the journal *Japan Film* (*Nihon eiga* 日本映画) that film has the characteristics of epic poetry (叙事詩) while theater has the characteristics of lyric poetry (抒情詩). According to Takamatsu, this not only accounts for their difference, but also helps account for the popularity of film over theater.[27] Chiba Akira also sees these forms as ontologically separate (本質を異にした二つの芸術).[28] This theory is played out in practice as Murayama remembered early *rensa-geki* productions from his youth. Murayama spoke about older *rensa-geki* as being a fairly simple progression of clearly demarcated scenes. In other words, live and filmed sequences were closed units separated by a musical interlude played by a flute, a practice borrowed from scene changes in kabuki performance, while the screen was raised and lowered. The live and mediated portions of the narrative formally had little to do with one another, even though they both served to advance the same narrative.[29] This approach to film-stage hybridity had parallel approaches in contemporary Europe as well. Iwamoto Kenji describes how European avant-garde performances featuring simultaneous film and theater highlighted the rupture inherent in the juxtaposition of liveness and mediation. He notes the work of Erwin Piscator and other European avant-gardists, who deliberately and overtly created a disparate montage of genres and media influences. Iwamoto says:

> This tight relationship between stage and film—in other words inserting onto the stage film that is specially made for the stage—was attempted in *Sturmflut* (written by Paquet, premiered at the Volksbühne on [tr. note: February 20] 1926). Paquet was born in Frankfurt and was a journalist, and from the standpoint of observing the Russian Revolution, it is said that his work showed a strong familiarity with Meyerhold's stage. *Sturmflut* itself was revolutionary theater on the theme of the Russian Revolution. This play included a large screen in the background in front of which six projectors were lined up that projected floods, the ocean, naval battles, mobs, and the like on what was called a "living wall". Even though the projections were connected to the themes on the stage, and even though they projected scenes of contemporary reality, they can be termed "atmospheric images". Arabesque, collage, montage, etc, **rather than being linked with the narrative, they are linked with the topic; and they do not stop at the closed contents of the fictional story but rather intend to open up the audience's eyes to the reality of the outside world**. [emphasis added]

舞台と映画とのより緊密な連係——つまり舞台のために特に製作された映画を舞台に挿入すること——は、次の「津波」（＝「海嘯」、パクエット作、一九二六　年、民衆劇場）によって試みられた。作者のパクエットはフランクフルト出身の　ジャーナリストで、ちょうどロシア革命を目撃する立場にいて、メイエルホリド　の舞台にもよく通じていたらしい。「津波」そのものがロシア革命をテーマにし　た革命劇である。この芝居の映像的処理としては、背景に巨大なスクリーンを置き、六台の映写機を並べて、洪水・海・海戦・群衆等々を映写して"生きている壁"を作り出すことにあった。映像は舞台とはテーマ的につながっていっても、　また同時代の事実を写し出してはいても、一種の巨大な「環境映像」的処理とも言える。アラベスク、コラージュ、モンタージュ等々、それは物語上の「連鎖」　よりも、主題の「連鎖」であって、虚構の物語内部に閉塞するのではなく、現実の世界へとめを開かせるべく意図された舞台であった。[30]

128 *Shinsengumi live!*

In other words, at a very fundamental level, this *rensa-geki* functions to question the boundaries and role of the live in an increasingly mediated world. By taking an opposite approach to this question to that of *Laughing Letter*, *Shinsengumi: A Talkie Rensa-geki* demonstrated artistic choices which struck at the heart of the ontology of performance itself, with consequences for the Proletarian Theater Movement as a whole. After all, the Proletarian Theater Movement was grounded in ideals of performance that foregrounded the live and politicized the unscripted, improvisational, un-repeatable nature of performance.[31] In this approach the political agenda of their theater was dependent upon a specific understanding of performance.

Thus, while these foreign examples that influenced Japanese experiments highlight the disconcerting rupture between liveness and mediation, others espouse continuity between the elements. In the aforementioned early example of the form, *The Incursion of Imperial Forces into Russia*, the production demonstrates elements that would continue to make the genre popular by expanding the range of storytelling techniques. This early production featured film scenes that would have presented traditional stage directors with enormous challenges—for instance, one scene showed a Russian soldier (played by the head of the Shinmyōza, Sasaki Takejirō) riding a horse around a mountain while being bombarded by Japanese guns. By using film, he was able to realistically portray this scene with only about 200 shaku (about 200 feet) of space and less than five minutes of time. With disparate elements of the scene blended into a single narrative, *rensa-geki* overcomes the limits of liveness by bridging spatial and temporal elements in the performance environment. Unlike Senda's *The Laughing Letter*, Kubo's and Murayama's *Shinsengumi* represents this understanding of the elements of *rensa-geki*.

In his treatise titled *An Introduction to Proletarian Film* (プロレタリア映画入門 1928), Murayama Tomoyoshi actually goes so far as to argue that *rensa-geki* is the ideal proletarian performance genre. He points out that film offers the ability to represent special effects and scenery that would be very difficult to render on stage. In turn, the staged scenes featured sound, color, and most importantly, liveness (現実感). No matter what technical advances the future brings, Murayama says film will never be able to match this latter characteristic of the live stage. Because of this, he sees the form as representing a combination of strengths with no downside. Indeed, even after nearly a century of stunning technical achievements in mediation, it is not hard to see the appeal of what is in effect a super high definition 3D performance experience that never pixilates and doesn't require glasses or VR headgear. Thus, while Murayama acknowledges the rift between liveness and mediation, he sees this rift as bridgeable. The organizing principle in Japanese *rensa-geki* was to apply this potentially jarring multi-media mix in a way that prioritized a seamless narrative experience. As Shibata Katsu explains it:

> *Rensa-geki* was valued as a new production method which merged live and film performance and facilitated scene changes. In other words, when scene changes were called for which could not be represented on stage, such as car chases, airplanes in flight, and battles on the water, these scenes could be

Shinsengumi live! 129

rendered on film and connected to the live performance. Further, the audience was not burdened with long intervals between acts, and the production was characterized by a smooth progression.

連鎖劇というのは、一つの劇の中に映画と実演とを適宜に組み合わせて場面の変 化を求めるつまり舞台で現わし得ない場面、たとえば自動車の追跡とか、飛行機の飛んでいるとか、水中の格闘とかの場面をフイルムに撮影して実演の舞台に接続する新しい演 出法と認める価値がある、また舞台劇に於ける長時間の幕間という不愉快をかんずることもなく劇がスムーズに進行するという特徴がある。[32]

In other words, he sees *rensa-geki* productions as holding narrative and production continuity as guiding principles. In short, it was an attempt to fuse liveness and mediation. Indeed, even Chiba Akira, cited earlier as conceiving of film and stage as fundamentally different, still held that they should be fused in a way that created an organic sense of continuity (有機的に関係し合い且つは同時的に進行しからみ合う). He notes that theater in itself is a hybrid art form, and adding one more element to the mix does not fundamentally change what theater is. He goes on to criticize *The Laughing Letter* for its confusing insertion (挿入) of film on the stage in a way that does not add anything of value to what is already being presented on stage.[33] Unlike the European avant-garde multi-media performance model, which made use of chance and surprise, this competing vision saw the form as one of seamless complementarity. However, in both instances, there is meaning created in the juxtaposition of live action and projected images. The 1937 discussion prefigures the scholarly debate over liveness and mediated narrative with the rise of so-called new media, as argued most prominently on the one side by Peggy Phelan. Phelan famously argues that:

> Performance's only life is in the present. Performance cannot be saved, recorded, documented, or otherwise participate in the circulation of representations *of* representations: once it does so, it becomes something other than performance. To the degree that performance attempts to enter the economy of reproduction it betrays and lessens the promise of its own ontology. Performance's being, like the ontology of subjectivity proposed here, becomes itself through disappearance.[34]

Phelan juxtaposes the non-reproducible ontology of performance with that of the written word. The written word's curious ability to represent someone else's speech as our own, and simultaneously to represent the same referent over and over—to always represent the same thing every time it is read—fixes its speech act status as one of Austin's constative utterances (statements that describe). By contrast, the live and performed utterance is pregnant with the possibility of being, for an elusive moment, a performative utterance (a statement that achieves something by virtue of it being said aloud). Some scholars of Japanese film—particularly of

130 *Shinsengumi live!*

the related performance practice of the *benshi* narrator of early Japanese cinema—saw the act of adding multiple media into the experience as impacting the mode of reception itself by interfering with the diegetic effect of the film.[35] Indeed, liveness in performance with or without mediated elements presents the audience with multiple sources of information that are not funneled through the media of just the screen and speakers. It is here in this performative imbrication of past, present, and future—the performative moment that moves from anticipation to instantaneous realization to non-existence—that the Meiji Restoration Plays of the Shinsengumi found their cultural and political resonance for 1930s Japanese radicals.

The hard ontological distinction between liveness and mediation quickly breaks down in the production of multi-media performance. Iwamoto argues that *rensa-geki* eschewed the jarring rupture represented by the Dadaist experiments in contemporary Europe—ones which foregrounded the seeming incompatibility of live and recorded art. As Shibata and Murayama saw it, *rensa-geki* was a means to complement the features of the two art forms and produce a seamless narrative. This was particularly true during the heyday of *rensa-geki* in the late 1910s.

These seamless productions foreshadow the kinds of performances that Philip Auslander cites which trouble the live/mediated dichotomy.[36] In his argument, mediation defines our experience of live performance, and live performance is often fundamentally dependent upon mediation for its reception. Decades before many of the examples that Auslander cites in the mid to late twentieth century, his analysis describes the Zenshinza's approach to their *Shinsengumi* productions. Situated in a curious position between Murayama's novel and the Zenshinza's movie version of the Shinsengumi story, Kubo's and Murayama's *Shinsengumi: A Talkie Rensa-geki* is an inter-semiotic translation (to use Jackobson's term) that troubles the boundary between stage and film and makes an attempt to confuse the dichotomy of liveness and mediation.

Shinsengumi: a talkie *rensa-geki*

The narratives of Kubo's Shinsengumi stories (*Shinsengumi* and *Goryokaku*) bookend the history of the group, but his *rensa-geki* did not enjoy an actual production. The project had developed to an advanced stage, as attested to by the level of detail in stage directions in the script and the fact that filmed scenes for the *rensa-geki* had already been produced.[37] However, negotiations with the Kadoza Theater that was scheduled to host the production broke down at the last minute, and the Zenshinza was left without a venue. Undeterred, the Zenshinza continued negotiating with the same theater, and in November 1937 it put on a new *rensa-geki* production with the same title as Kubo's, this time written by Murayama Tomoyoshi. In conjunction with this performance, the Zenshinza released a film, also titled *Shinsengumi* and written by Murayama Tomoyoshi, directed by Kimura Sotoji (1903–1988). The narratives of Murayama's two scripts are largely identical, and some of the filmed scenes in the *rensa-geki* came from the film version (the *rensa-geki* script indicates the scenes that utilize footage from the film).[38] The two Shinsengumi *rensa-geki* shows highlight these ontological distinctions in

Shinsengumi live! 131

both their formal and narrative elements. Kubo's production begins with a filmed opening credit introductory sequence that speaks about the production in a strikingly self-referential way. It is essentially the kind of introduction that early film received from a live lecturer, but in this case it is presented from within the film itself. It begins by showing a train passing across the screen with the actors (not in character) looking out the windows at the audience and addressing them directly. Chōjūrō, the Zenshinza actor, looks out the window and says, "Ladies and gentlemen, we are heading to the filming location. What you are about to see is an ambitious project that we have worked long and hard on". Then the next train window passes by, and another actor looks out the window and says, "This is a new form of combining theater and talkies". The next actor's window comes into view, "This is a new project, so we are both nervous and excited about how it will turn out". The cast is then introduced, and the train arrives in Otsu and becomes part of the diegesis. Kondō Isami disembarks and helps an obviously ill Okita Sōji to a teahouse to rest. It then transitions to a scene performed live:

> While this is happening, using a trick, the projection begins to fade, and with the projection still on the screen, the screen is raised and the projection falls on the *sha no maku* behind. From outside the frame, a spotlight shines in from the side, two figures wearing the same clothes [as Kondō and Okita] are illuminated and the image shifts to the living people. At this moment, the spotlight rotates, and the light vibrates to create the effect of a shift.[39]
>
> The frame folds up, opening up the stage, and there is the normal frame around the stage.

> この間に、トリックによって、スクリーンの映像うすれ、映写のまま スクリーン　が巻き上げられ、映像そのうしろの紗の幕にうつる。さ らにフレームの奥にサイ　ドからスポットライトがはいり、同じ服装 の二人が照り出され、映像は生きた人間に移り変る。——その時のス ポットにホウィールをかけて廻転し、ライトを顫　動させて、移り変 りの効果をたすけること。
>
> 　フレーム、折りたたみの仕掛で、四方に開き、舞台のいつもの枠 となって納まる。[40]

The *sha no maku*, called a scrim in English, is a kind of drop that is opaque when lit from the front and transparent when lit from behind. Used as it is in this scene, the filmed sequence appears to magically dissolve into the live scene behind it. So right from the start with the actors breaking the fourth wall of the screen and then morphing into live actors, there is a very powerful visual cue that troubles the line between live and mediated narrative. In a later scene, the transition comes from the other side of the screen, as the actors end a live scene by transitioning onto the screen behind it: as Kondō is summoned to the Aizu daimyo's quarters in Kyoto, the scene change calls for him to stand in front of the screen, with his recorded-self projected on top of his live-self (近藤の姿にダブる) in the transition to a filmed scene.

132 *Shinsengumi live!*

Indeed, just as *Goryokaku* represents an intersemiotic translation of text to stage, the audience can view in real time the almost magical translation process from live to film and back again. Yet this process calls into question important assumptions about where the locus of authority of the translation is—the source or the target? In the case of *Goryokaku*, that authority is ostensibly vested in the text, but the live performance outlived the textual sources that grounded each act, and the script has had much less cultural resonance than the live production. In the case of this *rensa-geki*, it is not even clear which is the source, and in fact the key takeaway is that the barriers between the two are effaced. It is, in other words, one of the curious category of translations without an original. When others in the Proletarian Theater Movement at the time were speaking of fracture in the face of an onslaught of government oppression, these productions scripted by Kubo and Murayama utilized this new genre of the talkie *rensa-geki* to perform unity in a time of chaos through the use of sound as an artistic mechanic that fused disparate artistic elements and political ideals.

Film and live theater share many obvious properties, a fact highlighted by the flow of technical, acting, and production talent back and forth between stage and screen. They are often presented in the same venues, and this genre of the *rensa-geki* (literally "linked theater") actually brought the two forms together into a single performance with alternating filmed and live sequences. Film is not a better, more technologically advanced, and more efficient method of representing stories told by performing actors. If it were, this mixed format would have been moot in the 1930s, and live theater would be as rare now as telegrams or typewriters. Yet what exactly is the relationship between film and theater is not a settled question. The fact that live theater has not been eclipsed by film and is still a vibrant cultural presence more than a century after the advent of cinema highlights what some in performance studies see as the unbridgeable ontological divide between liveness and mediation. Others, however, point to the continued close relationship of film and theater to argue that the differences are actually not so great. In 1930s Japan, the performance world was still in the early stages of understanding and negotiating that complicated relationship when a new twist was thrown into the mix courtesy of the dazzling new technological advance that allowed audiences to actually hear the actors on screen speak in their own recorded voices.

Even though regulations in the early 1920s reduced the number of performances compared with *rensa-geki*'s heyday in the 1910s, the genre was still vibrant enough that a production would not turn heads simply by virtue of combining film and live performance. As innovative as the visual techniques in these particular instances were, it was the notion of incorporating the talkie's recorded sound in the *rensa-geki* that was indeed novel. It was also not an obvious production choice. After all, to the extent that *rensa-geki* existed as a technical solution to the limits of silent film, live theater's spoken voice was rendered redundant through the technology of recorded sound. Yet the re-invention of the *rensa-geki* for the sound era elicited an enthusiastic critical response in the media. In other words, addressing the technical limitations of film was not essentially Murayama's aim in tackling the *rensa-geki* form. Both Murayama's writings about *Shinsengumi*

Shinsengumi live! 133

and the production's wider critical response demonstrated new interest in emerging possibilities available in blending liveness with mediation precisely because of the advent of recorded sound in film. Critics and the promotional materials for *Shinsengumi* cued in on this key feature in the various responses to the work in print media, and the show prompted critical discussion on both sides of the production's generic divide. As an example, the responses to the production appeared in both the theater journal *Engei gahō* and the film journal *Nippon eiga*. The consensus opinion of these critics was that the talkie *rensa-geki* represented something fundamentally new (a "new genre", 新しいジャンル) and conceptually innovative, and by extension something different from a traditional *rensa-geki*.

Both Kubo's and Murayama's *Shinsengumi* talkie *rensa-geki* went out of their way to make liveness and mediation interact in their own productions by playing with and overlapping the scene transitions. This is demonstrated in their visual choices as shown earlier, but aurality also played a key role in the transition between live and filmed scenes. It served to draw the elements together rather than divide them as Murayama saw with the flute interlude in previous practice. Thus, rather than obviating the need for live voice, the advent of recorded sound actually allowed for greater artistic possibilities than had previously existed. *Shinsengumi* as a talkie *rensa-geki* has at least four different options to contrast liveness with mediation by overlapping the two during the scene changes. The transitions could (and did) feature the following juxtapositions: live sound with a live image, recorded sound with a live image, live sound with a projected image, or recorded sound with a projected image. Murayama even went further in complicating the interaction between liveness and mediation by combining the visual live and mediation as well as aural live and mediation at the same time, as will be seen later. The fact that Kubo and Murayama embraced the possibilities of mediation with the advent of recorded sound was key to this experiment in liveness, and in this instance their artistic interests meshed well with the Zenshinza troupe. Although the troupe was made up primarily of trained kabuki actors, they were keenly interested in the possibilities of film—the Zenshinza had recently opened up a rehearsal space that they billed as a "theater and film research center" which they used for both modes of performance. In addition to their active theater repertoire, they also experimented in the production of feature-length films.

In the three examples that follow from Kubo's 1934 and Murayama's 1937 scripts, aurality acts as a key element to probe the questions outlined in the surrounding political and artistic discourse on the talkie *rensa-geki*. Each one of these transitions utilizes sound to create continuity over what might otherwise be irreconcilable logical gaps of time, space, and ontology. This may sound like too great a burden for this new technology of recorded sound in film to bear, yet such a view would underestimate the power of mediated sound. As Michel Chion points out, sound among all the available effects at the disposal of the film maker has the greatest ability to defy the bounds of logic and disbelief.[41] The first transition that highlights this particular use of aurality in these two Zenshinza talkie *rensa-geki* comes early in Kubo's 1934 version. The scene recounts the often-told episode in the history of the Shinsengumi where Serizawa Kamo, in a

134 *Shinsengumi live!*

pique, burns down a building in a village they are traveling through. Yamanami and Harada, in a film sequence, hear an alarm bell sound that alerts them to what Serizawa has done. The recorded sound that begins in the filmed sequence of the fire continues into the live sequence and connects one temporally contiguous but spatially separate episode from screen to stage:

> [On screen] *Yamanami splashes his face with water and cocks his head, listening. "Harada, be quiet." Harada stops singing. The sound of alarm bells.* "It's a fire!" . . . *The screen fills with a flaming pile of timber. Appearing in the flames, Serizawa stands waving his iron fan with Hirayama. Serizawa says in a loud voice,* "If anyone disturbs this fire, I will cut you down". *Out of the public bath comes running with kimono half untied or wearing loincloths: Yamanami, Tōdō, Nagakura, and Harada. They run out through the hall. Fade out.*
>
> [On the stage] *The alarm bell continues. From the dark stage running along the hanamichi comes Kiyokawa Hachirō. As the curtain rises, Ishizaka Shūzō enters onto the hanamichi, and the spot focuses on the two.*[42]

A second scene in Kubo's script utilizes these transitions to fuse a temporal gap. The setting is the day after Kondō has killed Serizawa on the orders of the Aizu Daimyo. On stage, Kondō hears the sound of rain as the scene changes to film, and the following scene is a flashback to when Kondō was working to isolate Serizawa from the power structure of the Shinsengumi. In this scene, the sound of the rain begins just at the end of the live scene, and as Kondō walks out the door and the rain continues across the change into a filmed sequence, the scene that follows is a jump backward in time. In other words, the aural cue creates continuity across the rupture of a temporal jump. It provides both a conceptual and sensory link as the scene jumps into the past.

Sound of heavy rain.

KONDŌ: Raining again? Storming just like last night. Immediately after the Hamaguri Rebellion, I and six others who guarded the coffin were quickly summoned to the Aizu Daimyo's residence and were told directly that recently Serizawa's violence had reached the ears of the shogun. He is damaging the reputation of our group, and I was ordered to kill him. That night I secretly received the order, it was a heavy summer rain.

While he says these lines, the frame closes, and only Kondō's figure remains. Using an effect, this figure changes to a filmed image. Gradually, his figure is layered over by the image of Kondō wearing a kappa [rain gear]. The evening rain pours down incessantly.[43]

Figure 4.3 Kondō Isami played by Kawasaki Chōjūrō in the final scene of Murayama Tomoyoshi's *Shinsengumi*. The projected image of Kondō appears on screen at the same time as the actor performing the same scene live

The end of Murayama's production sees not a bridging of temporal or spatial divides but rather a fusion of disparate genres. Kondō has been captured, and the Shinsengumi has been obliterated. As he is being taken away, there is a projected image of him simultaneous with the live actor appearing on stage (played in both instances by Kawasaki Chōjūrō) (Figure 4.3). The recorded

136 *Shinsengumi live!*

image then speaks in place of the live actor, drowning out his voice with the final laugh:

> KAGA: We will go together to our main camp. Walk!
> *Kondō, who is bound, stands up and begins to walk.*
> KONDŌ: I will not be defeated by these cowardly fools. There will undoubtedly be a chance to escape. I will think of something! Have no fear, have no fear. Hijikata, I still have tricks up my sleeve. Hahahahaha!
> *Kondō on stage, suddenly begins to laugh in concert with Kondō on film. The projected image enlarges and the voice becomes louder, and as the curtain drops, the image is layered over the image on stage (ダブってうつり).*[44]

> 加賀 ：本陣まで御供致さう。お歩みなさい！
> 近藤縛れて立ちあがり歩き出す。
> 近藤 ：こんなうじむしのようなやつのために、おれがひねられてしまふなどといふことがあるものか。まだまだ必ず逃げれる道がある。おれは考へるぞ。大丈夫だ。大丈夫だ。土方まだまだ、何とかやってみせるぞ。アハハハ
> 舞台の近藤、突然、映画と同時にアハハハと笑ふ。映画が最後にニューと大きくなり、声も拡大され、緞帳がさがっても、それにダブってうつり。[45]

As the final curtain falls, live and mediated sound and image co-exist temporally and spatially through the uncanny blending of live and recorded sound and image. The use of sound in these two productions is particularly noteworthy when compared with Murayama's feature-length talkie which was released in tandem with this talkie *rensa-geki*. In the film version, sound is never used in transitions in the way it is in these examples in the *rensa-geki*. This is true even though the *rensa-geki* relied primarily on footage from the movie for its filmed sequences.

However, certain scenes were re-filmed and, more importantly, sound was re-recorded specifically for use in the *rensa-geki*. In the feature film version of *Shinsengumi*, there are no examples of sound bridging scene changes—although there are instances in which incidental sound continues across cuts, these only occur when those cuts are part of the same scene. Thus this use of sound in transitions in the *rensa-geki* is a deliberate choice for this performance mode. In each of these instances, sound functions to create continuities across space and time.

Having the show end with this striking co-presence forces the issue over the place of liveness in the face of this new technology of recorded sound, and it anticipates the discussion in contemporary performance studies over the ontology of liveness and performance. In each of the examples here, recorded and live sound functions to create continuities over disparate space, displaced time, and across the split of a live/mediated actor. These aural bridges create continuity that complements the visual bridges, and through sound and visuals these productions are asking whether liveness and reproduction can be fused.

Shinsengumi live! 137

This confluence of liveness and mediation bridges rifts that are bigger than simple generic distinctions. They reach across ruptures in artistic and political ideologies that come in the context of unprecedented threats to the live from new media and from political pressure. These threats would require fundamental rethinking of political artistic ideologies as a result of this probing of the place of liveness in the performative and political world and the dichotomoy between liveness and mediation.

In prior chapters, this book examined politically motivated paratheatrical performances like the sōshi theater and the Trunk Theater troupe that occurred outside the scopes of traditional theater space and standard theater histories. Those performances relied on a liveness dependent upon a fluid and unrehearsed quality. Those performances sometimes occurred beyond the province of the censorship apparatus, as in the case of the drawing room dramas of Shakespeare's Roman Plays. Likewise, in unpacking the semiology of sōshi theater, Ayako Kano sees the spoken sign as unencumbered by fossilized *kata*, foregrounding the role of chance and improvisation in their performances. That is, it represents a form of embodiment that approaches the spontaneous, unmediated, immediate act.[46] In utilizing these spaces and this style of dramaturgy, these performances directly flouted the authority of state censorship in ways that diverged from the economic interests of many major theater houses.[47] In either case, the ideological success of these performances must be attributed in part to political qualities of the spoken sign over the written sign, and of the ideological value of liveness. The performances in this chapter, by contrast, place liveness and mediation in dialog.

It is not surprising then to see these modes of paratheatrical performance brought forward into the Proletarian Theater. Writings in *Theater News* speak of taking performance out of the theater by creating a space with found objects in freely available spaces. In the same publication, Murayama Tomoyoshi borrows from Western Proletarian Theater models by advocating for "living newspapers" (*ikitashinbun*) which free production from the constraints of a standard script. More radically, writings in *MAVO* advocate for a theater that completely eschews standard theatrical conventions. They argue for guerrilla theater in public places such as shops and street corners that incorporate passersby and onlookers as unwitting "actors" in their productions. The values attached to these kinds of paratheatrical performances resonate with the approach adopted by the sōshi theater a half century earlier.

Yet such extreme experiments were not the only kind of performance in the Proletarian Theater world. Moreover, adherence to the spoken, unrehearsed, immediate sign was not the only possible approach to liveness. The productions examined in this chapter focus on the Shinsengumi and the losing side of the Meiji Restoration and represent a stance towards liveness and performativity that is at odds with more radical theatrical experiments. These productions ultimately embrace performances that circulate in the "representation of representations *of* performance".

Goryokaku and *Shinsengumi* situate their inter-semiotic translations within the lacuna between liveness and mediation in ways that address the crisis of live

138 *Shinsengumi live!*

performance *vis a vis* new and old forms of mediation. The value of live performance was especially challenged by the advent of recorded sound in movies. Indeed, the *benshi* narrators who had been so popular in early Japanese cinema were becoming obsolete because of the existence of mediated sound. Yet these two plays trouble the line between liveness and mediation in ways that resonate with current scholarly debate. In fact, as Auslander explains, both he and Phelan are attempting to reconcile the existence and necessity of live performance in the face of the threat of new media and market forces, and this is exactly the challenge that faced proletarian performance in the early 1930s.

In the face of these challenges, Murayama, Kubo, and the Zenshinza carved out a space that effaced the ontological divide between the mediated and the live. In creating a seamless narrative in which there is fluid exchange between a live and mediated stage space, Kubo and Murayama foreshadow later experiments that work to confuse these categories. In seeking out a space for live performance between the poles of the old media of the written word and the new media of cinema with recorded sound, Kubo was seen as placing live performance within an innovative form (発展的形態) that coexists between and overlaps with these mediated boundaries. These theoretical concerns continue in a very different iteration in the next chapter, where the focus turns to postwar representations of the Meiji stage. Performances, including those of Sudō Sadanori as represented in the film *Sōshi gekijō*, foreground the unscripted quality of sōshi performance as a mechanism of political agency.

Notes

1 The word *rensa-geki* (連鎖劇) is made up of characters that transliterate as "linked theater", and was a hybrid performance genre that mixed film and live performance.
2 Keene writes, "The proletarian movement in the late twenties became the dominant form of Shingeki; it was even averred that Shingeki that was not proletarian should not be called Shingeki at all" (Donald Keene, *Dawn to the West: Japanese Literature of the Modern Era*, 1st Owl Book ed. (New York: H. Holt, 1987). 458).
3 Yoshie Inoue and Sakae Kubo, *Kubo Sakae No Sekai* (Tōkyō: Shakai Hyōronsha, 1989), 151.
4 Ibid., 154.
5 Ibid., 157.
6 Other members included author Iketani Saburō, the artist Yoshida Kenkichi, Okada Sōzo, Ichikawa Sadanji's student Ichikawa Danjirō, Murase Sachiko (1905–1993), later known for her final role as the grandmother in Kurosawa's 1991 film *Rhapsody in August*), Itō Sen'ichi, Abe Tomoji (1903–1973), Funahashi Sei'ichi (1904–1976), Furusawa Yasujirō (1902–1983), and Uchiyama Inokichi. Sakamoto Tokumatsu, *Zenshinza* (Tōkyō: Ōdosha, 1953), 21–22.
7 With both working in German as a second language and both being fans of Kaiser, Murayama and Kubo competed with each other over the privilege of translating scripts for production by the troupe. In one case, much to the annoyance of Kubo, Murayama was allowed to translate *Juana*. As a consolation prize, Kubo was awarded the following translation, *Die juedische Witwe* (ユーヂット).
8 Ibid., 22.
9 The play was censored, and production was canceled the day before it was scheduled to open.

Shinsengumi live! 139

10 Tokumatsu, *Zenshinza*, 34.

11 Inoue, *Kubo Sakae no sekai*, 84.

12 Ibid., 120.

13 Gennifer S. Weisenfeld, *Mavo: Japanese Artists and the Avant-Garde, 1905–1931* (Berkeley: University of California Press, 2002), 31–32.

14 Kubo Sakae debuted at Tsukiji Little Theater in 1926 (the same year Sasaki Takamaru started the Trunk Theater) with his translation of "Die Hose" (ホオゼ) by Carl Sternheim [tr. note: recently adapted into English by Steve Martin with the title "The Underpants"]. This connection to German expressionism defined his early years with the theater. In the ten years after he was graduated from Tokyo University in 1925, he produced about 30 translated scripts, including Georg Kaiser's *The Burghers of Calais* and *Nebenneinander* (平行) while also producing original scripts such as *The Blood Oath at Goryokaku* (五稜郭血書). See Inoue, *Kubo Sakae no sekai*, 174.

15 For more about the fuzzy line between historical fact and historical fiction of the Shinsengumi, see: Miyachi Masato 宮地正人, *Rekishi no naka no Shinsengumi* 歴史のなかの新選組 (Tōkyō: Iwanami Shoten, 2004).

16 Kubo Sakae, *Kubo Sakae zenshu, vol 12*, (Tokyo: San'ichi Shobo, 1963), 370.

17 Kubo Sakae, *Toki rensa-geki shinsengumi* in *Kubo Sakae Zenshū* (Tōkyō: San'ichi Shobō, 1961), 345–346.

18 Murayama Tomoyoshi, "Kōshite shinario wo kaita," *Nihon eiga* (December 1937), 558–565.

19 Gekidan Mingei. *Kubo Sakae Kenkyū*, Vol. 11 (Tokyo: Hakkōjo, 1959), 3.

20 This was the same stance issued in the 1927 theses as recounted in Chapter 2, but in this case the ramifications of this reiteration were less devastating to the leftist movement than the first announcement six years earlier.

21 Kubo Sakae [Azuma Kenkichi], *Goryōkaku kessho: Gomaku* (Tōkyō: Nihon Puroretaria Engeki Dōmei Shuppanbu, 1933), 220.

22 György Lukács, *The Historical Novel* (Lincoln: University of Nebraska Press, 1983).

23 Incidentally, this was a prominent theater in the Shinpa world. While it is perhaps not surprising that cinema would rely upon the infrastructure of the theater, it is important to remember the degree to which these art forms were intertwined at every level of the creative and consuming process. If we can in fact say that these forms occupied separate conceptual and ontological spaces, this is only true in very specific ways.

24 Yet for the most part this is simply a matter of nomenclature. While the word *rensa-geki* has disappeared from common Japanese use, liveness and mediation remains tightly imbricated. In the postwar period, there were even pink films (soft-core pornographic films) that were performed and billed as "*rensa-geki*".

25 In contemporary times, the Japanese troupe Dumb Type is a prominent example of experimenting with new media on stage. In live shows by Kyary Pamyu Pamyu, recorded video content is often an integral part of the performance. In her shows, the video often seemingly leads the dance moves of the live performers. Other examples such as *The Rocky Horror Picture Show* still show regularly around the world. In other words, this mix is widespread in both high and low art.

26 In fact, it is often unclear exactly what is live and what is not. In the presumably "live" event at the Oscar ceremony in 2015, for example, the orchestra that scored the event played in a remote location yet performed in coordinated time with the main event. It is entirely unclear in cases such as this where liveness ends and mediation begins.

27 Takamatsu Yoshie, "Eiga to engeki," *Nihon Eiga* (September 1937), 18.

28 Chiba Akira 千葉昭, "Engeki to eiga no ketsugo" 演劇と映画の結合, *Nippon eiga* 日本映画 (October 1937), 99.

29 However, this description overlooks *rensa-geki* practices such as *kageserifu*, in which actors spoke lines of dialog from behind the screen (and, of course, *benshi* performance in which live performance existed in parallel, or overlap, with film). These alternate methods for contrasting liveness and mediation, which Murayama does not discuss

140 *Shinsengumi live!*

as characteristic of *rensa-geki*, actually foreshadow Murayama's own *Shinsengumi* experiment. However, this was not how Murayama himself remembered productions he saw as representative of the specific form of *rensa-geki*, and it was this construct that he was working against in bringing the talkie *rensa-geki* to the stage.

30 Iwamoto Kenji, *Sairento kara toki he: Nihon eiga keiseiki no hito to bunka* (Tokyo: Shinwasha, 2007), 70.

31 Murayama was typical of many in the Proletarian Theater Movement in seeing the expensive infrastructure of traditional theater as a barrier to proletarian performance. Beginning in the 1920s, Murayama was affiliated with the Trunk Theater, a troupe which, as opposed to making audience members travel to a theater, brought their performances to striking workers and other local venues to provide entertainment and encouragement. His avant-garde group MAVO advocated for what they termed the "anti-theaters movement" which along with a radical rethinking of the performer-audience relationship, sought to put performances near mines and places easily accessible to workers. This dramaturgical philosophy reappeared frequently in Murayama's critical and creative work. In the December 1931 issue of *Engeki shinbun* (*Theater News*), Murayama advocated for creating theater spaces in non-traditional venues with easily accessible materials. Likewise, he advocated for the practice popularized in the West of creating "living newspaper" performances, so even lack of scripts would not act as a barrier to workers staging Proletarian Theater.

32 Shibata Katsu, *Jitsuen to eiga rensageki no kiroku* (1982), 1.

33 Chiba Akira 千葉昭, "Engeki to eiga no ketsugo" 演劇と映画の結合, 102.

34 Peggy Phelan, *Unmarked: The Politics of Performance* (London: Routledge, 1992), 146.

35 Aaron Gerow notes that Burch, in *To the Distant Observer*, "argues that a film shown with a benshi differs from a Hollywood text that functions as a transparent window into a univocal world: the benshi splits the fictional source of enunciation by assuming the role of narration and thereby purges the text of narrative itself . . . spectators are unable to enter the world of the diegesis because they remain aware of the film as something to be read, as only a text. Burch contends that Japanese prewar filmgoers did not succumb to the fictional effect of the film but instead treaded spectatorship as the simultaneous viewing of both the spectacle of the text and the reading of the film". Aaron Gerow, *Visions of Japanese Modernity: Articulations of Cinema, Nation, and Spectatorship, 1895–1925* (Berkeley: University of California Press, 2014), 134.

36 Philip Auslander, *Liveness: Performance in a Mediatized Culture* (London: Routledge, 1999).

37 Iwamoto Kenji, *Sairento kara tōkī e: Nihon eiga keiseiki no hito to bunka*, (Tokyo: Shinwasha, 2007), 362.

38 Just as the choice of this format was a complicated mix of political and artistic ideals, so too the choice of content might not at first glance seem like an obvious one for everyone involved. Shinsengumi was perhaps a natural choice for the politically ambivalent Zenshinza. An outgrowth of the troupe's dual interest in historical dramas and film, the release of *Shinsengumi* followed the Zenshinza's first period film *Humanity and Paper Balloons* (人情紙風船, 1937). Both are films that starred Kawasaki Chōjūrō, and were produced with the help of Toho and PTO film companies, respectively. See Kawasaki Chōjūrō, "*Shinsengumi* zakkō," *Nippon eiga* (December 1937), 528.

39 This meta-acknowledgment of a transition between mediation and liveness mirrors a common technique in contemporary Hollywood film. When moving through a video screen so as to join the "live scene shown on a monitor, directors often insert a ripple effect when moving through the pane of the screen. This piece of cinematic vocabulary has become so widely utilized that it appears in films as thematically and generically different as the *Matrix* movies and *The Cabin in the Woods*. It highlights the awareness that film makers today still have with materiality of their medium that was shared even in this 1937 production.

Shinsengumi live! 141

40 Sakae, *Toki rensa-geki shinsengumi*, 282.
41 Michel Chion, *Film: a Sound Art* (New York: Columbia University Press, 2003), 239.
42 Sakae 久保栄, *Toki rensa-geki shinsengumi* トーキー連鎖新選組, 341.
43 Ibid., 350.
44 Murayama Tomoyoshi 村山知義, "Shinsengumi" 新選組, in *Gendai gikyoku dai 6 kan* 現代戯曲第 6 巻 (Tokyo: Kawade shobo, 1940), 470.
45 Murayama Tomoyoshi. *Shinsengumi* (Tōkyō: Kawadeshobō, 1937), 470.
46 This does not mean, however, that the spoken word and the unrehearsed gesture are devoid of materiality. Kano's view is rooted in a tension between what Terry Eagleton attributes to Walter Benjamin's description of the *Trauerspiel*: an ideological tension between performativity, orality, and the materiality of the sign. Whereas Derrida cannot overlook the materiality of the sign, and Saussure makes little distinction between the spoken and written sign, Eagleton notes that Derrida speaks of an "absolute proximity of voice and being, of voice and the meaning of being, of voice and the ideality of its ideological labour there". Unlike Kano, these views see the oral sign, by virtue of the physicality required for its production, as inhabiting and becoming materially part of both the performers and the audience.
47 Although there were exceptions to this, such as when Kawakami Otojirō's *Oppekepe* achieved enough popular success to make it financially viable for larger theater houses.

5 The last sōshi

In a scene late in the 1947 film *Sōshi Theater* (壮士劇場 *Sōshi gekijō*), Sudō Sadanori, the leader of his eponymous theater troupe, bemoans the state of the nation in the wake of the promulgation of his long-sought-for Meiji Constitution. A member of his troupe says after the creation of the constitution, "It sure looks like people are coming around to our beliefs, doesn't it?" (吾々の理想も民衆の支持をうけるやうになりましたな) To which Sudō replies, "No, we're not there yet. Even though the people are more politically aware, the current election laws are laughable . . . the people still aren't free. We have to re-write the constitution" (未だ駄目だ。民衆が政治に興味を持つやうになっても、現在のやうな選挙法ぢや話にならんぢやないか . . . これでは、未だ国民の自由はありつこないよ。君、吾々は身を持って、この憲法の書替をやらなければならぬのだ).[1] The claim here, one that is tied to the key message of the whole film, is bold on several fronts: it locates the motivating source of the Meiji Constitution—indeed, the origins of Japanese liberty and the national project itself—in the efforts of the socially marginalized ragtag group of sōshi; in doing so, it works to revive the respectability of the term *sōshi*; and it suggests a role for the sōshi theater of the early Meiji Period as a historical model, both performatively and politically, in the national reckoning following 1945 when the film was released.

As described in preceding chapters, Kawakami Otojirō and Sudō Sadanori achieved fame during the Meiji Period as sōshi performers. Yet history has not been kind to their legacy. In contemporary Japan, they have been almost completely written out of the popular narrative of the Restoration Period. Sudō has been forgotten entirely in popular history and the contemporary stage, and with very few exceptions, since the 1970s any attention that Kawakami Otojirō receives tends to be for his later non-political theater—his tours of the United States and Europe, and in his connection with his famous wife, Sadayakko.[2] Indeed there are exceptions to this collective amnesia. There is, for instance, some degree of local pride in Kawakami's hometown of Hakata for his fame achieved as a sōshi. Nonetheless, examples of remembrance of the sōshi in recent decades are vanishingly rare. This elision from popular memory is in stark contrast to the public fascination with even less reputable figures from the early Meiji Period such as the Shinsengumi (see Chapter 4 for prewar interest in performance of the Shinsengumi), and it speaks to a deep ambiguity towards the means and methods of sōshi performance in the creation of the new Japanese nation.

The last sōshi 143

Yet this public forgetting perhaps represents an improvement over prewar conceptions of the sōshi. Despite the keen interest in the Rights Movement by members of the Proletarian Theater Movement, neither Kawakami nor Sudō appear in any of their Restoration Plays. In fact, as recounted in Chapters 2 and 3, for a group that 1920s and '30s leftists could conceivably have seen as fellow resistance fighters, the term *sōshi* itself had come to have surprisingly negative connotations. In Sasaki Takamaru's *Itagaki Taisuke*, it is used exclusively to describe traitorous characters, and in Sasaki's *Secret Account from Tsukuba* it is the foes of the Rights Movement forces in the battle on Mount Kaba who are called sōshi. In other words, the word had become something of an epithet among these politically active performers, and there was little nostalgia for them in society at large. Yet sandwiched between prewar antipathy and recent apathy, there was a moment during the rebuilding after 1945 when the sōshi represented a vision of a past which allowed for the kind of narrative continuity which helps to rationalize the present that national histories require.[3] With fidelity to historical fact eschewed in favor of that narrative, the performance of the sōshi became the subject of a variety of narratives.

This chapter examines the way that the live, unscripted nature of Meiji Period sōshi theater is re-examined on stage in the postwar years. These performances question the staid, codified dramaturgy of postwar shingeki during the two decades after the war, and they look to the promise of politically resistant theater which breaks the norms of fourth wall–embracing passive viewing. The works in this chapter span a decade and a half of performance from Inagaki Hiroshi's film *Sōshi Theater* in 1947, to Misho Kingō's unproduced screenplay *Oppekepe: Kawakami Otojirō the Sōshi Actor* (オッペケペ：壮士役者川上音二郎) in 1957 to Fukuda Yoshiyuki's play *Oppekepe* in 1963 (with many subsequent revivals).[4,5]

Despite the differences in their backgrounds and ideologies, Inagaki, Mishō, and Fukuda all presented resonating views of the dramaturgy of the sōshi that were grounded in their common postwar political and performative context. These performances utilize the sōshi theater to recall a politically potent performative past which offers a model for a counterfactual history and alternative presents and futures. Surprising as it may be from a contemporary viewpoint, when the very existence of the sōshi has largely dropped from popular memory, Inagaki's, Mishō's and Fukuda's representation of Sudō's and Kawakami's troupes are part of a pattern of postwar performances about the sōshi which attempted to resituate the agency of performativity and to postulate an alternative historical trajectory that begins with the Restoration and grapples with dual conceptualizations of sōshi culture in the context of post-1945.

Performing sōshi history

The sōshi as initially conceived in early Meiji was on the one hand a gendered metonym for Japan's hoped-for future strength and status. Alternatively, they also were viewed as uneducated degenerates who were not worthy of the national future that they were pivotal in ushering in. In other words, as described in earlier chapters, the

144 *The last sōshi*

term houses a conflicting set of referents describing a person who both embodied and failed to live up to the promise of the new nation. Even more than youth generally do in all times and places, the coinciding of the emergence of the term *sōshi* with the run-up and promulgation of the new constitution meant that the sōshi represented simultaneously the promise and threats of an entirely new subjectivity.

In the theoretical ideal of sōshi put forth by Rights Movement thinkers, the sōshi stands as an idealistic Meiji youth, active in the politics of the Freedom and People's Rights Movement that would shape Japan into a modern nation on a Western model. As such, the label was used for students of thought leaders in the Rights Movement such as Nakae Chōmin and Itagaki Taisuke. Likewise, as described in preceding chapters, the term was used for young men (and some women) who brought new political philosophies to a broad swath of the populace through political speechifying, popular political *enka* songs, and their political theater known as *sōshi shibai* that would later be recognized as the origin of modern Japanese theater.

One formative early account of this demographic category ran in a series of articles titled *On Sōshi* (壮士論) from January 22 to February 23, 1889 (Meiji 22) in the newspaper *Daybreak News* (東雲新聞).[6] Featuring prominently in the paper, with each entry appearing in the first column at the top of the broadsheet, the series represented a message important to the editors of the paper and, by extension as the paper's owner, Rights Movement leader Nakae Chōmin himself. Seeking to define the Japanese sōshi and situate them within a national and global historical context, *On Sōshi* makes the case for the sōshi as a crucial component of national development. Establishing the model of the sōshi followed in Inagaki's *Sōshi Theater*, the column argues for a role for the sōshi as an essential component in navigating the transition through the Meiji Restoration to a modern nation with a constitution. This process ideally results in a state of enlightenment (*kaigo*) for the entire nation. *On Sōshi* sees the bravery and vitality of the young sōshi as the mechanism that allows for the possibility of a nation of the Orient to achieve this kaigo. Despite having no historical experience or expectations of incorporating liberal democratic rights into their social contract—rights which citizens of Western nations had come to expect as a starting point in philosophy of government—Japan's future looked bright to this unnamed newspaper columnist because the sōshi would help to establish a modern nation and a new political subjectivity.

Thus, according to *On Sōshi*, it is not the great men at the top of government who are leading the nation into the grand promise of modernity, but rather it is the unsung brave youth of the new nation who operate on the front lines of securing and maintaining liberal democratic rights for society. The *Daybreak News* series goes even further to argue that the sōshi are not a uniquely Japanese phenomenon. Sōshi have existed and served as a motivating force for democracies everywhere, appearing in all Western societies that have struggled to maintain liberty for its citizens. The sōshi existed in France, and they even appeared as far back as ancient Rome.[7] In this view, then, the sōshi are essential components of a liberal (and presumably modern, despite their existence in antiquity) democratic state. This heroic image of the sōshi offers a second, competing model with which to categorize these youth, and this Jekyll/Hyde nature plays out in the postwar performances in this chapter.

Postwar representations of the sōshi borrow from both the *On Sōshi* version of the sōshi and the more critical representation. Fukuda Yoshiyuki's (福田善之 1931–) *Oppekepe* is less sanguine about the character of the sōshi than Inagaki is in *Sōshi Theater*, but he still saw in their performances a model of political activism that was lost in contemporary postwar shingeki theater. The play was first performed by the Shinjinkai at the Haiyūza Theater in 1963 (with multiple restagings in subsequent years) (Figure 5.1). In this bastion of the mainstream, shingeki theater, Fukuda attempted to break the confines of postwar shingeki theatrical practice in order to rethink the role of the past through the performative lens of the present—and he hoped to change theater in the process. A pupil of Kinoshita Junji (1914–2006), Fukuda inherited a dramaturgical tradition of socialist realism. Despite his training within mainstream shingeki modes of modernist performance, Fukuda was drawn to the radical politics and disruptive performance practices of the contemporary underground theater and broke with the prewar shingeki theater of his mentor.[8]

Sōshi Theater, by contrast, came at its subject matter from a very different context. Released in 1947, it was directed by Inagaki Hiroshi (稲垣浩, 1905–1980), whose prolific body of work includes the highly acclaimed prewar *Muhōmatsu*

Figure 5.1 Scene from Fukuda Yoshiyuki's *Oppekepe* (1963); Shiroyama performs for his audience in this play-within-a-play that is itself within a play

Source: Reproduced with permission from the Tsubouchi Memorial Museum.

146 *The last sōshi*

no isshō (無法松の一生, 1943) and the *Samurai* trilogy (1954–56) based on the novel *Musashi* by Yoshikawa Eiji and which won an Academy Award. Coming just a few years after a string of pre-1945 critically and popularly successful films, including winning picture of the year under the Imperial censorship regime for very different historical pictures and Restoration Period films, *Sōshi Theater* represents a navigation of a new ideological landscape for Inagaki. Under the eye of the Allied Occupation, Inagaki filtered very similar historical subject matter through a very different lens. Facing a newly imposed ideology, a new conception of liberty prominently on display in the new (translated) constitution and enforced in the theater world through a stringent censorship system, Inagaki looked to a historical moment when the notion of liberty had been fresh and new. Rather than representing a shift in his own ideology, however, Inagaki saw his script primarily as subject matter which would meet the approval of the Occupation's censorship regime.[9]

Inagaki's treatment of the Restoration in *Sōshi Theater* stands in stark relief to his work immediately before the end of the war. Only three years earlier, while working with Daiei in 1944, Inagaki produced a film set during the run-up to the Meiji Restoration titled *Signal Fires over Shanghai* (狼煙は上海に上がる *Noroshi wa Shanhai ni agaru*). Starring the popular actor Bando Tsumasaburō (with whom Inagaki had recently produced *Muhōmatsu no issho*), the film tells the story of the historical voyage of Japanese diplomats to China just after the Harris treaty was signed and just before 1868.[10] Just as his postwar film would do for the Occupation, *Fires over Shanghai* served as political propaganda that (as evidenced by its large budget and production permissions) obviously pleased the Imperial censors. In short, these two films are separated by only a short period of time but are divided by the war to create very different takes on similar subject matter. In *Signal Fires*, set just before 1868 and produced just before 1945, Inagaki tells a story of the Restoration as harboring the promise of pan-Asian unity in the face of European infidels. He then manages to negotiate an entirely different official ideological agenda by following this with *Sōshi Theater*, set after 1868 and produced just after 1945, which paints the Restoration as a failed opportunity for a free and democratic society.

Fitting the ideals of the new censorship regime, *Sōshi Theater* draws a picture of the sōshi theater congruous with that argued for in the *Daybreak News*. Inagaki's portrayal sees Sudō's troupe as representing the democratic promise of the Meiji Restoration—a potentiality that is portrayed in the film with decidedly unsubtle storytelling techniques. In one example, when Sudō's troupe is forced to disband because of financial pressures, they hold a closing party in which Sudō breaks a mirror and gives a piece to each of the members of the troupe as a memento. Later in the film, Sudō has been attacked in the street by ruffians and drops his piece of the mirror that he has always carried with him. Fortunately for Sudō, a blind musician being led down the street is (inexplicably) able to see the reflection of the sun in the mirror and is drawn to pick it up and return it to Sudō (Figure 5.2). The image of a blind man who sees the light of the sun in this metonymic remnant of the sōshi theater is so plainly spelled out that it leaves little work on the part of the audience to unpack. Artistic subtlety taking a back seat under Occupation censorship protocols is perhaps not surprising. However, it is remarkable the degree to

Figure 5.2 A blind shakuhachi player sees Sudō's lost mirror in Inagaki Hiroshi's *Sōshi gekijō*

148   *The last sōshi*

which this representation of sōshi theater places the political and national promise of the early Meiji Period in the hands of those at the lowest rung of society rather than the elite figures such as Itō Hirobumi, Fukuzawa Yūkichi, or Itagaki Taisuke, who are more commonly credited as the founding fathers of the modern Japanese nation.

As Frederic Jameson observes, historical fiction is never actually about the past. It is rather a statement about the present, and when it ceases to be a comment on the present it loses cultural relevance. Inagaki's vision of the sōshi as voices in the wilderness who were ignored by mainstream society and the elites writes a historiography of the prewar historical trajectory that offers a way to think through Inagaki's present. Likewise, Fukuda's *Oppekepe*, initially staged 16 years after *Sōshi Theater* in 1963 and restaged multiple times in succeeding years, offers a different view of the sōshi but with a similar eye towards explaining the truths of the present through the performative prewar history of sōshi theater. In making a distinction that resonates with Hayden White's "real" versus "true" history, reviewers saw in the play a historiography with significant deviation from actual fact but a powerfully explicit comment upon the contemporary postwar moment. One *Yomiuri News* review, for example, commented that "the playwright has skillfully deviated from history and snuck in a contemporary voice".[11] This "contemporary voice" spoke, among other things, to an acknowledgment of a more problematic history of the sōshi theater than is acknowledged in Inagaki's portrayal. Yet this complicated history offers a more useful narrative through which to understand the troubled history of liberal democracy in Japan.

This idealization of the sōshi and their theater in the *Daybreak News* that *Sōshi Theater* builds upon is one that obfuscates the fact that in actual practice the term was used to describe a great many youth who were not motivated by artistic concerns and were only nominally or not at all politically inclined. Many engaged in gambling, crime, and marginally sanctioned violence.[12] Recent scholarship adds complexity to Inagaki's and *Daybreak*'s image of sōshi as a heroic and principled youth by examining an alternative (and commonly held) portrayal as little more than just rowdy thugs covered by a thin veneer of political principles, or simply as jingoistic supporters of empire.[13] The sōshi of actual history existed on the margins of society. While they often called themselves "students" (*shosei*), they were rarely well educated. Jason Karlin has demonstrated the way violent masculinity was central to the self-conception of the sōshi, an identity that expressed itself in both behavior and fashion. Eiko Maruko Siniawer shows how this violence extended across the often imperceptible line between the political and criminal worlds and how in both of these iterations they became one of the "violence specialists" who went on to make up the organized political and criminal actors of the modern Japanese nation. The violence that permeates sōshi culture was not surprisingly a key component of their theater, as attested to in scholarship by Egashira Kō, in reflections by sōshi actors themselves, and in visual representations of sōshi theater (see Chapter 3 for a selection of representative descriptions). Violence was an integral component of the performative event for sōshi, which is underscored

The last sōshi 149

by the way that Kawakami spoke about casting actors not for their performative skill but for their physical stature, giving them the ability to withstand the abuse of the crowd. Visual representations of sōshi performances invariably show an audience that is at best just rowdy and at worst engaged in full-scale violence—the degree to which this was anticipated and an expected part of the performance is highlighted by one widely reproduced image in *Liberty Illustrated News* (絵入自由新聞) which shows an audience member during a production drawing a dagger that had been brought into the theater in advance. More significantly, the political ideals that they propagated were problematic at best from the standpoint of mid-Showa middlebrow theater.

Mishō Kingo's (御荘金吾 1908–1985) *Oppekepe: Sōshi Actor Kawakami Otojirō* is perhaps a less influential example of postwar representations of the sōshi than either Fukuda's or Inagaki's.[14] Published in 1957, before Fukuda's production and after the release of *Sōshi Theater*, it is a scenario that never saw production. Yet it did receive a ringing endorsement from Murayama Tomoyoshi, who had emerged from the war with even more clout in the theater world than he had in the 1930s. More important than this script's level of impact for my purposes here is the fact that its image of the sōshi theater resonates with that of both Fukuda's *Oppekepe* and Inagaki's *Sōshi Theater*. In all three narratives, the sōshi theater is represented as a violent site of resistance to the Meiji authorities. At the beginning of Mishō's script, Kawakami takes the stage during his brief time as a rakugo storyteller and immediately goads the police into closing the show, inciting the audience to violence against the authorities, and ultimately provoking said police to arrest him.

Yet, despite these commonalities among all three representations, Mishō's play also evinces a skepticism of the political ideology of the sōshi that resonates with Fukuda's telling and contrasts with Inagaki's vision of the sōshi as a heroic ideal of the Restoration which the nation failed to capitalize on. Act I of Fukuda's play begins in the early years of the movement, a time when Kawakami is shown as idealistic and young, not unlike Inagaki's Sudō in *Sōshi Theater*.[15] In Act II, set several years later at the beginning of the nationalistic mania that surrounded the run-up to the first Sino-Japanese War, the play charts the troupe's abandonment of the ideals of the Freedom and People's Rights Movement and the troupe's devolvement into a jingoistic embrace of imperialism and war-mongering. The central thematic concern is in asking how the ideals of the Freedom and People's Rights Movement could devolve from a focus on liberal democracy to ethnocentric nationalism.

Despite this contrast in representation of the sōshi, Inagaki, Mishō, and Fukuda all ground their production in the performative nature of sōshi theater, with an emphasis upon a specific kind of audience-performer relationship. All are backstage dramas, and Fukuda's production amplifies this trope by creating a multilayered framing device: the play is about a play about a theater troupe that puts on plays in the course of the show. This framing device serves as yet one more mechanism to focus the production on the performativity of sōshi theater and specifically on the role of audience in their performances.

150   *The last sōshi*

Performing in the third space

This interest in the relationship of the audience to the performers is played out in the way that the sōshi theater's conceptualization of the performance space contrasted sharply from the expectations of Inagaki's, Mishō's, and Fukuda's audience. In short, these postwar performances wrestle with the relationship between theatricality and the everyday and the potentiality for political agency in performance in ways Peter Brook and Victor Turner, working half a world away but in a contemporary context, can help explain. The sōshi saw the stage as unbounded by a restrictive fourth wall, and audiences were unencumbered by norms proscribing rambunctious, disrespectful, and other interactive behavior in the theater space. By contrast, in postwar period theater, the house/stage divide is architecturally telegraphed and enforced with the adopted Western structure of the proscenium and other physical features and cultural practices. These practices reformulated means of audience participation from theater that is actively participated in to something which is silently observed. Premodern modes of audience-stage interaction (which sōshi theater clearly drew upon) were also largely done away with by the postwar years, even in traditional performance.[16] Victor Turner saw the performative event as a cultural practice that was removed from the everyday and which allowed for transgressive participation by all involved. These features of performance are acknowledged in the normative practices of theater as typically performed after the advent of modernity. Separated by the fourth wall, it is the actors alone who are permitted the privilege of transgressing societal norms, and the modern performance space tends to overtly encompass only those within the diegetic frame of the narrative. While these norms were firmly ensconced in mid-Showa mainstream Japanese theater practice, the notion of the apron of the stage as an impermeable, if invisible, fourth wall was unknown in popular Japanese theater.[17] In the lack of normative confines of the performance space and the fourth wall, in other words by bringing real-world consequences into the entire theatrical space, sōshi performance eschews the separation of performance from the audience. As a result, the kind of stage space represented on the sōshi stage expands the "third space" into one which is more in line with the kind of expansive experience Turner sees as the potentiality of the performative event. In other words, the audience joins rather than views a space that exists "beyond the bounds of reality" which, in other examples of the third space (including ritual) encompass all participants but is (often physically) separated from the normal social world.[18] The function of this third space, according to Turner, is to serve as a mode of redress of "social dramas", to think through the past in the present, and to be a space in which "performances are represented which probe a community's weaknesses, call its leaders to account, desacralize its most cherished values and beliefs, portray its characteristic conflicts and suggest remedies for them, and generally take stock of its current situation in the known 'world'".[19] Turner sees this challenge to the status quo as a politically efficacious and socially therapeutic practice which serves a real and valuable function in society. Yet Turner still sees theater locked in the "cultural subjunctive", and

The last sōshi 151

views it as an inherently conservative cultural force. It is difficult to construct, under this model, a theater of resistance.

It is in this treatment of the stage as a sequestered third space where Mishō Kingo's *Oppekepe* draws the strongest distinction with both Inagaki's and Fukuda's representation of sōshi performance. Early in the narrative, after Kawakami has been released from jail over a confrontation on stage with the police, Kawakami resolves to give up the kind of confrontational, resistant performance that defines sōshi theater in both Inagaki's and Fukuda's narrative. Yet unlike in Fukuda's narrative, in which Kawakami simply abandons his political principles for popular jingoistic theater, Kawakami attempts to transform his theater into an artistically sophisticated theater on a modern Western model. In Mishō's telling, Kawakami shifts his dramaturgy in order to pursue a higher artistic (rather than political) calling. In explanation of his giving up the resistant norms of sōshi theater, he says, "You can't win the hearts of the people from a jail cell". The climax of the script highlights this clash of political with artistic ideals. As Kawakami's troupe is on the cusp of performing at the large Nakamura Theater in Tokyo, his production is ambushed by local sōshi in the audience. Unlike stories from sōshi contemporaries of Kawakami, Mishō's Kawakami feels consternation at the breakdown of theatrical and legal norms in his production. This breakdown represents a setback in this narrative for Kawakami's artistic aims.

In other words, the disconnect between Meiji and Showa methods of constructing the third space drives the plot of each of the performances at play in this chapter. All of these narratives take as a central focus the subject of the performance in which the Meiji stage space is inclusive of the audience and the police censors and everyone else within the theater building. This expanded stage space allows for the sōshi theater a role in political meaning making, a fact which becomes the object of inquiry with re-performance as a source of reconciling with the past through embodied memory. Further, this representation of the stage allows for the historical possibility that sōshi theater was central in establishing a new national subject in the early Meiji Period. Expansive use of a liminal stage space drove the popularity and political efficacy of the sōshi theater. Yet these performed narratives in *Sōshi Theater* of an artistically and politically sophisticated drama wrestled with the historical fact that the term *sōshi* was not only applied to sincere students of liberal democratic ideals with a sophisticated dramaturgical agenda. It was also applied (and self-applied) to thugs, grifters, and gamblers, and to those who saw theater as a way to make easy money and gain popularity. Because twentieth-century Japanese theater history scholars made value judgments based on what the sōshi lacked, that is, formalized training and artistic rigor, the sōshi have been largely elided from modern Japanese theater history.[20] And because their politics was tinged by thuggery, crime, and the status of the participants as relegated to the outskirts of society, they have largely been left out of social and political histories.

This messy, complicated sōshi lifestyle and dramaturgy resonates with what Peter Brook calls "Rough Theater", a theater with limited resources and a level of interaction with the audience that distinguishes it from "Holy Theater".[21] Brook describes Holy Theater as one with resources, one which fastidiously preserves

152 *The last sōshi*

the unities, and one which maintains a formal audience-performance relationship. "Rough Theater", on the other hand, makes due with insufficient resources and, when necessary, gives a "holler at the trouble makers" in the audience.[22] As Brook describes it, Rough Theater is lively and improvisational in ways that define the key characteristics of the sōshi theater, and Holy Theater speaks to postwar modern theater-viewing practices. Yet, while Brook contrasts the Holy Theater and the Rough Theater, he does not set them in a hierarchical relationship, a key distinction with the way that sōshi theater was seen both during the Meiji Period and in the mid-Showa performances examined here. Brook sees the opportunity for powerfully affective theater in the Rough, a possibility that was clearly evident in the sōshi stage, even if not widely appreciated in its contemporary Japanese theater world. Perhaps most importantly from the standpoint of the Rights Movement's goals in the Meiji Period, Rough Theater worked in a space that was "revolutionary" by being inherently close to the people. Perhaps not coincidentally, reviewers of Fukuda's *Oppekepe* (contemporaries of Brook) literally referred to sōshi theater as "rough" (粗雑), and their use of this Japanese word in their descriptions resonate with Brook's notion in English. These reviewers equated this "roughness" with what they complained was sōshi theater's lack of "class" (品), and they set it in opposition to more sophisticated postwar theaters in ways very similar to Brook's Rough/Holy Theater juxtaposition.

While the tone of *Sōshi Theater* is much more laudatory of the performers as people than is either Mishō's or Fukuda's, the performances all foreground the active role that audience plays in performance. Publicity stills of *Oppekepe* such as Figure 5.1 almost all include "spectators" (actually actors that are part of the diegetic frame of the performance) within the representations of the performance. Usually these audience members block what is ostensibly the subject of the photo. Scenes in these narratives which feature performances that invariably receive their plot arc not from the staged narrative but rather from the actor-audience interaction. The audiences in these representations of Rough Theater are contained within a larger performance in which audiences conform to the norms of Brook's Holy Theater—they attend a theater experience defined by a strict dress code, fancy chandeliers, and a reverent silence towards the performers on stage. The Holy Theater, in short, manifests in material and normative ways, which in the case of all three of the representations of the sōshi stage here results in a contemporary audience with a stance towards the act of performance which conflicts with that of the Rough Theater from the Meiji Period which they are observing.

The performance spaces of Inagaki's and Fukuda's narratives (and Mishō's, presumably, had it been performed), the cinema and the Haiyūza theater, perform in the space and in the mode of Brook's Holy Theater. By representing the performance of the sōshi within the confines of the Holy Theater, both performances contain the more spatially expansive third space of the Rough sōshi theater within the more spatially restrictive third space of the Holy mid-Showa cinema and Haiyūza theater. Yet this containment undermines the very mechanisms which sōshi's political performances utilized to exorcise the problems of the everyday. This containment risks neutering the political potency of the theater

The last sōshi 153

which ostensibly served as the sōshi's raison d'etre and reduces the performance into something close to the common English usage of "political theater" as a euphemism for neutered, meaningless, or even disingenuous action. The theater of Sudō and "Shiroyama" (the stand-in for Kawakami in Fukuda's play) employs a dramaturgical approach towards political theater that resists containment. It is a dramaturgy which metonymically strives for the liberty that the characters within the narrative are seeking, yet it remains cloistered within the liminal space of Holy Theater. It subverts efforts for real-world consequences. This contained focus on audience-performer interaction, in some instances to the exclusion of attention to the narrative ostensibly being performed, highlights the tension between competing notions of liminality and the performative objectives of the sōshi.

This dynamic of containment of the Rough within the Holy is present throughout the narrative of Inagaki's *Sōshi Theater*. One example of the foregrounding of the dramaturgy of Rough Theater in the film comes during a scene of Sudō's production of a courtroom drama where a woman is on trial for prostitution. The scene begins with a wide establishing shot that includes the proscenium and the audience in the foreground, and the camera then sweeps in on a crane to isolate the action on stage with the performance already taking place. In the scene, the judge is interrogating the accused woman. The action on stage is then interrupted by a drunk audience member who insults the play and the actors on stage. The camera then pans back as Sudō walks out on the hanamichi and confronts the rowdy audience member. To the delight of the crowd, he pulls the rowdy man up onto the stage and proceeds to put *him* on trial in front of the audience. When the judge asks the audience what punishment he deserves, the crowd cheerfully plays along by yelling out "beat him!", "give him the death sentence!" etc., and the judge ultimately sentences him to an actually enacted punishment of banishment from the theater. The crowd hoots and jeers as the man is escorted down the hanamichi and out of the auditorium (Figure 5.3). What is particularly notable is that the filmed scene ends here and does not map with either the beginning or the end of the scene that is being enacted on stage. Rather than return to the scene on stage to resolve the fate of the woman accused of prostitution, the arc of the filmed sequence is resolved with the removal of the rowdy audience member. Although this interruption might be seen as a disaster in other theatrical contexts, as the actors file into the dressing room and take off their costumes and makeup, two of them say "Wow, the audience loved it!" "Yes—it went really well!" Even for the actors themselves, the actual scripted drama barely registers as a significant component of the performance. Instead, the artistic and political work of the performance in Inagaki's representation exists beyond the stage and outside of the drama, a fact that is highlighted in the directorial choices of camera use and in the script writing with having a scene arc that does not correspond to the beginnings and endings of the play on stage.

The sōshi theater undermines the social practices of the Holy Theater and probes its community's weaknesses in a liminal social space that expands beyond the stage space and is in turn intruded upon by the world of the everyday in the form of police censors. Despite whatever value offering "redress"

Figure 5.3 In this four image sequence from *Sōshi Theater*, an intoxicated audience member disrupts the troupe's performance, is subjected to a "trial" on the stage, and is sentenced to banishment from the theater in *Sōshi gekijō*

Figure 5.3 (Continued)

156 *The last sōshi*

in the third stage might serve society generally, the theater of the Meiji sōshi works to move beyond the distinction that Turner labels as the "cultural subjunctive" of the theater world into the "cultural indicative" of the world of the everyday. In Turner's view, theater's resolution of social dramas both large and small serves valuable social functions but with fundamentally conservative ends. In the wake of the Restoration when important new Western concepts of "liberty" and "revolution" in a Japanese context were being thought through in embodied discussion on the sōshi stage, the sōshi were not hoping to resolve social dramas at all but rather to effect radical social change. This goal is in stark contrast to a view of theater that Turner describes as having a built-in lack of agency (or at least a lack of consequences) in the world of the everyday. As a place of opposition and resistance, the culturally subjunctive space of the Meiji stage was necessarily limited in its efficacy by the degree of control that extended over the stage. By maintaining a strict (and in practice highly arbitrary) pre-approval censorship process through local authorities— an institution that dates back to the Edo period and hints at the mostly invisible censorship of the Occupation—the terms of redress in this liminal space were very deliberately constrained. Local authorities then reinforced this restriction of the pre-approval process by placing police on or in view of the stage (these censors are included in all three of the performances discussed in this chapter and can be seen in Figure 5.1 from *Oppekepe*). This two-step censorship process provided a visual reminder of the authorities' ability to grant and rescind permission for performance and to ensure that the performance adhered to the approved script. Theater in this context appears neutered of its political efficacy and as a tool for resistance.

In actual practice, having police officers sitting visibly on or near the stage blurred boundaries and encroached on the liminal space, making the divide from reality more slender and easily traversable in Meiji sōshi theater than it otherwise would have been. By placing the representation of the object of resistance right on the stage, and thereby attempting to police the third space, the authorities made it more likely that critique would move from the liminal world of the performance space, where alternative realities could be thought through, into the world of the everyday with forms of resistance that were strictly proscribed. Rather than encouraging obedience, they encouraged resistance. Accounts of actual performances indicate that this was in fact a key appeal of the theater. In one instance, Kawakami Otojirō is said to have goaded the police on stage into shutting down his performance by insulting them with an ad-libbed humorous monologue ostensibly about goldfish but that in fact was directed at the censors. Indeed, historian Yanagi Takenao speaking in a recorded dialog recalled the exchange between Nakae Chōmin and Sudō when Chōmin suggested he should become a sōshi performer. When Sudō replied that he had practice giving public speeches but that he was not an actor, Yanagi says that Chōmin replied, "But you can fight, right? Just get up on stage and fight, and the people will love it!" As demonstrated in the plays in this chapter and in prior chapters, Yanagi's description is not as preposterous as it might initially have sounded.[23] Likewise, Kawakami's reputation

The last sōshi   157

as a sōshi performer was built partly upon the large number of real-world, actual arrests he had on his record.

In scenes in *Sōshi Theater* which follow the aforementioned scene of the interrupted performance, the narrative performs ways of stepping outside of the fourth-wall confined liminal theatrical space. This dramaturgical spatiality increasingly provokes confrontation and real-world consequences outside of the stage. By stepping beyond the bounds of the cultural subjunctive, actors come in conflict with the police who are placed there to maintain the divide between the approved alternate world with alternate rules and the real world in which the audience and censors exist. Since scripts were limited in their political messages during the pre-approval process, performers used improvisation in the actual performances as a space of resistance. In the second scene of *Sōshi Theater* that features a performance by the troupe, Inagaki utilizes similar strategies to those in the first scene described previously. The scene begins with the actors voicing concern about the presence of the officers in the theater, which is a marked step up in the level of control exerted by the authorities from the scene represented earlier in the film. The camera then cuts to the scene already in progress, again panning across the audience before focusing on the performers. In this scene of their play, the hero is a sōshi-like figure who comes across a corrupt official in the street and proceeds to denounce him. The official's goons attack him, but the hero proves too much for them. In the melee that follows, one actor is tossed into the front rows of the audience (who then bows to the audience members in apology before climbing back onto the stage). The hero pauses dramatically in mid-fight to denounce the corrupt authorities: "The citizens suffer under your oppression, and now you use violence on a man of justice. What cowardice! These are the true colors of the authorities! This is the true nature of the Meiji government!" (権力によって人民を苦しめ、今また正義の者に暴力を以てするとは怪しからぬ。これが官吏の正体だ。これが明治政府の真実の姿なのだ！）[24] The police in the theater have had enough and rush onto the stage and engage in a real fight on the stage and run off stage to arrest Sudō. The troupe is next shown held without charges and without interrogation in jail in Hakodate. When the troupe is finally released from prison and prepares to stage a new performance, the troupe appears on the apron of the stage before the show in front of the closed curtain to offer what seems to be a coerced statement by the authorities as a prerequisite for approval of the performance. He begins his direct address to the audience in contrite fashion, saying that they always obey the authorities and that only a savage would break the law. However, his speech quickly turns to a direct denunciation of the authorities, saying that the injuries they have suffered from the abuse by the police is a violation of human rights. When the police officer shouts a warning to him, Sudō tells him, "Shut up! This is what freedom of speech is!" The audience cheers Sudō on, and he continues addressing them saying, "This is not just my fight . . . for the sake of the twenty-five million citizens of Japan, we must overthrow this oppressive government and create a new one for the people!" (黙れ、言論は自由だ！． . . 諸君。これは一角藤定憲のみの問題ではない . . . 二千五百万の人民に対し 〖 〗 政府を打倒して、速やかに民

158 *The last sōshi*

衆のための政府を . . .)[25] The authorities then jump in and shut down the performance before the play has even begun. While the theater is shut down and the members of the troupe are stranded in Hakodate in winter, Sudō is ultimately able to get the chief of police fired for abusing his office. The theater space here is not represented as a locus for empty political bloviating, and it is not a space for the cultural subjunctive mood where actions do not face consequences. Inagaki portrays sōshi theater as part of the everyday, capable of real-world, performative action. Yet, in ways that mirror the presentation of Fukuda's narrative, Inagaki's representation of an interactive audience plays out through the medium of film, which is unable to duplicate the performative practice in his narrative by virtue of film's mediation.

Oppekepe enacts a similar contemporary challenge to realistic modes of performance and uses the historical setting of the sōshi theater for its content. Beginning in Act I during the pivotal time for the Rights Movement in 1892, Shiroyama and his troupe advocate for civil rights shortly after the promulgation of the Meiji Constitution. At the start of Act III, however, the timeline has moved to 1895, and the troupe is in rehearsal for a play valorizing the Sino-Japanese War. His key historical conundrum is in explaining how the idealists of the Rights Movement became in just a few short years such full-fledged proponents of war and Imperial expansion on the continent. Or, as one reviewer puts it, the play examines how "The sōshi theater collided with the Sino-Japanese War, was blunted, then tumbled around until morphing into shinpa". The progression to nationalism is told through the theater history of the Meiji Period.

This nationalism manifests in a complete breakdown in the final act of the play. The unity of the theater troupe, so strong in the first act of the play, has fractured in the intervening years. Tatsuya sees the war in China as antithetical to the liberal democratic ideals for which the troupe once stood. Ultimately, their performances are broken up by a rival sōshi gang in the audience and by Tetsuya crashing their militarist play by singing pacifist songs. Yet, in both cases, the focus of the performance is a meta-theatrical commentary upon theatrical viewing practices. Indeed, the reflexive nature of the play is foregrounded from the very beginning, which starts with an actor on a bare stage under simple work-lights practicing lines for *Oppekepe* before beginning what is ostensibly a rehearsal. In other words, it is a play within a play in which the scenes in the play are part of a rehearsal within the play being performed for the audience (see Figure 5.1). This reflexive, meta-theatrical drive of the play is again highlighted at the conclusion during the final performance of Shiroyama's troupe. As Tatsuya enters singing pacifist songs, the stage on which the actor-audience sits rotates 180 degrees, such that both Shiroyama and his audience are looking through the fourth wall at the real audience in the Haiyūza theater. Such an engagement with the audience, after modeling a rambunctious and interactive mode of viewing theater, represents a challenge to their audience as to the aims and ends of theater. Fukuda envisioned an "anti-realist" theater (非写実的) which was at odds with mainstream shingeki. This theater was one that was political and that worked in the "cultural indicative" mood to effect real and progressive change.

Beyond the third space

Turner's view of the theater as a sequestered third space resonates with common notions of the positionality of translation in a liminal space "between". The notion of an in-between-ness of translation carries intuitive appeal to a modern, Western sensibility, as Maria Tymoczko has pointed out.[26] After all, interpreters often physically locate themselves between the two people for whom they are facilitating oral communication; language transfer often occurs across spatial gaps on the map; and the etymology of the word "translation" itself is rooted in the movement of physical objects and bodies of knowledge. Yet Tymoczko takes this conceptual construct of translation to task, showing that in fact there is no "between" space in which languages and translators can be situated. The translator, like an anthropologist, "can never stand in a neutral or free space between cultures, but of necessity operates within some cultural framework, notably the constraints of his or her own primary cultural system".[27] Perhaps more importantly she argues, in ways which resonate with Naoki Sakai's view of language, that in looking at languages from the standpoint of systems theory, there is never a space between linguistic codes. There are only larger frames within which smaller frames or systems are nested. In other words, rather than a location between languages, a translator is situated within a larger systemic frame which encompasses *both* language systems.

The key problematic of this notion of "between", then, is that it places the translator in a rarified space occupied by perhaps the odd Romantic genius but which is otherwise sequestered from the world in which it operates. This hermetic seal serves an identical function to the fourth wall and Turner's notion of third-space performance in the way that both push performance and translation into the cultural subjunctive mood. Thus, it creates what Turner sees as an inherently conservative social force with little or no space for resistant cultural discourses. Indeed, as noted in earlier chapters, performance is widely seen as empty, insincere action (see locutions such as "political performance" or "kabuki dance" used on the floor of the United States Congress to devalue the motives of competing partisans). Any conceptual model which removes or marginalizes the role of key stakeholders (i.e. translators and theater professionals) from the cultural discussion around performance and translation risks missing the vital role that previous chapters of this study demonstrate was crucial to the discourse on how to translate the new concepts of liberty and revolution in the Meiji Period.

These two models of nesting performative and translation systems both play with notions of liminality and betweenness that speak to the plays in question here. Inagaki's representation of theaters in which there is no "between" the audience and the actor, and Fukuda's nesting of a larger third-space Meiji Asakusa Theater building within a smaller third-space postwar Haiyūza Theater stage works to sequester the performance space. This is much like Tymoczko's "Chinese nesting doll" model of translation that places all three operators (translator, target text, and source text) into direct contact. In the latter model, we see a role for translation that resonates with the embodied translation of liberty and revolution on the performance stage seen in all of the chapters of this study.

160 *The last sōshi*

Thus, the spatial metaphor fails in important ways to explain a model of translation which is as universal as it is often portrayed. It struggles to explain the performance as translation outlined in this book as well as by placing the translation process within a communal space in which there can be no solitary model of meaning transfer. Richard Schechner, along with Peggy Phelan and other performance studies scholars, have located the essence of performance not on the stage, but have similarly seen performance as something that involves everyone, every day. In Schechner's view, almost any social situation can be studied "as performance" because performance is not a thing which is contained on a stage. Rather, performance is a mutual creation of at least two people. In other words, performance exists between a performer and an observer (who can also, of course, be a performer within the performance). As in Tymoczko's Chinese nesting dolls, there is never anywhere to observe a performance from outside a frame of reference in which we are not a part of the performance, and every participant is a player in the translation. Kawakami's notions of liberty, explicated in performances that appear in Chapters 1 and 3, relied upon but also competed with dominant translations of the term in textual versions such as Nakamura's *On Liberty*. Likewise, Sasaki's notions of revolution on stage in Chapter 2 engaged with the larger debates between the Fukumotoists and the Yamakawaists. It is in this fact where Fukuda sees the value in Meiji sōshi performance—that is, as a way to recover a dramaturgy in which the collaborative nature of performance, one which is just as much a collaboration between the stage and the house as one between the varied members of a theater troupe.

One hundred years of sōshi

With these twin interests in history and performative agency driving the popularity of the sōshi in the early postwar years, it is perhaps then not hard to explain the disappearance of sōshi theater from cultural relevance in more recent decades. The distance of time has perhaps reduced the felt urgency by some of explaining the failure of the Pacific War, and contemporary political expression in Japan is tame in a way that does not demand for the kind of violent confrontation which the sōshi performed.[28] Even during the prewar period, the sōshi's guerilla theater tactics embodied a dramaturgy and a social philosophy at odds with the theater-viewing practices and ideals of many in the politically resistant theater of the prewar Proletarian Movement. This is even more true in theater in more recent years. It is true that these practices flew in the face of the more conventional cinemas and mainstream theaters where *Sōshi Theater* and Fukuda's *Oppekepe* were performed. But modes of political protest in the 1950s and '60s, which informed the *angura* (underground) theater that influenced Fukuda, highlighted the degree to which theater was out of step with the political activism of the time. Mid-Showa theater viewership practices had radically changed from the early Meiji Period. The Western-style proscenium arch had become a fixture of the Japanese theater experience, visibly codifying and marking off from the audience a liminal "third space" for performance. This

The last sōshi 161

architectural barrier stood at odds with the free-wheeling exchange between actor and audience in early Meiji dramaturgy. Foregrounding the liminal nature of the theater within the "third space" of the performance, these postwar narratives highlighted the violence of the sōshi while simultaneously neutering that violence by containing it within the diegetic frame of the stage space. In other words, the performances utilized the sequestered quality of the performative event in order to constrain and explore the spatially expansive liminality at the heart of sōshi theater. By containing the transgressive power of the third space, and by de-naturing the disruptive power of sōshi performance, Showa theater challenges the audience's role in the agency of political performance. Probing subjects with larger national implications for viewers in the postwar era, these performances explore how the idealistic youths of the Freedom and People's Rights Movement could also be the same violent, petty criminals who would transform into the jingoistic supporters of the war on the continent during the first Sino-Japanese War. Yet simultaneously, it mourns the postwar, mainstream shingeki loss of a theater, with real-world consequences.

Inagaki, Mishō, and Fukuda all foreground a sōshi theater which relies on the live, unscripted dramaturgy at the heart of Rights Movement political theater introduced in earlier chapters. The sōshi theater described in the performances in this chapter and in earlier chapters housed both the liberal and revolutionary ideals of the Enlightenment and the virulent nationalism that led to a jingoistic war with China and then Russia, but they also represented a brand of resistance theater which required audience engagement for its political efficacy. It was a theater with a dramaturgy, if not a politics, that resonated with that of the contemporary underground theater which Fukuda saw as offering a politically and theatrically vital alternative to the staid realism that mainstream shingeki had become.

For the century of performances traced in this and preceding chapters, the Rights Movement served as a metonym for the Restoration and the introduction of Western political philosophy after 1868, including the introduction of the Meiji Constitution. Inagaki, Mishō, and Fukuda locate the sōshi as the embodiment of the promise of the Meiji Restoration, a stance that is evident with the quote that begins this chapter from *Sōshi Theater*. It also comes across in a song released in 1966 by Moriya Hiroshi titled *One Hundred Years since Oppekepe* (百年目から オッペケペ).[29] The recording is a rewriting of *Oppekepe* just before the centenary of the Meiji Restoration that, despite Kawakami's song not being 100 years old in 1966, stands as an assessment of the critique of the Restoration laid out by Kawakami and his fellow writers of *Oppekepe* in the late 1880s. Moriya sees an obsession with Western goods and culture, which by implication is at the expense of attention to Japanese goods and culture, that mirrors the Western materialism which Kawakami satirizes in the Meiji Period. Yet Moriya's song sees failure where Kawakami hinted at promise. Moriya begins his song with "Even with the progress of Civilization and Enlightenment/We're just as obsessed with foreign stuff as we used to be:/ Perfume, lighters, and wrist watches, and/ "If it ain't jazz, it ain't music" (文明開化は進んでも/ 舶来好みは変わらない/ 香水ライ ター腕時計/ ジャズでなければ歌じゃない). Perhaps one of the key official

162 *The last sōshi*

slogans of the Meiji government, in other words, has failed to produce the self-confident, powerful culture for which it was clearly intended to effect. Yet unlike Kawakami, who wanted to make "enemies of people's rights chug shots of liberty booze", liberty is not the solution for Moriya. In fact, it is quite the opposite. The first lines of his song ring a very different tone: "Freedom, rights, and opportunity/ Everyone chasing their own self-interest/ Japan is you and me together/ *Oppekepeppo peppopo/ Oppekepeppo peppopo*" (自由だ権利だ開放だ/ みんながそれぞれわがままを/ 日本あって君と僕/ オッペケペッポ　ペッポッポ/ オッペケペッポ　ペッポッポ). Moriya's refrain of "oppekepe" evinces not a plucky and snarky challenge to the establishment, but rather a claim that the Meiji experiment has failed. Liberty is symptomatic of rather than a cure for the small-minded, self-centered pursuit of individual interests which undermines the collective good of a vibrant Japanese nation. Compared with their Meiji predecessors, seeing culture as moving at a rapid speed into the future, Moriya sees Japanese culture as being in retreat: "A century has passed since Meiji, but our psychological culture is going backwards" (明治は百年たったけど/精神文化は逆もどり). The pursuit of Western philosophy and culture so evident throughout this study has failed to move Japan into the future. Moreover, these failures are not just domestic: "We are a people who has mastered mechanics, science, and physics/ But the elephants and bears wonder why/ We're still fighting barbaric wars. . . . Why have we not achieved world peace? We're no different than the ancient past" (力学　化学　物理学/ これほど進んだ人類が/ 野蛮な戦争なぜするの/ 象さん　くまさん　不思議がる. . . . 明治は百年たったけど/ 精神文化は逆もどり/ 世界の平和はまだこない/神代の昔と変わらない).

A century after the Restoration, the function of *jiyū* in Moriya's *Oppekepe* is turned on its head from Kawakami's Meiji Period original. No longer is *jiyū* even a site of resistance as an aspirational ideal—the wake-up call that Kawakami saw it against economic and political injustices. Whereas the characters satirized in Kawakami's version of the song, detailed in Chapter 1, are misguided rubes who mistakenly equate their materialistic Western airs with political and cultural sophistication, Moriya's critique does not disambiguate liberty from crass obsession with money and status. Perhaps recalling earlier connotations of the character compounds floated in early Meiji as possible translation words, Moriya sees liberty and rights as indicative of a self-centered individualism that also manifests in social injustice and discord. Forcing the populace to pound shots of "freedom booze", as is Kawakami's prescription for Meiji society's ills, would have no therapeutic effect for Moriya. Liberty isn't the solution to society's problems, in other words. Liberty *is* the problem. Even more striking, the pursuit of liberty has lost its place as a goal and motivator of resistance.

It is perhaps unsurprising that Moriya produced his song as the sōshi and the Rights Movement lost their hold on the cultural memory of the Meiji Period. The centenary of the Restoration marked an ending of the cultural relevance of these stories treated in this book. The three backstage dramas in this chapter, along with novels and short stories from the same period, represent the last boom of popular narratives of the Rights Movement in performance and as performance.

The last sōshi 163

While later generations, including and especially the current one, still wrestle with the meaning of liberty and the locus of national and personal rights, after the 1960s the Freedom and People's Rights Movement ceased to be a trope through which these debates were mediated. Moriya's assessment of the achievements of 1868 mirrors those of Inagaki, Mishō, and Fukuda: the sōshi embodied the promise, but by corollary, the failures of the Restoration.

Notes

1 Yahiro Fuji, *Sōshi gekijō: kenpō kinen eiga* (Tokyo: Daiei Kyoto Satsueijo, 1947), 4–11.
2 Fleeting references to the performances of his youth do exist, such as an appearance in the film *Waga fuyu no uta* (dir. by Seiichirō Yamaguchi, 1977) when Kitamura Tōkoku attends a performance of his biggest single hit, the song *Oppekepe bushi*. Yet even narratives dedicated primarily to Kawakami elide his identity as a sōshi during the time of *Oppekepe*. The Takarazuka show about Kawakami, titled *Yoake no jokyoku* (夜明けの序曲 *Prelude to the Dawn*, 1982), has Kawakami sing *Oppekepe* as his friends send him off on his trip to the United States (1899–1902), well after his days as a true sōshi. Mitani Kōki's *Osore wo shiranu Kawakami Otojirō ichiza* (恐れを知らぬ川上音二郎一座 The Fearless Otojirō's Company, 2007) dispenses with Kawakami's political theater in an opening montage with a benshi-like narrator before moving on to the main story line of the performance of his trip to America. Additionally, the 1985 NHK taiga drama *Haru no hato* primarily told the story of Kawakami's later life with his wife, Sadayakko, whom he met at the tail end of the sōshi's popularity.
3 Thomas Keith notes in *Religion and the Decline of Magic* that during times of violent change, "all societies seek to establish links with their own past" (p. 505). This postwar Japanese search for continuity was not unique to the theater, and the object of the search was not limited to the early Meiji Period. In the wake of the loss of constitutional and sovereign integrity after 1945, society at all levels searched for evidence of a throughline of the cultural narrative. Naoki Sakai, for example, shows how Watsuji Tetsurō scrambled to find national continuity in the postwar period with the newly weakened emperor system (*Translation and Subjectivity: On Japan and Cultural Nationalism* [Minneapolis: University of Minnesota Press, 1997]).
4 Other examples include Mishō Kingo's screenplay *Oppekepe: Sōshi yakusha Kawakami Otojirō* (おつぺけぺい：壮士役者川上音二郎他一篇) (1957), for which Murayama Tomoyoshi wrote a glowing introduction, and Naoki Prize–winning author Hozumi Miharu's novel *Sōshi ichidai* (*Sōshi: A Life*). 御荘, 金吾. おつぺけぺい：壮士役者川上音二郎他一篇 (Tōkyō: Bungaku Hyōronsha, 1957).
5 Fukuda Yoshiyuki 福田善之, *Oppekepe and Hakamadare wa doko da: Fukuda Yoshida dai ni sakuhinshū* オッペケペ：袴垂れはどこだ：福田善之第二作品集, Dai 1-han. ed. (Tōkyō: San'ichi Shobō, 1967).
6 Sudō Sadanori worked for the *Daybreak News* for a time, and it was run under the supervision of Rights Movement leader Nakae Chōmin.
7 Neither of these examples is expounded upon with specifics, suggesting that the readership would understand the historical references. Based on creative and philosophical works cited in earlier chapters that would have been familiar to *Shinonome shinbun* readers, presumably the French example would draw on 1789 and the Roman example would be either at the beginning of the Republic or the transition to the Empire.
8 Kan Takayuki 管孝行, "Kono 20 nin no engekijintachi no kōzai-3-Kinoshita Junji, Fukuda Yoshiyuki, Miyamoto Ken この20人の演劇人たちの功罪—3—木下順二、福田善之、宮本研". *Teatoro* 632, no. 8 (1995), 21–26.

164 *The last sōshi*

9 Takase Masaharo 高瀬昌弘, *Waga kokoro no Inagaki Hiroshi* 我が心の稲垣浩 (Tōkyō: Waizu Shuppan, 2000), 242.

10 For more on this film, see Chapter 10 from: Fogel, Joshua A. Maiden Voyage. University of California Press, 2014; also see O'Reilly, Sean D. Reviewing the Past: The Uses of History in the Cinema of Japan, 1925–1945. PhD diss., Harvard University, 2015.

11 「作家は器用に歴史ばなれをして現代の声をしのびこませている」(Ozaki Kōji writing in the Nov 16, 1963, *Yomiuri shinbun*, quoted in the 1963 *Oppekepe* playbill).

12 Recent scholarship in both Japanese and English, such as Egashira Kō, Jason Karlin, and Eiko Siniawer, uncovers the degree to which perceptions of the sōshi varied in the images conjured up by the new Meiji Period demographic category of sōshi.

13 For the sōshi theater's support of expansion of empire, see: Ayako Kano, *Acting Like a Woman in Modern Japan: Theater, Gender, and Nationalism* (New York: Palgrave, 2001).

14 Mishō Kingo, *Oppekepei: Sōshi yakusha Kawakami Otojirō* (Tōkyō: Bungaku Hyōronsha, 1957).

15 In fact, Inagaki initially intended to center his story on Kawakami but switched because his father had been a fan of Sudō. These figures were, in other words, largely interchangeable for Inagaki.

16 Even practices such as *kakegoe*, where the audience members of kabuki plays shout out their appreciation for certain actors or particularly moving scenes, has in practice become codified and restricted in its use to highly trained audience members.

17 Noh theater, of course, features a strong fourth wall, typically using a small gravel border between the audience and stage to function where Western stages use a proscenium. However, noh was primarily an aristocratic performance genre. Bunraku is perhaps an exception here, since it is both a popular performance art and also resists audience stage interaction.

18 Victor W. Turner, *From Ritual to Theatre: The Human Seriousness of Play*, Performance Studies Series, 1st V (New York City: Performing Arts Journal Publications, 1982), 15.

19 Ibid., 11.

20 Theater historian Akiba Tarō, for example, when describing Kawakami Otojirō's career, wrote that while he was performing sōshi shibai (sōshi theater), he was not actually an actor (*haiyū*). It was not until sōshi theater became more formalized into what is now considered *shinpa* theater that Kawakami could be considered to be "acting".

21 Peter Brook, *The Empty Space* (New York: Athenium Press, 1968).

22 Ibid., 66.

23 From a taiwa (dialog) with Yanagi Takenao dated March 1981, www.ncbank.co.jp/corporate/chiiki_shakaikoken/furusato_rekishi/hakata/015/01.html. Accessed July 25, 2019.

24 Yahiro, *Sōshi gekijō*, 3–2.

25 Ibid., 3–10.

26 Maria Tymoczko, "Ideology and the Position of the Translator: In What Sense Is the Translator 'In Between'," in *Apropos of Ideology: Translation Studies on Ideology: Ideologies in Translation Studies*, ed. Maria Calzada Pérez (Abingdon, UK: Routledge, 2002).

27 Ibid., 195.

28 This is not to say that protest and resistance are completely dead in Japan. Yet there is a vibrant if small commitment to resistant performance in contemporary Japan, most visibly seen in reactions to the Fukushima disaster. See Noriko Manabe, *The Revolution Will Not Be Televised: Protest Music After Fukushima* (New York, NY: Oxford University Press, 2015).

29 The song was re-released on CD in 2014 on the Crown label as a single with a recording of the bakumatsu period song *Ei janaika* as the b-side.

Index

advertising 12, 91–92
Aihara Naobumi 80–82
Akiba Tarō 82, 84, 88, 90–91, 164
Akita Ujaku 63
Ange Pitou (The Triumphal Song of the French Revolution) 54
anti-realist theater (*hishajitsuteki*) 158
Arendt, Hannah 47–51
Armored Train 14–69 116
Arts Theater (*Geijutsa-za*) 62–63
Association for Theater Reform (*Engeki kairyō kai*) 26
Atsuko Ueda 29, 41
audience 6–7, 13, 19–20, 31–33, 46, 58–59, 61, 74, 96, 126–127, 129–130, 140; audience-performer relationship 73, 150–152, 157–161; violence 83, 94–95, 149; *see also* performance, audience
Auslander, Philip 130
Avant Garde Theater (*Zen'eiza*) 9, 10, 62–64, 102, 111–115, 117; Proletarian Arts (Purogei) 64–65; Worker's Arts (Rōgei) 64–65, 79; *see also* MAVO
Ayako Kano 7, 88–89, 101, 137, 141

bakufu 49, 83, 92, 119, 125
Bando Tsumasaburō 146
Battle Records of the Shinsengumi, The 120
benshi 10, 70, 116, 130, 138–140
Bentham, Jeremy 14
Blood Oath of Goryōkaku, The 45, 112, 119, 122–125, 131–132, 137–139
Boat Heading to Shore, The 45
Brandon, James 85
Brook, Peter 150–152
Brothers of the House of Oki, The 45, 61, 77
Buchner, Georg 60–61
Bungei Sensen see Sower, The (Tanemaku hito)
Burghers of Calais, The 139

Carlson, Marvin 2
censorship 6, 13, 38, 41, 83–85, 94–95, 106, 156–157; resistance 30–31, 33, 92, 137–138, 146, 151, 153
Chiba Akira 126, 129
Chikugai Koji 26
Chūshingura 65
Collection of Liberty Poems 54
comic storytelling (*rakugo*) 33, 46, 54, 90, 92
Communism 9, 60, 73, 76; *see also* Fukumotoism; Marxism
Conditions of the West 15
Considerations on the Causes of the Grandeur and Decadence of the Romans 24
Coriolanus 8–10, 24, 29, 52, 54, 58; Itakura's translation *Liberty's Scourge and the Bonds of Affection: The Tale of the Greatest Hero of the Age* 17–18, 24–29, 55, 58–59
Crab Cannery Boat, The 8

Daigaku 51
Davis, Tracy C. 32
Dawn of Liberty in the East, The (Azuma nada jiyū no akebono) 86–87
Death of Danton, The (Danton no shi) 44, 60–61, 77
Decorated Scabbard of Liberty, The 86
Details of the Itagaki Tragedy, The (Itagaki sōnan tenmatsu) 91
Die Hose 119, 139

Edano Yukio 5
Egashira Kō 30, 148, 164
Eguchi Kan 116
Eiko Maruko Siniawer 30–31, 41–42, 148
embodied memory 1–7, 82, 54–55, 61, 101–102, 151, 159; historiography 2–3, 51

166 Index

enlightenment (*Kaigo*) 12, 49–50, 83, 144
Ennosuke 116–117

*Falling Cherry Blossoms at Inaba in the
Twilight* (*fubuki inaba no tasogare*) 86
Fascist Doll 122
film 6, 10, 112, 126–140; *see also rensa-geki*
*Forerunners of the Recent Port Openings,
The* (*Chikagoro minato no sakigake*) 83
Forerunner Theater (*Senkuza*) 63, 115, 117
Freedom and People's Rights Movement
(*jiyū minken undo*) 2, 12, 14, 16, 46, 89;
Daybreak News (*Shinonome shinbun*)
91, 144, 146, 148; factions 16, 29, 50,
106; performances of 1–10, 33, 39, 41,
107, 162–163; *see also* Itagaki Taisuke;
Nakae Chōmin; Sudō Sadanori; Ueki
Emori
Free Theater (*Jiyū gekijo*) 62
French Revolution, The 47, 49–50, 54–55,
59, 62, 69–72
Fujii Reisuke 87
Fukuda Yoshiyuki 6, 143, 145, 149,
151–152, 158–161
Fukumotoism 9, 64, 160
Fukumoto Kazuo 64; *see also*
Fukumotoism
Fukuzawa Yūkichi 15, 89
Furuhara Yoshiaki 22

Gekisen 73, 117
Grote, George 14–15
guerilla theater 10, 32, 39, 66, 137, 160;
see also liveness; Sōshi

Hakuōki 120
Hamlet 8, 17, 40
Harootunian, Harry 62, 78
Hatori Yukisato 105
Hijikata Toshizō 119, 122
Hijikata Umeko 114
Hirao Michio 119
historical drama (*jidai geki*) 6, 44, 81, 124
historiography 20–24, 39, 48, 51, 55, 82,
120; Restoration 2–3, 6, 19, 65, 105, 148
History 14–15
History of Greece 14
Hobbes, Thomas 14–16, 38
Hohlov, Nikolai 60
Hopkins, Lisa 52
Hoshi Tōru 30, 41
Howland, Douglas 7, 16
Humanity and Paper Balloons 140
Hutcheon, Linda 80

Ichikawa Danshū (Ichikawa Danjurō) 9,
26, 89, 92, 115
Ichikawa Emiya 117
Ichikawa Kodayū 117
Ichikawa Yaozō 68, 70, 117
Ii Yōhō 88
Iketani Shinzaburō 116
Inagaki Hiroshi 6, 10, 143, 145–153,
157–159, 161, 164
*Incursion of the Imperial Forces into
Russia, The* 126, 128
Inoue Tsutomu 40
Inoue, Yoshie 114–115
Internationale 63
Introduction to Proletarian Film, An 128
Itagaki Morimasa 109
Itagaki plays 80–82, 84–87, 91, 93, 96, 109
Itagaki Taisuke 1–2, 5–6, 10, 16, 73, 80–82;
see also Itagaki Taisuke; *Record of the
Saga Disturbance, A* (*Saga bodōki*)
Itagaki Taisuke 10, 44, 61, 77, 80–81,
102–107, 109, 143
Itakura Kōtaro 24–29, 39, 55, 58–59
Itō Chiyū 94
Iwamoto Kenji 127, 130
Iwata Atsushi 4, 11

Jiyūtō ihen 109
Julius Caesar 8–10, 17–18, 20, 29, 52–54,
58; Kawashima's translation *The Rise
and Fall of Rome* (*Rōma seisuikan*) 19,
21–24, 26; Shōyō's translation, *The
Amazing Story of Caesar: The Legacy of
the Sharpness of Liberty's Sword* (*Jiyū
no tachi nagori no kireaji: Shiizaru
kidan*) 18–22, 25, 28–29, 41, 52, 55–58

kabuki 13, 65, 79–80, 93–94, 116–117;
actors 61, 70, 86, 133; conventions
6, 26, 28, 40, 88–89, 93–94, 125;
Proletarian Theater Movement 68,
70–71, 79–80; traditionalism 13, 26, 65,
67–68, 82–83
Kagawa Susumu 68, 71, 73
Kaieda Susumu 22
Kaiser, Georg 116, 119, 138
Kanagaki Robun 40
Karlin, Jason 148, 164
Kawakami Otojirō 5–6, 13, 38–39, 42,
103, 156–157, 163–164; performance
30–33, 88–95, 106, 142–143;
representations 149, 151; *see also
Itagaki Taisuke*; *Oppekepe*
Kawano Hironaka 73

Index 167

Kawasaki Chōjūrō IV 115–117, 135, 140
Kawashima Keizō 18–19, 21–24, 28, 39,
  55–56, 59
Kawatake Mokuami 83
Keene, Donald 113, 138
Kobayashi Takiju 8, 9, 63
Kokoroza Theater 113, 116–117
Kondō Isami 112, 119–120
Kubo Sakae 10, 62–63, 111–112, 114,
  116, 118–120, 138–139; *see also Blood
  Oath of Goryōkaku, The*; Shinsengumi,
  Kubo's 1934 script
Kurahara Korehito 67
Kuwabara Takeo 50
Kyary Pamyu Pamyu 139

Land of Volcanic Ash, The 122
La nuit 114–115
Laughing Letter, The (*Warai no tegami*)
  126, 129
Les Miserables 71, 77
Levy, Indra 7–8
Lianeri, Alexandra 14
liberty (*jiyū*) 1–6, 8–16, 162–163; liberal
  democracy 12, 14–16, 21, 144–145,
  148–149; Liberty Party (*Jiyūtō*) 49, 52,
  57, 73–75, 80–82, 86–87, 105–106;
  in Shakespeare translations 17,
  19–24, 27–30; *see also* Itagaki plays;
  Oppekepe; translation, liberty
Literary Arts Society (*Bungei kyōkai*) 30, 62
Literature and Arts Theater (*Bungei-za*) 63
liveness 6–7, 81, 86, 101, 107; fourth wall 7,
  96, 131, 143, 150, 157–159; improvisation
  32, 102, 128, 137, 152, 157, 161;
  mediation 3, 7, 80, 111–112, 125–140,
  158; performance 10, 27, 125–129,
  132–133, 136–138; *see also rensa-geki*
Luongo, Robert 17

Madame Terese 54
Maki Toshio 66, 102
Marxism 9, 44–46, 59, 62, 77, 102–103,
  107; *see also* Fukumotoism
Masaki Yoshikatsu 65, 67
Mateo Falcone 71, 77
Matsumoto Kappei 82, 84
Matsumoto Shinko 82–84
MAVO 66, 102, 118, 124, 137, 140
Meiji Restoration 12, 33, 83, 107;
  aftermath 1–3, 45, 48; as Bourgeois
  Revolution 46, 62, 65, 76, 122; *see also*
  Freedom and People's Rights Movement
  (*jiyū minken undo*); Restoration Plays

Mencius 50
Merchant of Venice, The 40
Midsummernight's Dream, A 8
Mills, J.S. 4, 8–9, 14–15
Mishō Kingo 6, 10, 143, 149–150
Mitani Hiroshi 49–51
modernity 8, 9, 12, 46–47, 61, 65, 144
Modern Theater Society (*Kindai geki
  kyōkai*) 63
Mori Sankichi 93
Morita Kan'ya 83
Moriya Hiroshi 161–163
Morris, William 40
Muhōmatsu no isshō 145–146
Murayama Masao 54
Murayama Tomoyoshi 9–10, 111–112,
  149; writing 64, 102, 118–119, 128,
  137–138, 163; *see also Shinsengumi: A
  Talkie Rensa-Geki*
music 1–2, 93, 108, 158; political
  songs (*Enka*) 90, 144; and the Rights
  Movement 7, 71; singers of current
  events (*yomiuri*) 90; *see also Oppekepe*

Nakae Chōmin 1, 13, 46, 49–50, 91, 144,
  156, 163
Nakamura Kamematsu (Tsuruzō) 116
Nakamura Kan'emon 116
Nakamura Keiu 1, 4, 13, 15, 46
Nakamura Sōjūrō Ichiza 40
Nakamura Utaemon 117
Naoki Sakai 159, 163
Nebenneinander 139
Nero in Skirts 116
New History of All Countries, A 49
New School theater (*Shinpa*) 62, 88, 101
New Theater (*Shingeki*) 63, 88, 113,
  115–118, 138; *see also* Tsukiji Little
  Theater (*Tsukiji shogekijo*)
Nihon rikkenseitō shinbun 22–23; *Rikken
  seitō shinbun* 52, 92
Nihon Sheikusupia sōran 22
Nikkatsu 116

Ōi Kentarō 68, 71, 73, 95
Ōkuma Shigenobu 16, 29
old theater style (*kyūgeki*) 81–82, 88
One Hundred Years Since Oppekepe
  161–162
one night pickles (*Ichiyazuke*) 85–86,
  93, 106
On Liberty 4, 8, 13, 15, 46, 160
Ono Miyakichi 67, 117
Ono Tomojirō 25

168 *Index*

Oppekepe: Fukuda's 1963 play 10, 143, 145, 148, 152, 158, 160; Kawakami's song 6, 8, 33–38, 42, 91–92, 141, 161, 163; Mishō's 1957 scenario 10, 143, 149, 151; Moriya's 1966 song 161
Oriental Liberty Newspaper 50
Osanai Kaoru 63, 67, 113–115
Otani Takejirō 117

Peace Preservation Law of 1887 33
performance 1–3, 5–7, 39, 102, 107–109; audience 27, 39, 149–150, 152–153, 158; Meiji 26–31, 80–86; paratheatrical 10, 31–32, 39, 102, 107, 137; political 1–3, 5–7, 10, 31–32, 80, 85, 92, 152; Proletarian 102, 107, 111–113, 128–130, 137–138; third space 150–152, 159–161; *see also* liveness, performance; Sōshi, performance; translation, of performances
Phelan, Peggy 129, 160
political theater (*sōshi-shibai*) 31, 42, 102, 144
Popular Theater (*Taishūza*) 44, 62, 68, 70, 117
Postlewaite, Thomas 32
Proletarian Theater Movement 7–10, 44–47, 65–68, 113, 128; and the Rights Movement 62, 82, 107, 111–112, 142; Trunk Theater 7, 63, 79, 102, 113, 115, 117, 140; *see also* Avant Garde Theater (*Zen'eiza*); Tsukiji Little Theater (*Tsukiji shogekijo*); Zenshinza
Puroretaria Geijutsu 64, 79

Record of a Gang of Thugs 122
Record of Itagaki's Tragedy, The (*Itagaki Taisuke sōnan tenmatsu jikki*) 87
Record of the Saga Disturbance, A (*Saga bodōki*) 96–101
Record of Two Generations of the French Revolution, A 49–50
Red and the Black, The 63
Reformed Theater (*kairyō engeki*) 88, 108
rensa-geki 7, 10, 105, 107, 126–130, 136, 138–139; *see also* Shinsengumi
Restoration (*ishin*) 47–51; *see also* Meiji Restoration
Restoration Plays 6, 9–10, 44–47, 60, 65, 76–77, 103, 105, 107, 111–112, 130, 142
revolution (*kakumei*) 5, 6, 9, 46–54, 62, 156; in theater 55–61, 74–78, 111, 160; *see also* translation, revolution
Romance of the Three Kingdoms, The 20, 56
Rurouni kenshin 120

Sadanji 116–117
Sadayakko 142
Saigō Takamori 51, 82, 96, 104–105
Sakamoto Ryōma 45
Sakurada Naosuke 83
Samurai trilogy 146
Sano Seki 67–68, 102
Sasaki Takamaru 6–7, 9, 46–47, 63–65, 67, 70–72, 76–77, 79, 114–115, 160; *see also Death of Danton, The* (*Danton no shi*); *Itagaki Taisuke*; *Secret Account from Tsukuba, The* (*Tsukuba hiroku*)
Satsuma-Chōshu 51, 122
Secret Account from Tsukuba, The (*Tsukuba hiroku*) 7, 44–47, 61–62, 65, 67–72, 77, 109, 117, 143
Seikanron debates 82, 96–101, 103–104
Selbin, Eric 46, 53–54, 61, 70
Senda Koreya 63–64, 115
Serizawa Kamo 119–120
Shakespeare 9, 17–18, 24, 28–29, 38, 52–53, 137; *see also Coriolanus*; *Julius Caesar*; translation, Shakespeare
Shimada Keiichi 103
Shimosawa Kan 119–120
Shinjinkai 145
Shinsengumi 45, 107, 111, 119, 137, 139, 142; representations 10–11, 112–113, 119–120, 122, 130, 140; *see also Blood Oath of Goryōkaku, The*
Shinsengumi: Kubo's 1934 script 112, 125, 130, 133–134; Murayama's 1937 film 112, 126, 130, 136; Murayama's 1937 *rensa-geki, Shinsengumi: A Talkie Rensa-Geki* (*Toki rensa-geki Shinsengumi*) 45, 112, 128–130, 133, 135–137, 139–140; Murayama's 1940 novel 112; *see also Laughing Letter, The* (*Warai no tegami*)
Shin Tsukiji Gekijō 103
Shiroyama 145, 158
Shōchiku 70, 79, 108, 116–117
Shunka-za 63
Signal Fires over Shanghai (*Noroshi wa Shanhai ni agaru*) 146
Skeleton Dance, The 8
Slain Senta (*Kirareta Senta*) 45
Social Contract 13, 50, 72
Soganoya Gorō 91
Sorori Shinzaemon 33
Sōshi 1–2, 6–7, 9–11, 30–31, 96, 109, 163; performance 13, 31–33, 84, 88–90, 108, 137–138, 156–157, 160–161, 164;

Index 169

representations 10–11, 75, 93–94, 142–145, 148–158, 160, 164; violence 30–33, 41–42, 94–96, 101, 105, 148–149, 161
Sōshi Enka and Revolution Songs of the Meiji Period 11
Sōshi Theater (*Sōshi gekijō*, 1947) 10, 138, 142–149, 151–155, 157, 160–161
Sower, The (*Tanemaku hito*) 63, 79
speech-meeting (*enzetsukai*) 54, 80, 85, 89–90, 92–94, 109, 143
Spy, The 70, 117
Stage Society (*Butai kyōkai*) 63
Sudō Sadanori 42, 88–89, 91–95, 109, 138, 156, 163; *see also Sōshi Theater* (*Sōshi gekijō*, 1947)

Taboo 120
Theater News (*engeki shinbun*) 65–66, 102, 137, 140
Thucydides 14
Tokugawa Shogunate 48–49, 82
Tolstoy, Aleksei 60
Toshirō Ihara 84
Toyoda Ichirō 29
translation 1–9, 89–90; analogy 46–47, 52–53, 55, 59–60, 76; liberty 4–10, 12–17, 19–23, 29, 33, 38, 43, 146; in performance 3, 7, 13, 89–90, 107, 159–160; of performances 118–119, 125, 138; revolution 9, 48–49, 57–60, 72; Shakespeare 2, 6, 8–9, 13, 17–33, 39–41, 46, 52
True Account of Itagaki's Tragedy at Gifu, The (*Itagakikun Gifu sōnan jikki*) 93
True Account of the Tragedy at Gifu of Liberty Party Leader Itagaki Taisuke, The (*Jiyūtō sōri Itagaki Taisuke shi sōnan Gifu jikki*) 93
Tsubouchi Shōyō 9, 19–24, 28–30, 39, 41, 52, 55–56
Tsuchitori Toshiyuki 1, 5, 11
Tsuchiya Momoko 85

Tsukiji Little Theater (*Tsukiji shogekijo*) 63, 44–45, 63, 112–117, 122, 139
Tsukiji Youth Faction 114–115
Turner, Victor 150, 156, 159
Tymoczko, Maria 62, 159–160

Ueki Emori 54, 71, 87, 103
Ukiyotei Marumaru *see* Kawakami Otojirō
Usuda Kenji 103

violence: audience 6, 31, 83, 94, 96–97, 151; Chichibu Uprising 7, 30, 71, 73–75; Gifu Incident 80, 85–88, 91, 101–103, 105–106, 109; performance 31, 94–95, 101, 148–149, 151; political violence 30, 45, 48; staged violence (*tachimawari*) 70, 93, 96, 101; *see also* Sōshi, violence

Wadagaki Kenzō 40
Warner, Michael 32–33
Weisenfeld, Jennifer 102
Westernization 1, 5, 13–19, 33, 82–83, 90, 144
What is Translation—Japanese and the Culture of Translation (*Hon'yaku to wa nanika—Nihongo to honyaku bunka*) 15
White, Hayden 148

Yamakawaists 9, 64, 78
Yanabu Akira 15–16, 42
Yanagida Izumi 29
Yanagi Takenao 156
Year 93 (*The Carnage in the Streets of the French Revolution*) 54
Yoda Hyakusen (Yoda Gakkai) 19–20, 26, 56, 88
Yose 6, 31, 83–85
Yoshida Tōru 11
Yoshie Takamatsu 126

Zenshinza troupe 111–113, 115–119, 122, 126, 130, 133, 138, 140

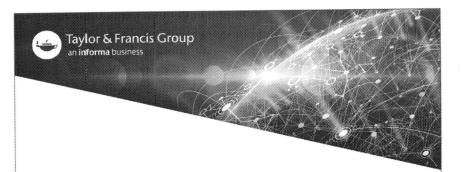

Printed in the United States
by Baker & Taylor Publisher Services